IMAGES
of America

DAVIDSON COUNTY

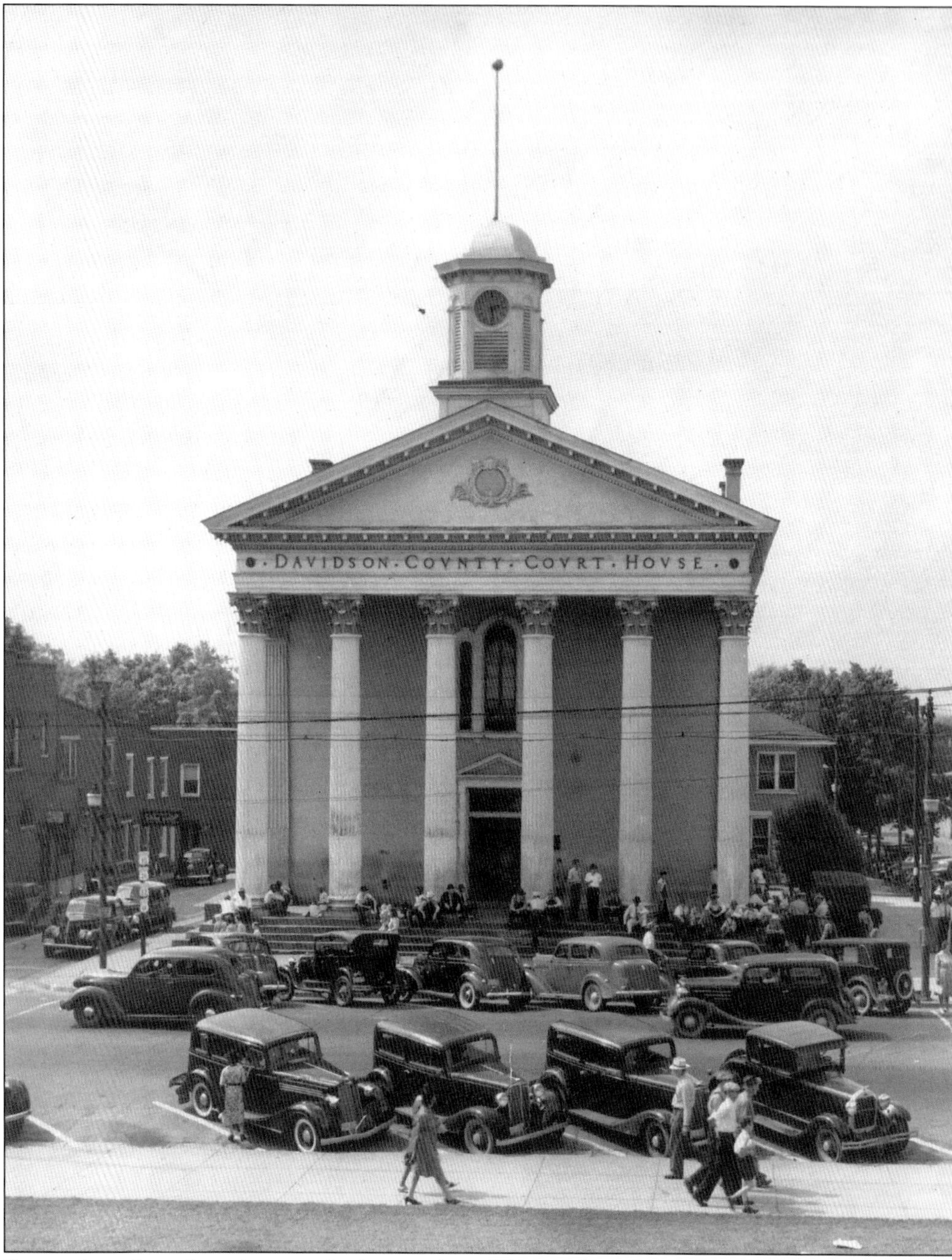

Remember when Saturday was the busiest day of the week in town? It must have been a warm Saturday afternoon when this picture was taken around 1930.

(*on the cover*) The Myers Family Reunion of 1939 was photographed at the Reeds home of Barton Myers.

IMAGES
of America

DAVIDSON COUNTY

Ray Howell
Davidson County Historical Museum

ARCADIA
PUBLISHING

ISBN 978-0-7385-0637-1

Published by Arcadia Publishing
Charleston, South Carolina

Printed in the United States of America

Library of Congress Catalog Card Number: 00-106477

For all general information contact Arcadia Publishing at:
Telephone 843-853-2070
Fax 843-853-0044
E-mail sales@arcadiapublishing.com
For customer service and orders:
Toll-Free 1-888-313-2665

Visit us on the Internet at www.arcadiapublishing.com

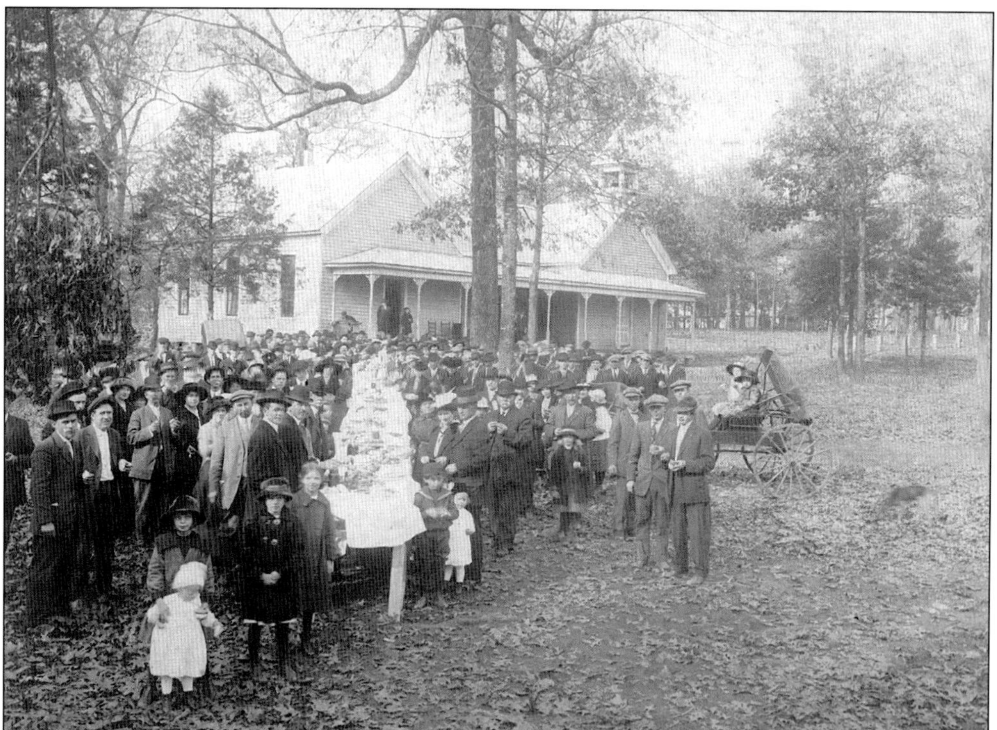

On Thanksgiving Day in 1914, these grateful Davidson County people gathered at Linwood School for an outdoor feast.

Contents

ACKNOWLEDGMENTS

Davidson County has been a collaborative effort with the Davidson County Historical Museum and the good people of this remarkable county.

Public response to the call earlier this year for old pictures was overwhelming. We apologize for the many pictures not included in the book. Nearly 400 pictures were collected, and we simply ran out of room. But each picture has been preserved in the archives of the museum for future generations. My hope is that this project will make people more conscious of the importance of preserving and sharing photographs of their family and community history.

This book would never have happened without the exceptional efforts of Museum Curator Catherine Hoffmann and staff members Pam Daniel and Tonya Sink. The museum staff prepared the materials for publication after they scanned, cataloged, researched, and did pre-production work on hundreds of photographic images in their permanent collection as well as those donated for this project. The technical work was possible because of the generous donation of a digital imaging system by the "Celebrate 2000" business group nearly two years ago. This millennium gift was designed to help make the Museum's permanent collection more accessible to the public, and *Davidson County* seems to fulfill that goal admirably.

Shortly after moving to Lexington in 1990, I was given a copy of Dr. J.C. Leonard's 1927 book *Centennial History of Davidson County North Carolina*. The book has been an inspiration to me, and I consider it an honor to add a footnote to Dr. Leonard's prolific history. *Pathfinders Past and Present*, published in 1927 by M. Jewell Sink and Mary Green Matthews, is an excellent resource filled with detailed information. Another important resource has been the *Dispatch*. Special editions from 1954, 1958, 1968, and 1972 contain a wealth of historical information on Lexington and the county. Joe Sink and his competent staff have been extremely helpful. In addition, the *Thomasville Times* was also very generous and their 1990 Centennial edition provided outstanding historical documentation. Our thanks go to Cinde Ingram for her help in searching their files for photographs. In addition, many pictures were collected and scanned at the Thomasville branch of the Davidson County Public Library—thanks to Librarian Crystal Baird and other helpful staff members.

This is not my first experience with historical photographs. The positive response to *False Alarm at Midnight*, presented at the Smith Civic Center in Lexington on New Year's Eve, 1999, was the catalyst for my involvement with this project. Many folks seemed hungry for more old photos and stories, but my primary inspiration came from people like Howard Mae Hinson, whose father, Howard Michael, was killed in the firetruck wreck of January 1, 1926. Her enthusiasm for the recovery of a fading history made me realize that history itself is a powerful and redemptive story.

We are indebted to the many, many wonderful people of Davidson County who have graciously and generously shared pictures and information, as well as their personal stories. I also wish to thank my church family for their support and encouragement in allowing me to undertake this project.

Finally, I want to thank my dear wife, Joyce, who gave me love, patience, and support—as well as technical advice! We consider it a privilege to call Davidson County home.

—Ray N. Howell III

INTRODUCTION

There is something remarkable about Davidson County, North Carolina. It is a good, rich land with rolling hills, flowing steams, lush forests, and lovely lakes. The Sapona Indians called this land home long before the white settlers appeared.

This is the land that attracted Scot-Irish immigrants in the early-1700s and the Protestant Germans a few years later. They settled at places named Jersey and Abbotts Creek and on the banks of the Yadkin River. Squire Boone brought his family here with his 16-year-old son, Daniel.

Those early settlers would not recognize the Davidson County of today. Sprawling subdivisions, interstate highways, railroad tracks, airports, radio towers, towns, villages, and an expansive lake—Davidson County has changed!

This book is a pictorial record of many of the changes over the past 100 years or so. For many of you, these pictures will spark your memory and bring back scenes and events that have been long forgotten. This is a journey through the lens of the past. Behind every picture is a story. Within each story is a person. Inside of every person is the gift of life. The pictures presented within these pages are full of life—the life we have come to know and love in Davidson County.

There are many more stories that are waiting to be told. Tucked away in boxes in the back of closets and attics are countless numbers of historic pictures that need to be preserved. This book is only the beginning. We will wait for the untold stories to be shared.

Yes, there is something remarkable about Davidson County. You will learn about our children's homes and mill villages; our landmarks and our claims to fame—but the remarkable truth about Davidson County is not found in what we have accomplished, it is found in who we are. We are the people who call Davidson County home.

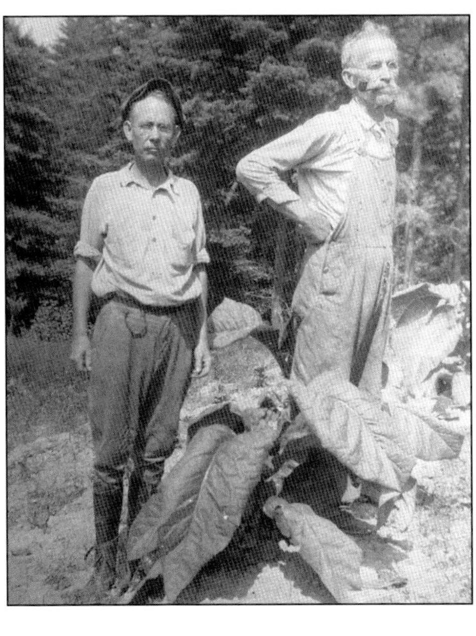

One

Around Court Square

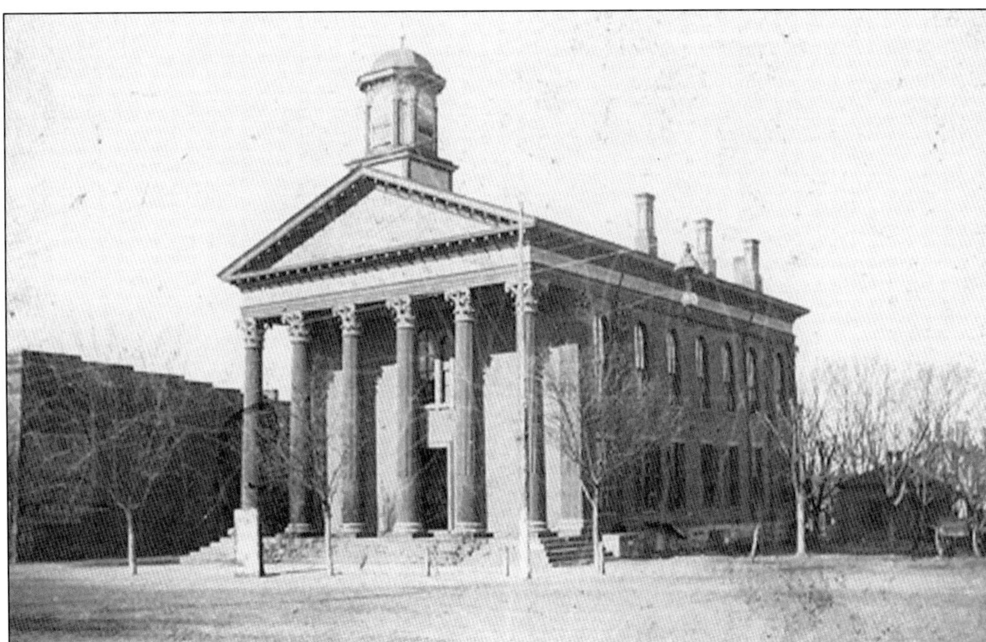

The old Davidson County Courthouse was completed in 1858 at a cost of $20,000. A disastrous fire in November 1865 necessitated repairs that were completed in 1868. The cause of the fire was never determined, although Union troops occupying the building were blamed. The imposing structure is of Greek Revival/Italianate Revival design, and it represents one of the best examples of this style in the southeastern United States. The large granite blocks on each side of the front portico were reportedly used for selling slaves before the war. The name of the building was not added until a 1918 remodeling. The building served as the county courthouse until 1958, and since 1976 has been home to the Davidson County Historical Museum.

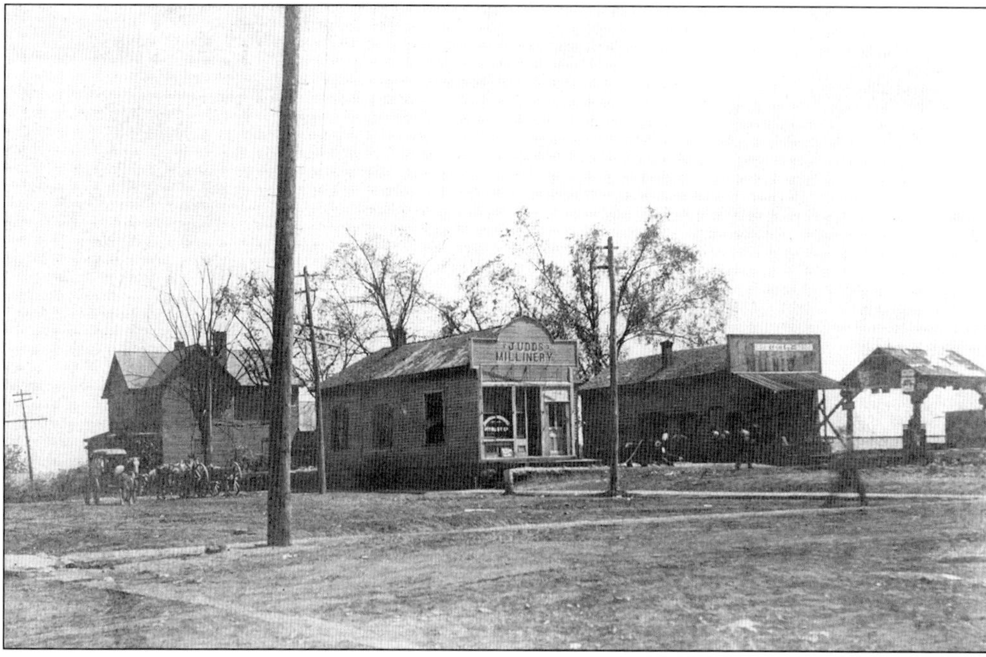

This is the southeast quadrant of Court Square in 1900. Lexington was a small town of 1,400 people at the turn of the century, but there was still a demand for hats. Behind Judd's Millinery is the home of J.H. Greer. Note the Coca-Cola sign on the store to the right.

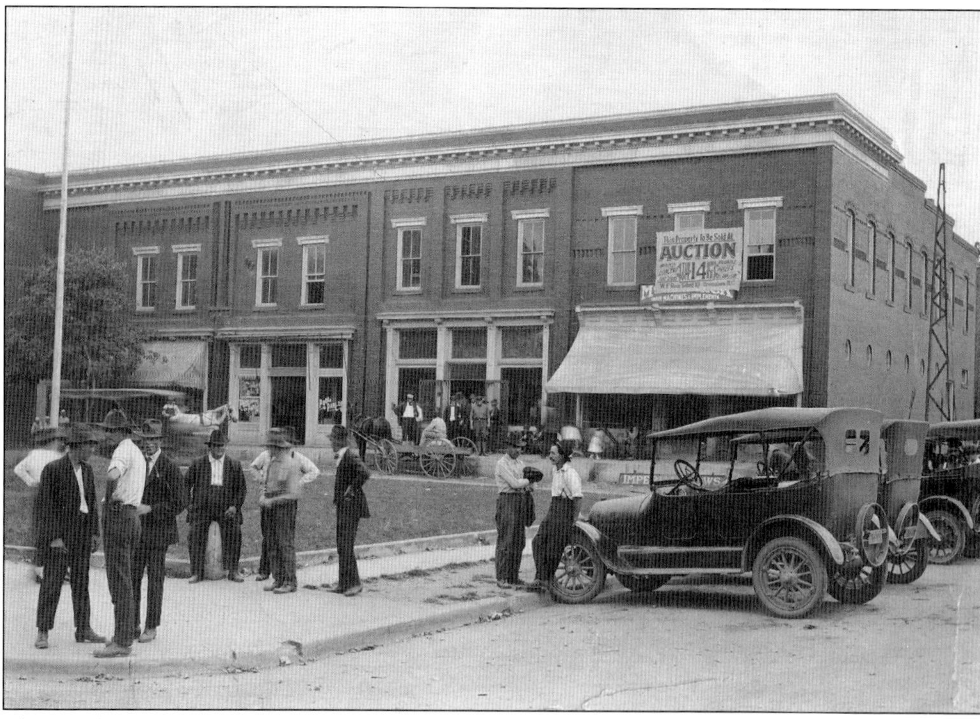

The northeast quadrant of Court Square is pictured here in the early 1910s. Note the mixture of horse-drawn buggies and horse-less carriages. The building on the right had been altered significantly by the 1920s, as is evidenced by the picture on p. 11.

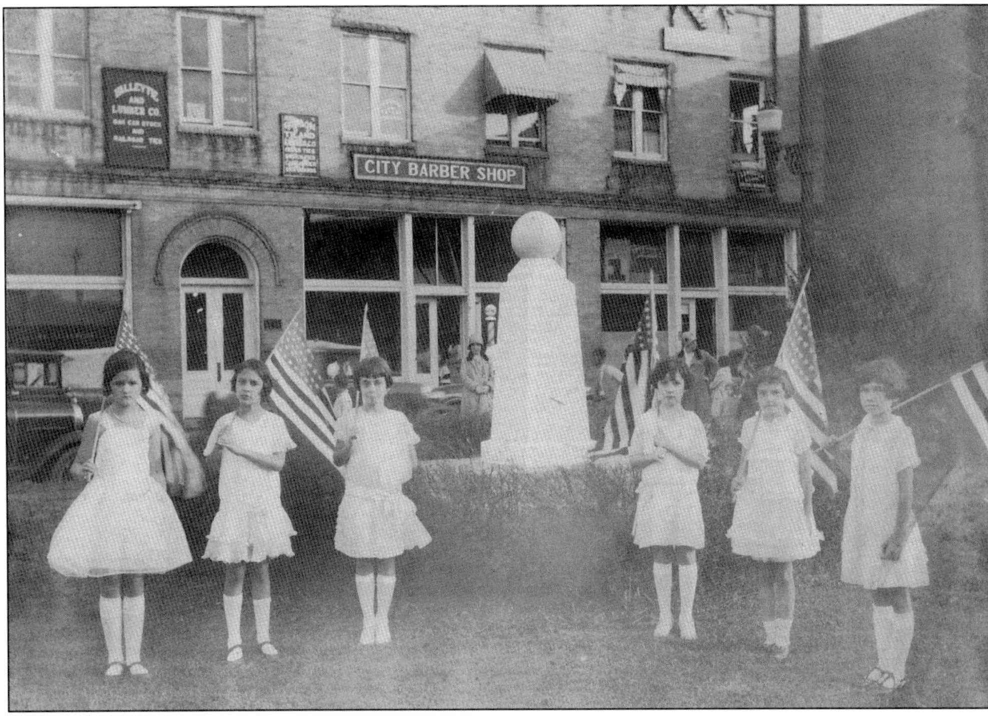

Lexington celebrated its centennial in 1928 with the unveiling of this monument on the southeast quadrant of Court Square. The patriotic girls in their pretty white dresses are, from left to right, Mary Martin Hinkle, Betsy Mountcastle Garrett, Mae Vestal Leonard Curtis, Margaret Spruill Smith, Jessie Clodfelter Moylette, and Jean Witherspoon. Behind them you can see the Development Building, which faces Main Street. The monument, minus the ball on the top, now rests on the northwest quadrant of Court Square.

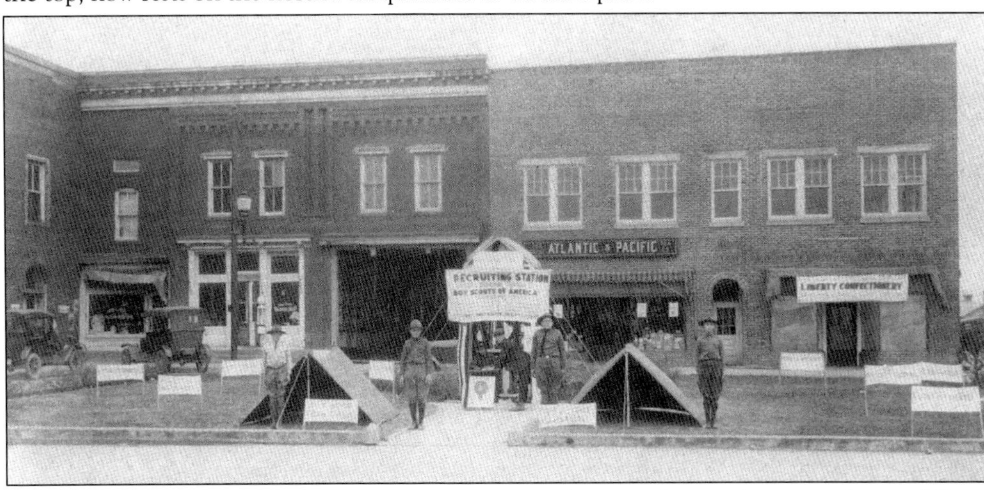

The Lexington Boy Scouts were recruiting new members on the northeast quadrant of Court Square in this early-1920s picture. Dwight L. Pickard recalled that in 1918 when he was 12, a group of boys met at the home of Mr. and Mrs. John Hunt on the corner of South State Street and West Fifth Avenue to discuss organizing a Boy Scout troop. Soon the first Boy Scout troop was formally organized at First Baptist Church on South Main Street. Mr. Pickard, who served as a lawyer with the state of North Carolina for many years, was a member of the original troop.

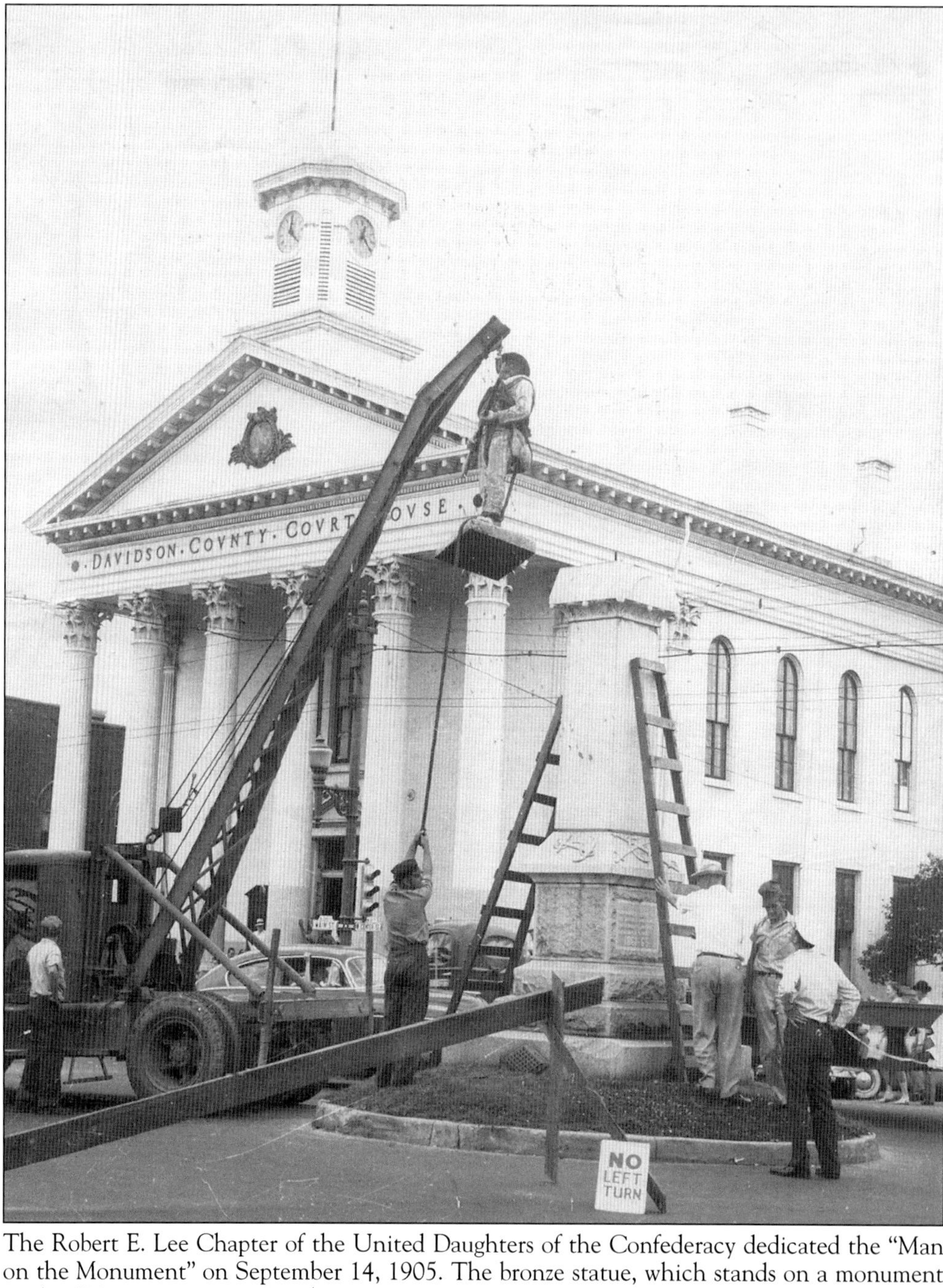

The Robert E. Lee Chapter of the United Daughters of the Confederacy dedicated the "Man on the Monument" on September 14, 1905. The bronze statue, which stands on a monument made of Vermont granite, cost $2,025. For 45 years, the old Confederate soldier stood watch in the very center of Court Square at the intersection of Main and Center Streets. In July 1950, the old soldier was moved out of the center of the square. He had suffered many indignities, being knocked from his 22-foot-high perch numerous times by careless drivers. Through the years, he suffered a broken head, broken arms and legs, and a broken musket. In 1993, the statue was cleaned and restored. He still stands watch today across the street from the courthouse that predates his war.

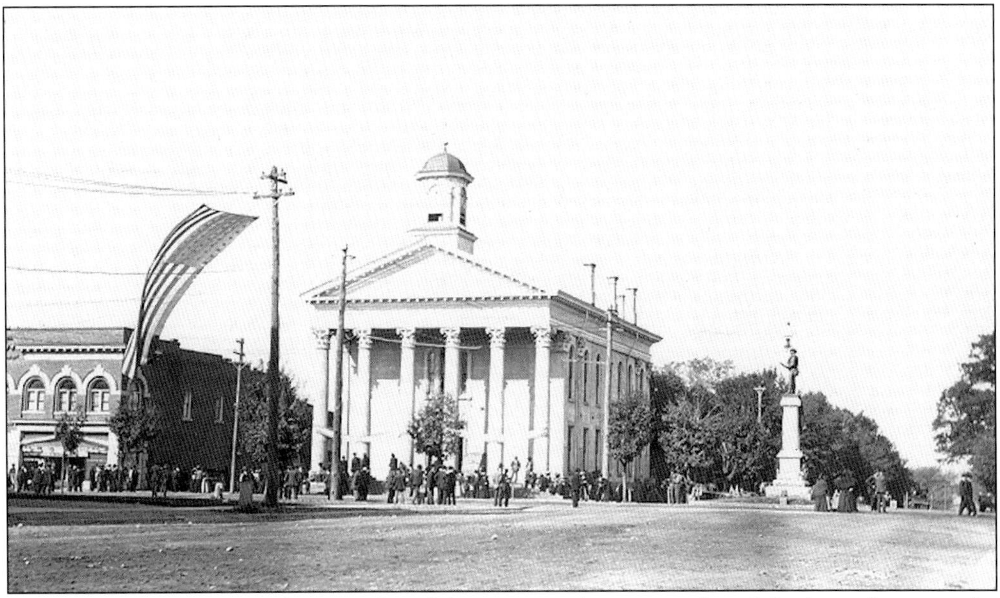

L.A. Martin, lawyer, legislator, and prolific writer, is best remembered for his column in the *Dispatch* "Around Court Square." He describes the old courthouse and Court Square with these words: "This old building has an atmosphere through the years that gives it the flavor of 'Town Hall.' Here I have attended all kinds of public meetings and rallies and political conventions. It was here I was first nominated for public office."

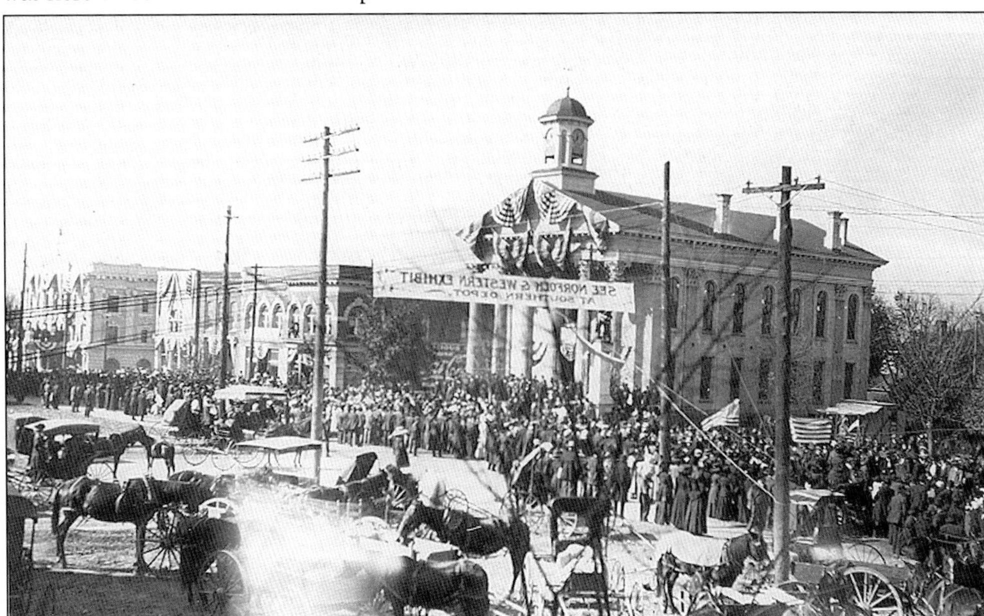

"Court Square is part of my being and I love it. I love even the scars of battle I have received here. I love the memories of the horse traders and the patent medicine vendors who until shortly after the turn of the century were a part of the scene around the watering troughs and the hitching posts on the Square . . . It was here I heard William Jennings Bryan deliver his famous lecture on the 'Prince of Peace.' It was here through the years I have known and loved my professional associates."

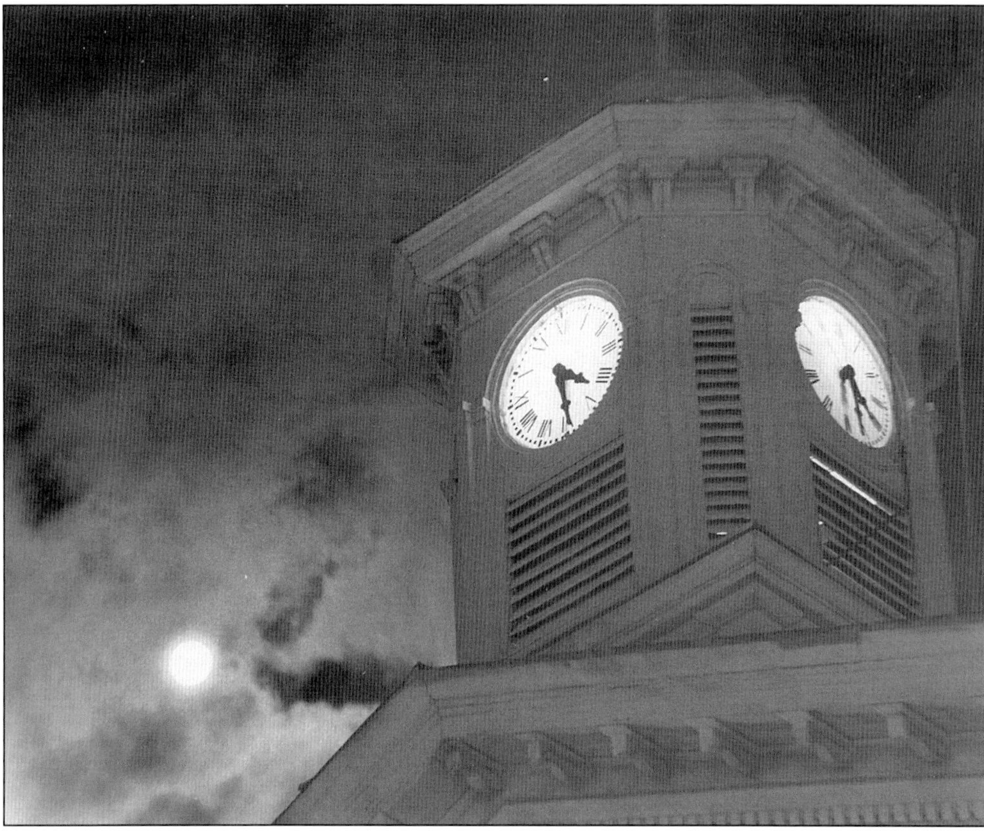

"I love the faithfulness of the old clock in the courthouse belfry, and its way of heralding out the time with its obliging sounds in the small hours of the night."

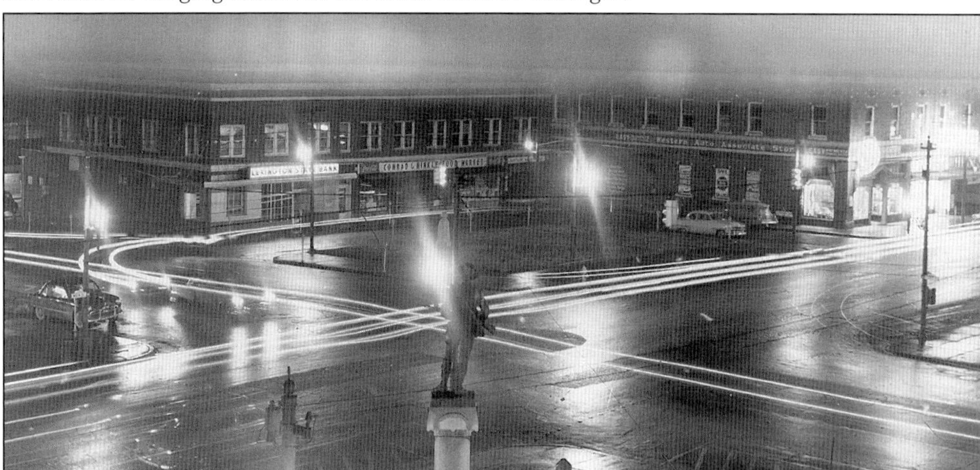

"Yes, my answer is simple and direct. I love Court Square because my life has been spent here. Professionally it opened here and professionally it will close here. Here I will die and close by I will be buried."

"And when I fall on sleep may eternity forbid that I shall ever forget or lose the tender memories I hold for Court Square, or let fade the love and affection I have borne for those with whom I have labored here!"

Two

DOWNTOWN

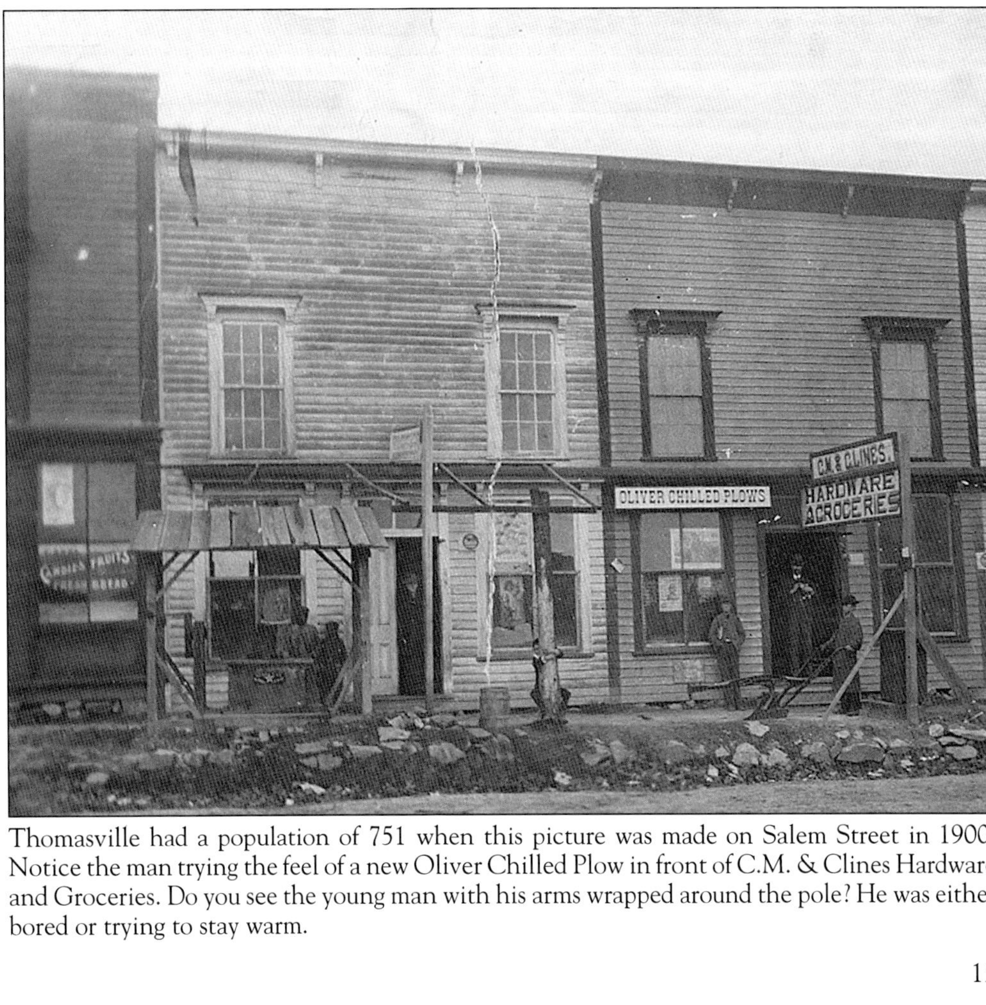

Thomasville had a population of 751 when this picture was made on Salem Street in 1900. Notice the man trying the feel of a new Oliver Chilled Plow in front of C.M. & Clines Hardware and Groceries. Do you see the young man with his arms wrapped around the pole? He was either bored or trying to stay warm.

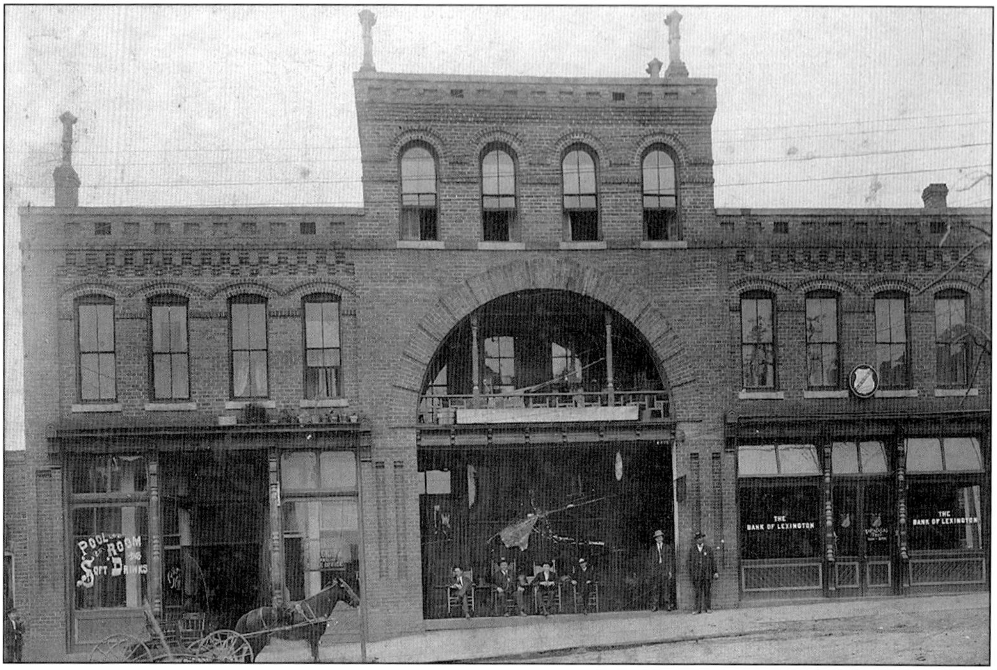

This is the old March Hotel in Lexington, built in the late 1800s. Shortly before the hotel burned in 1909, the Lexington Board of Trade held an extravagant luncheon to attract new business and industry. The international menu was designed to show Lexington's appeal to the world at large. The first course was grapes and bananas, which was followed by German dill pickles and three kinds of barbecue—lamb, pig, and opossum with Saratoga chips. Coffee and cigars made the meal complete.

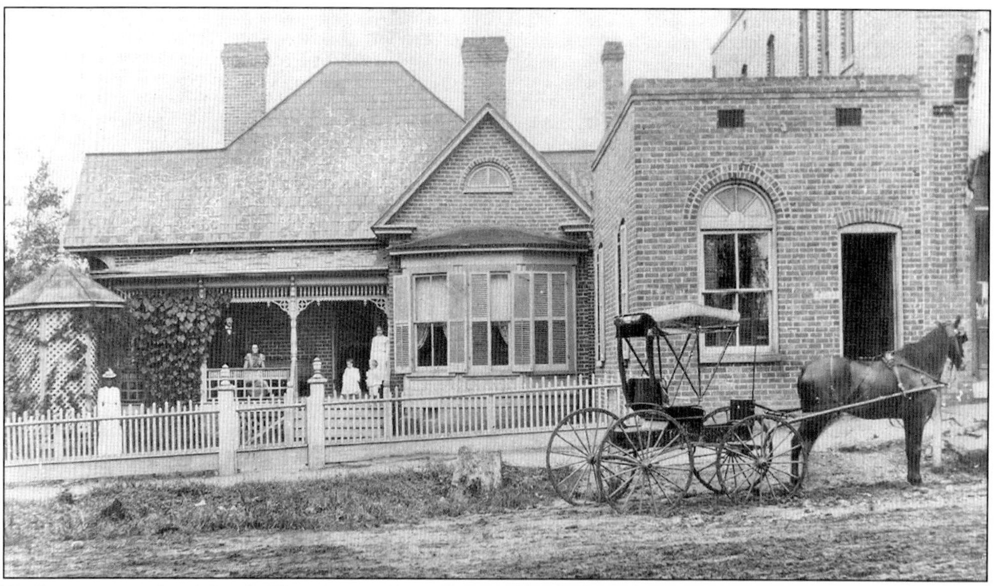

Right next to the March Hotel was the office of Dr. John Thomas, a general physician in the early 1900s. The brick home belonged to the Springs family, who were operating the hotel at the time. Miss Lillie Springs is standing behind the fence, with her family on the front porch. This picture would have been taken before 1909, the year the old March Hotel burned.

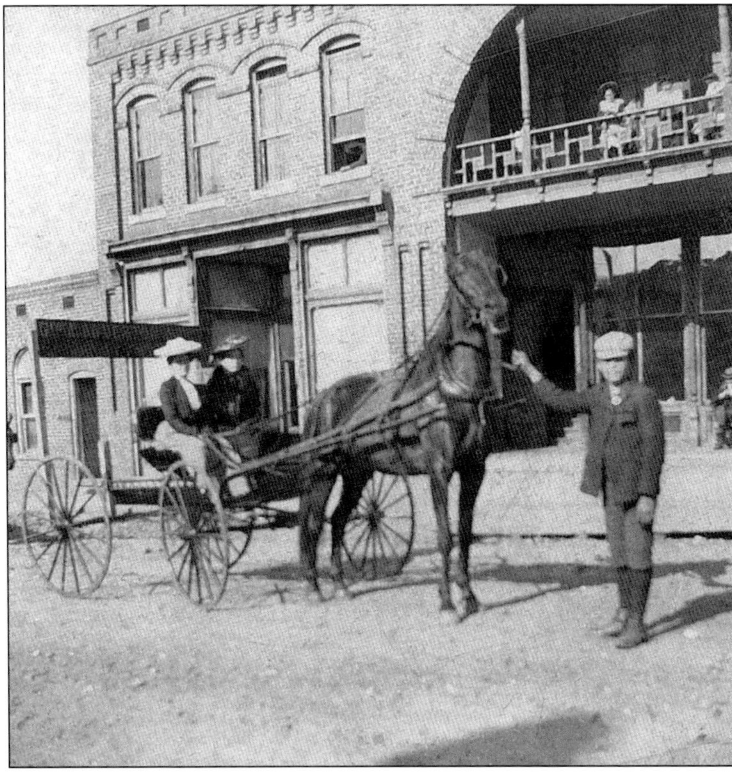

This is a rare picture of the old March Hotel in Lexington. There was actually an older March Hotel, a wooden structure on this site that burned sometime in the late 1800s. Seated in the buggy are Ida Beeson and Mag Slaughter. The young man holding the horse is unidentified. Note the ladies seated on the second-floor veranda.

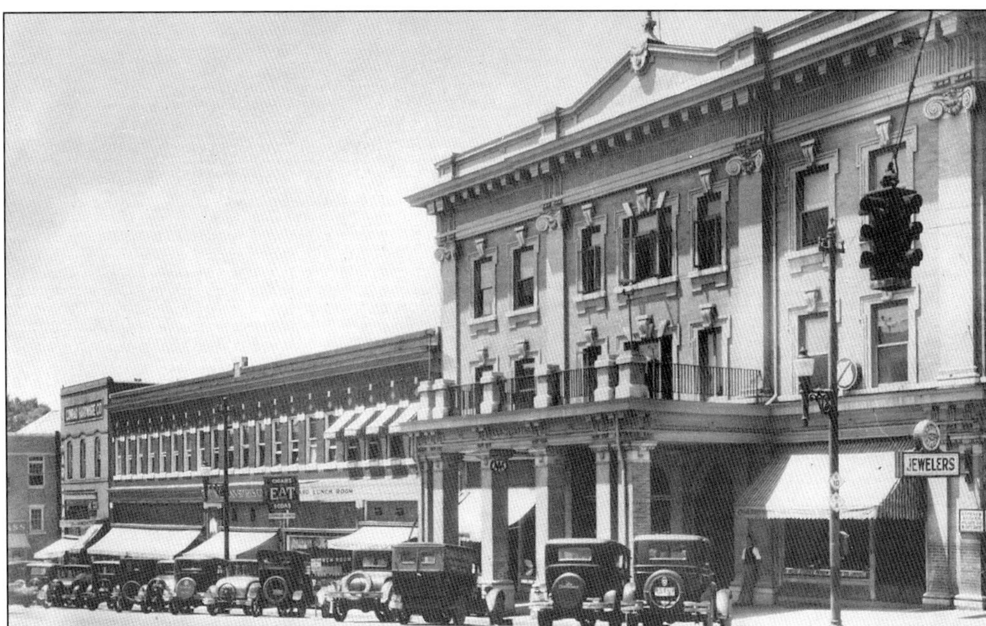

The "new" March Hotel, built following the 1909 fire, was a great social center in Lexington for well over half a century. The Rotary Club met here on Tuesdays and the Kiwanis Club on Thursdays. The building remains one of the most beautiful in downtown Lexington with its Renaissance Revival design.

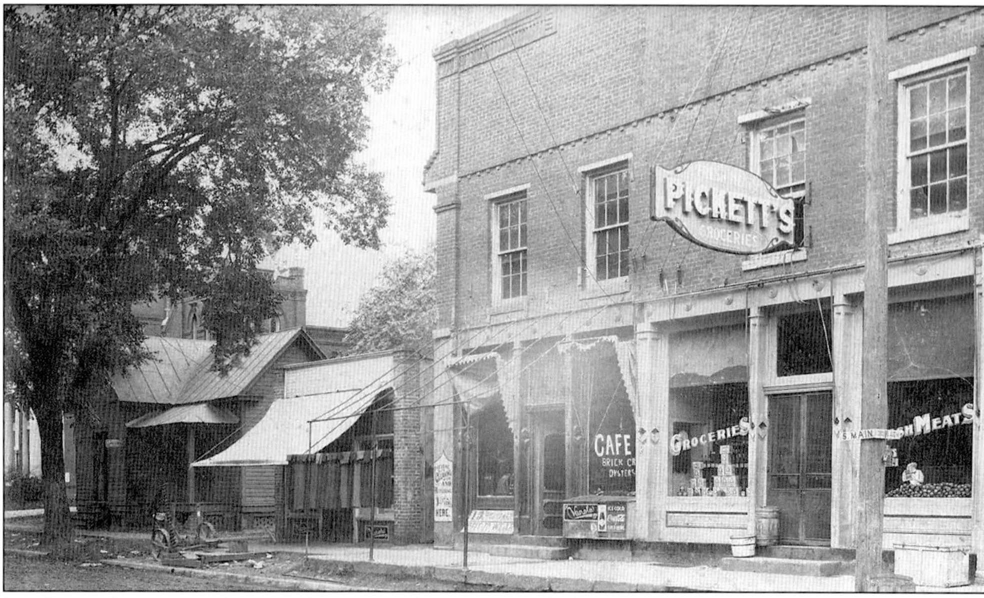

In the early 1900s, O.P. and E.A. Pickett operated this grocery store, which was a favorite shopping place for many Lexington residents. Pickett's Groceries was located at the corner of South Main and West Second Avenue. The building to the left with the awning was Dr. E.J. Buchanan's old office. He later built an office across the street next to his lovely home. You can see the old First Methodist Church beyond the tree. The Siceloff/Buchanan building stands today on the site of Pickett's Groceries.

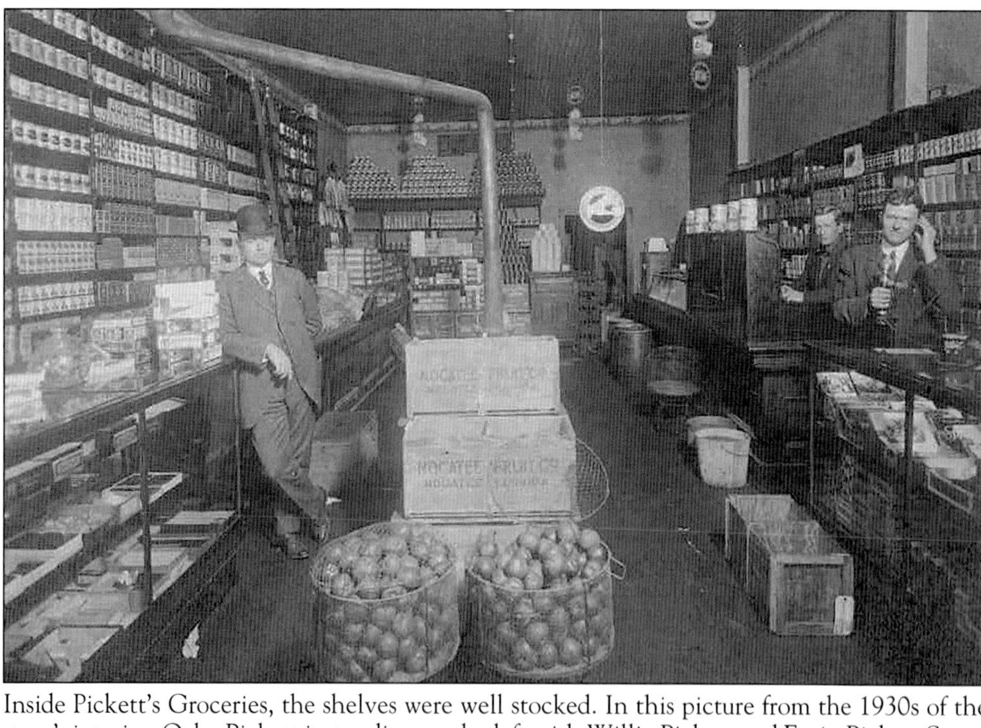

Inside Pickett's Groceries, the shelves were well stocked. In this picture from the 1930s of the store's interior, Ocko Pickett is standing on the left with Willie Pickett and Ervin Pickett Sr. on the right behind the counter.

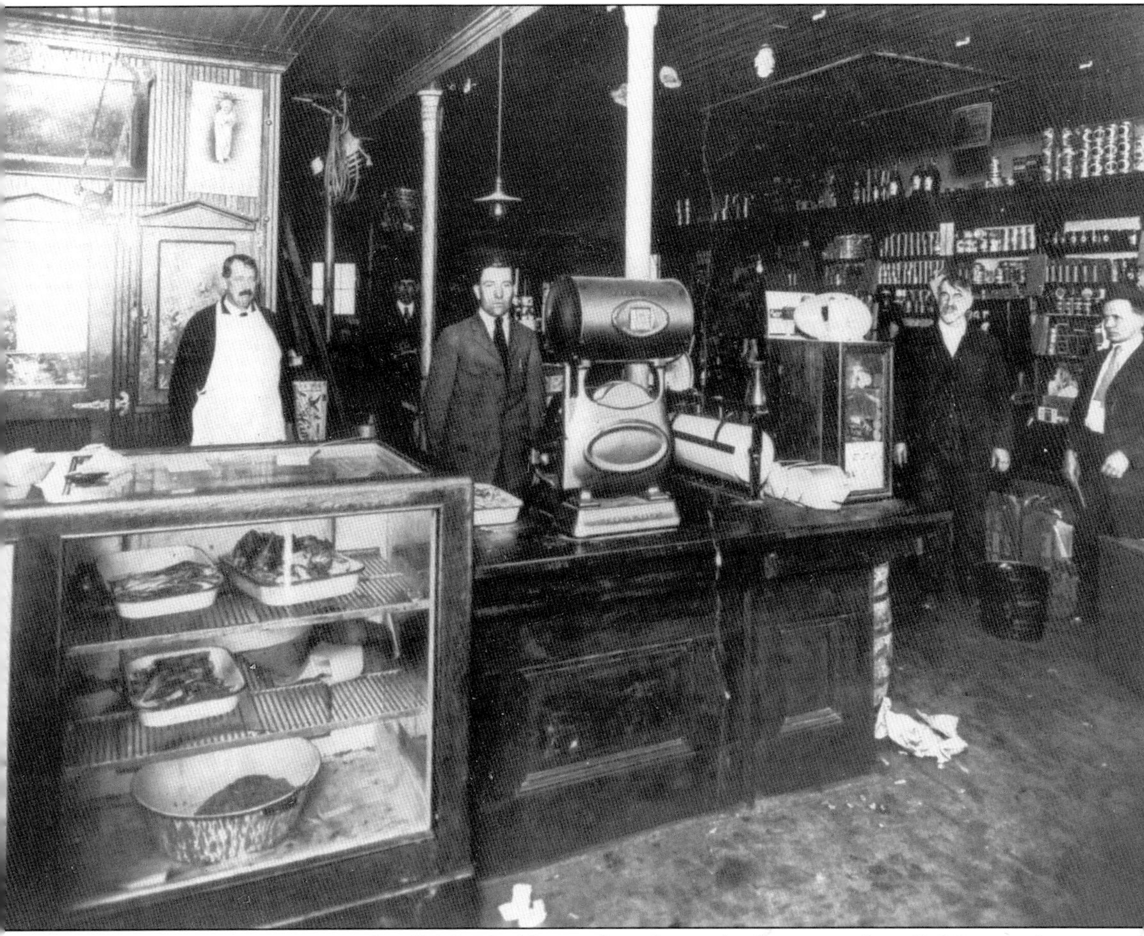

In February 1919, W.E. Conrad and E.O. Hinkle purchased a stock of groceries from R.I. Leonard and started a grocery store on the square. This is Conrad and Hinkle around 1927. W.E. Conrad (white apron) and Odell Hinkle (behind counter) remained as partners in the grocery business until 1934. Conrad and Hinkle were pioneers in frozen foods, becoming the first grocery store in North Carolina to install individual steel lockers in the large freezer and to process meat for individuals. The two men to the right in this 1927 picture are J.E. Link and S.O. Hege.

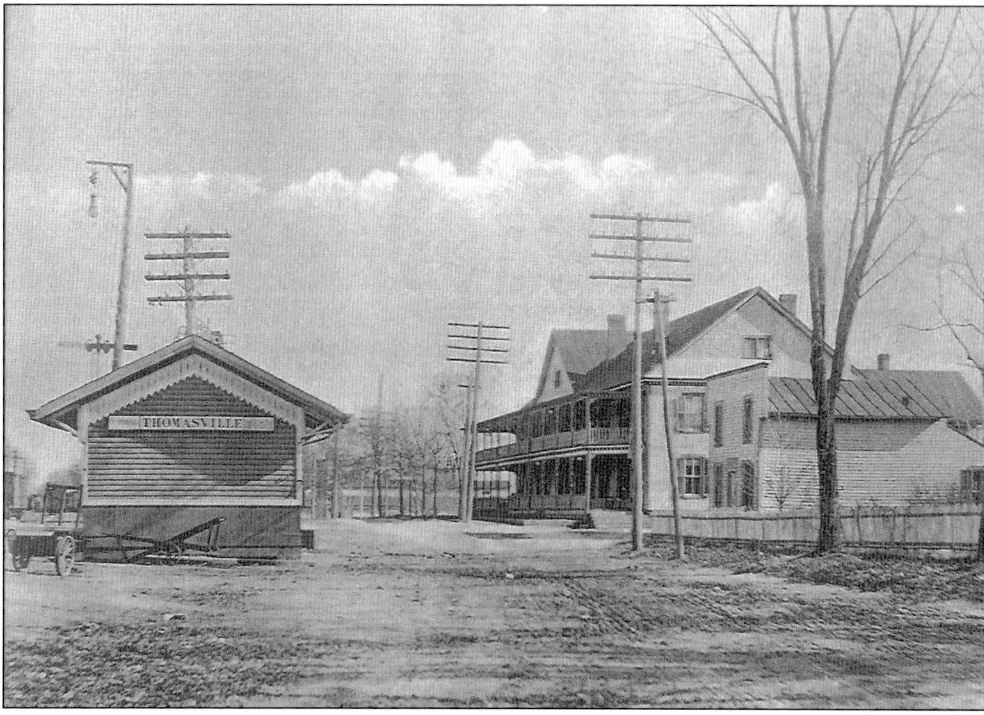

Thomasville was built around the railroad, completed in 1855. One of the first buildings in Thomasville was the Lewis L. Thomas Hotel, which also served as a ticket office for the railroad. In 1879, John A. Mock purchased a hotel from Mrs. Cynthia Clouse on the south side of the railroad. The Mock Hotel is pictured here following an 1890 renovation. This building, which had 40 rooms, burned in 1892.

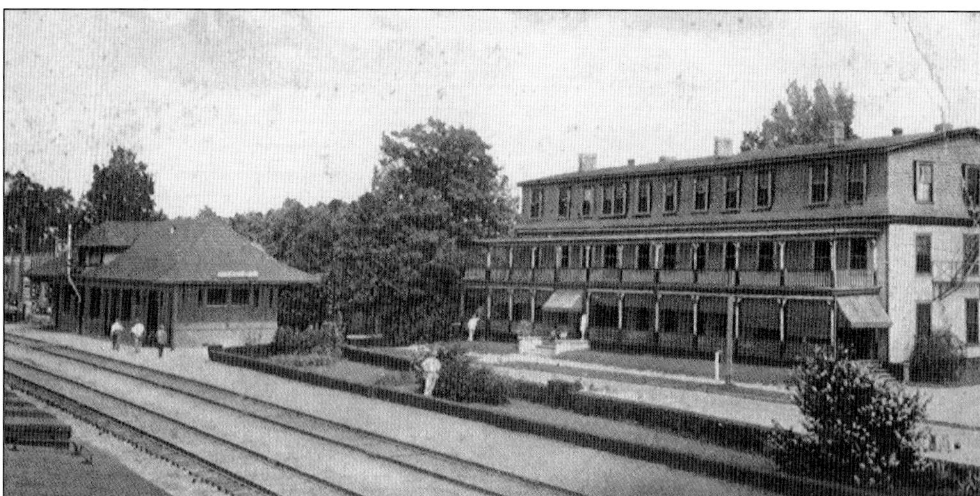

This is the new Mock Hotel, built in 1892 following the fire. Situated beside the passenger station, the Mock Hotel was the first stop for many visitors to the "Chair City" in the early 20th century. The Mock family operated the hotel until 1929, when it was leased to Mr. and Mrs. Dewey Skeen, who changed the name to the Baywood Hotel. On September 17, 1939, a fire destroyed the hotel completely. In 1947, the Skeens opened the Morning Glory on the site. The popular restaurant became home to the "Skeen Burger," a Thomasville tradition.

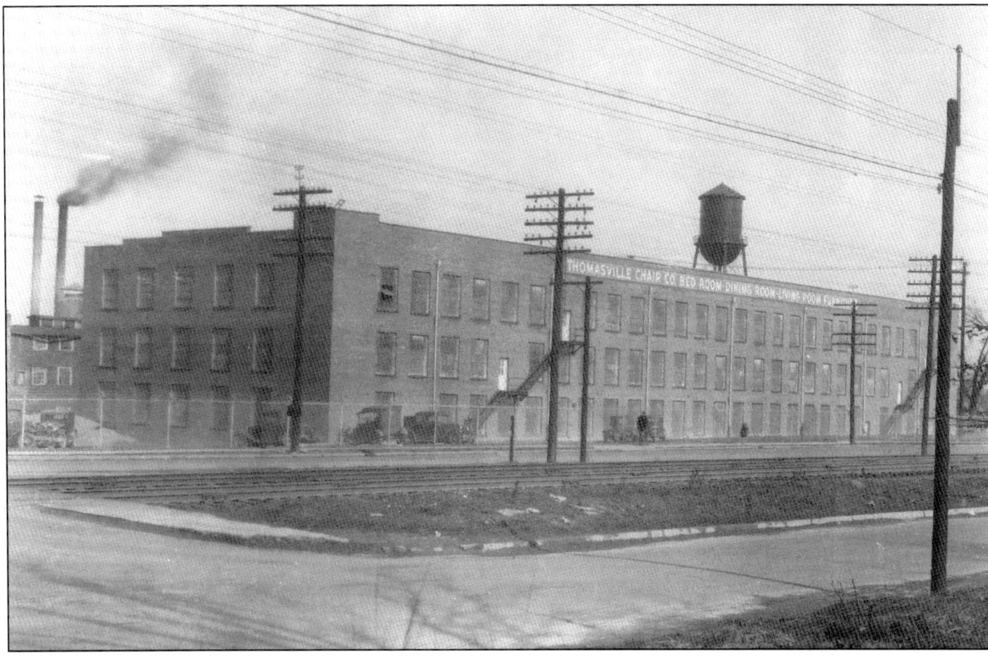

The Thomasville Chair Company was founded by the Finch family in 1904. The factory manufactured bedroom, dining room, living room, and dinette furniture and boasted over one million square feet of floor space.

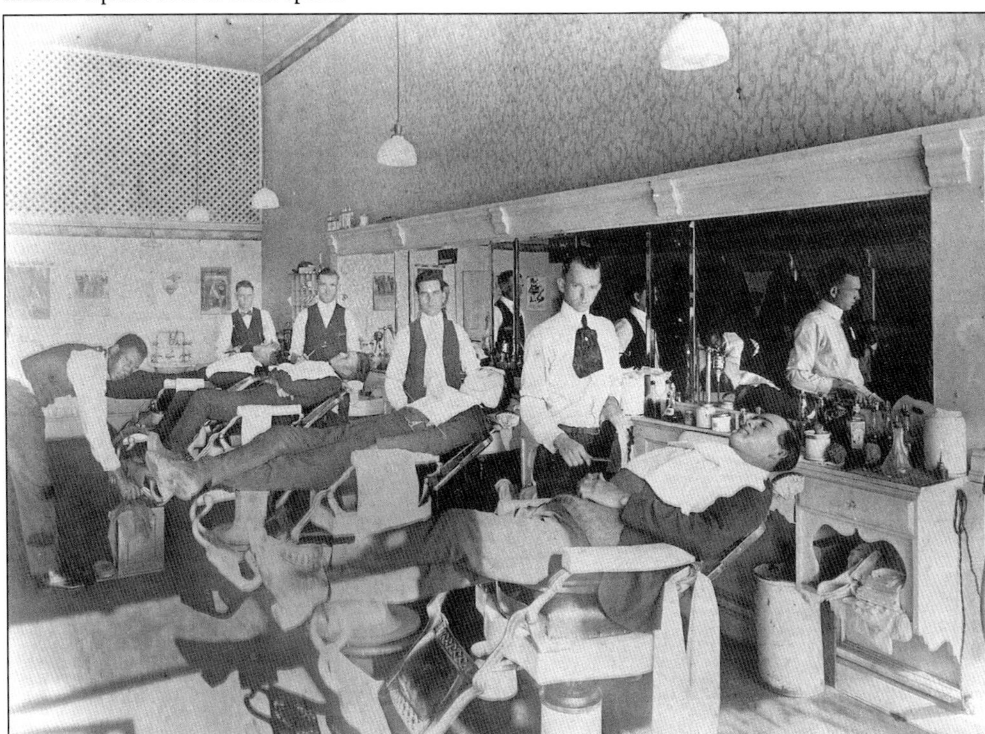

There is nothing like a shave and a haircut at the barbershop. Would you call this a barbershop quartet?

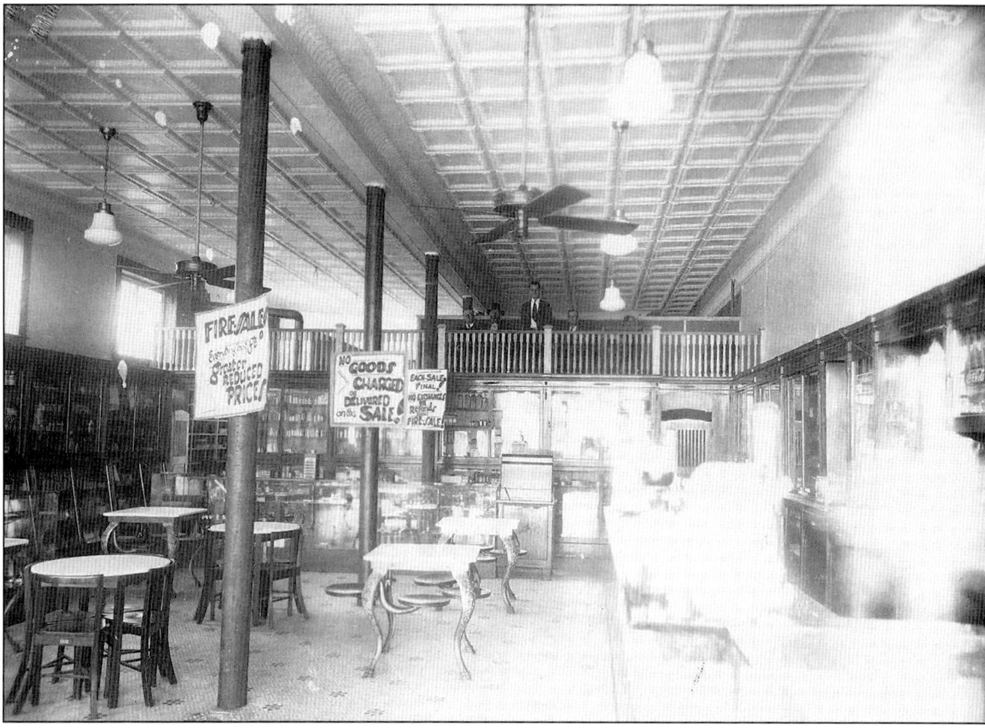

The Harville Drug Store stood on the corner of Salem Street and East Main Street in Thomasville. The store was a popular gathering place for local residents. In 1931, Mr. Harville sold his business to Mann Drug Company. The picture below shows the interior of the store in the 1930s.

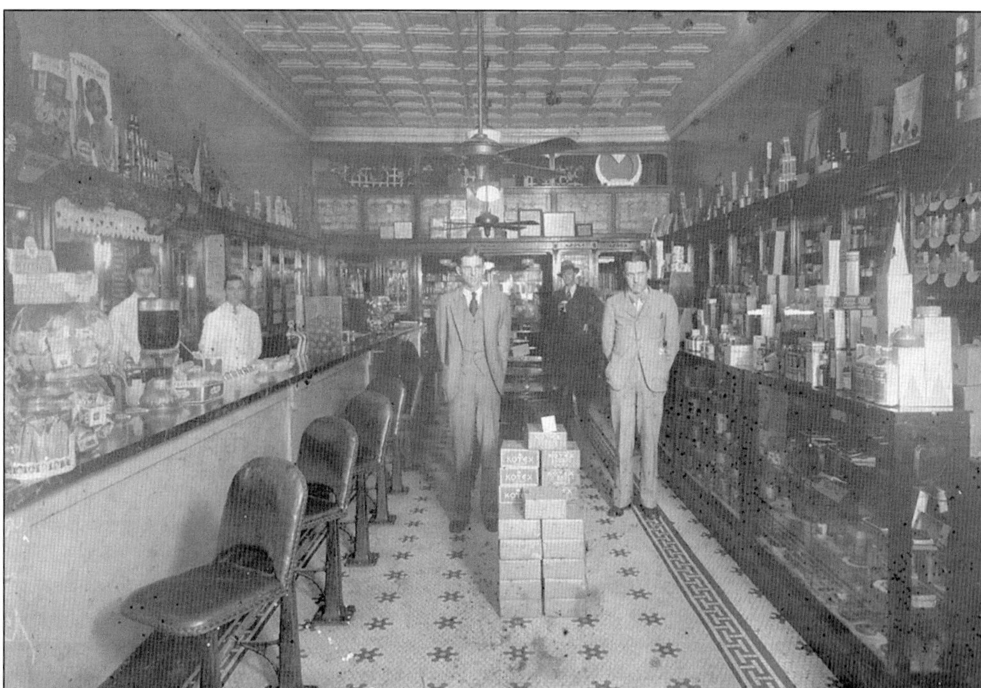

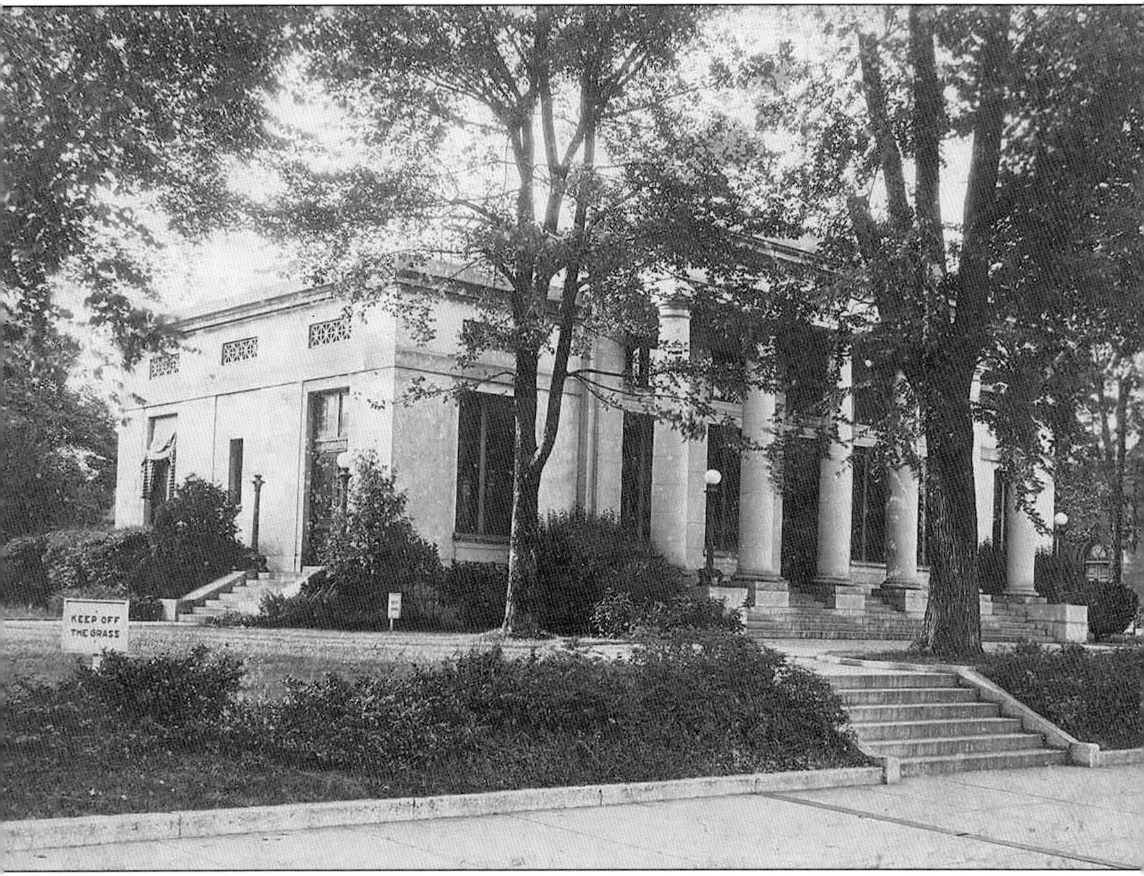

The old Lexington Post Office was built in 1912 on the site of the old Adderton house, which had been constructed before the Civil War. A bitter political fight resulted in Mrs. Martha Adderton accepting $15,000 for the lot at the corner of South Main Street and West Third Avenue. The house was actually moved across West Third Avenue behind the First Presbyterian Church. The Neoclassical Revival stone building cost $50,000. Six large Tuscan columns form a portico on the facade. The building housed the Davidson County Public Library from the mid-1960s until 1986. Today the old post office is home to Arts United for Davidson County.

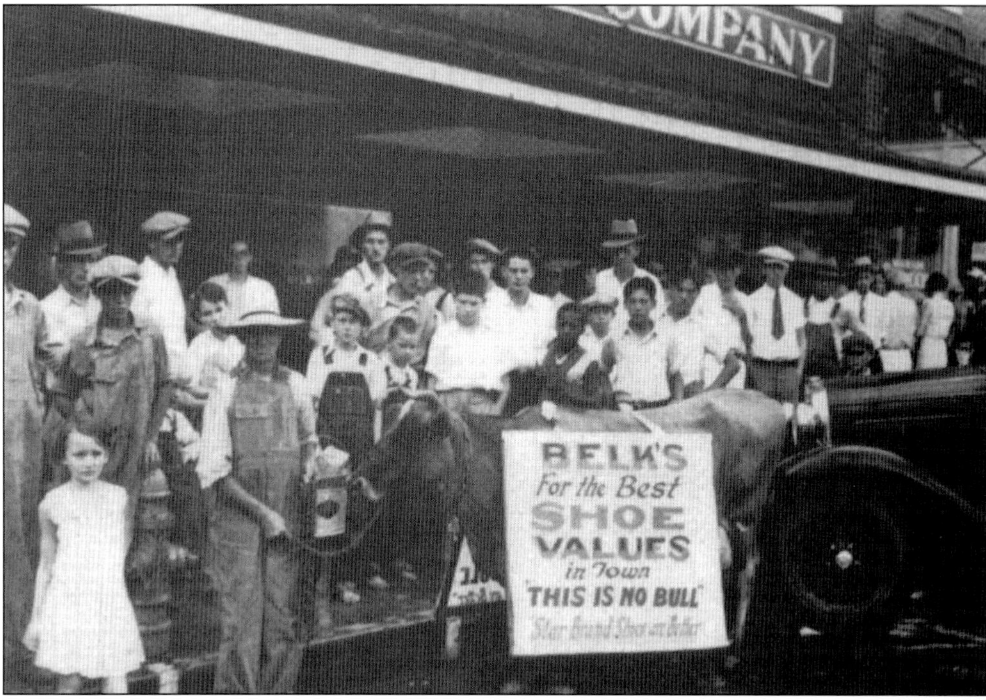

The bull appears to have drawn a crowd outside Thomasville's Hudson-Belk store in 1934. We don't know how many shoes were sold, but no one could ignore the sale!

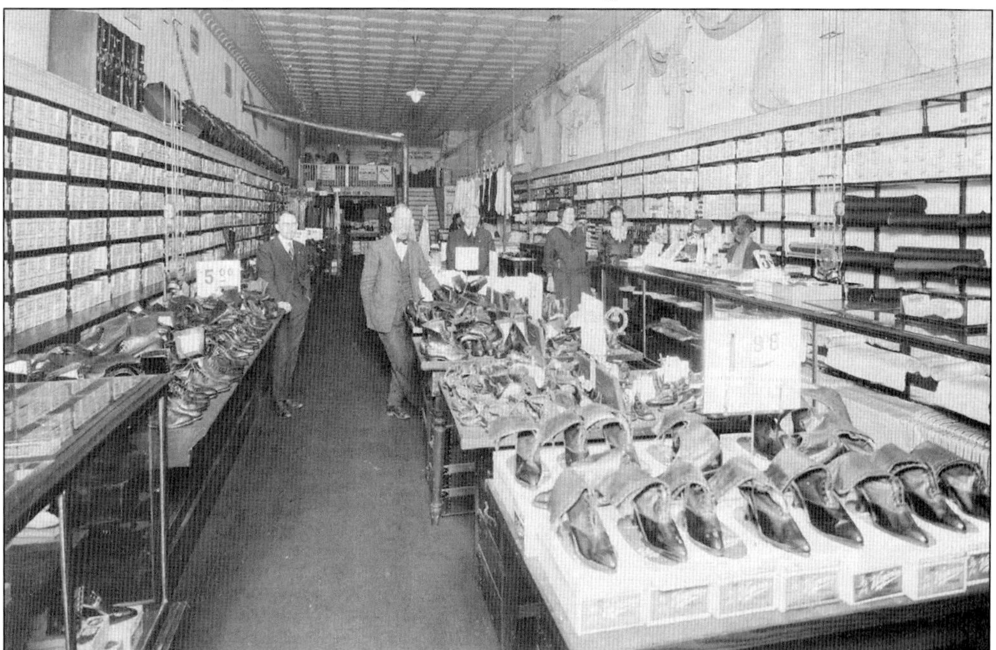

Efird's Department Store was a favorite shopping place for Lexington residents. Note the "tracks" on the walls used to send money and tickets to the office at the rear of the store. The first store opened in 1919 and in 1928 moved to a new store in the Buchanan-Siceloff block across Main Street.

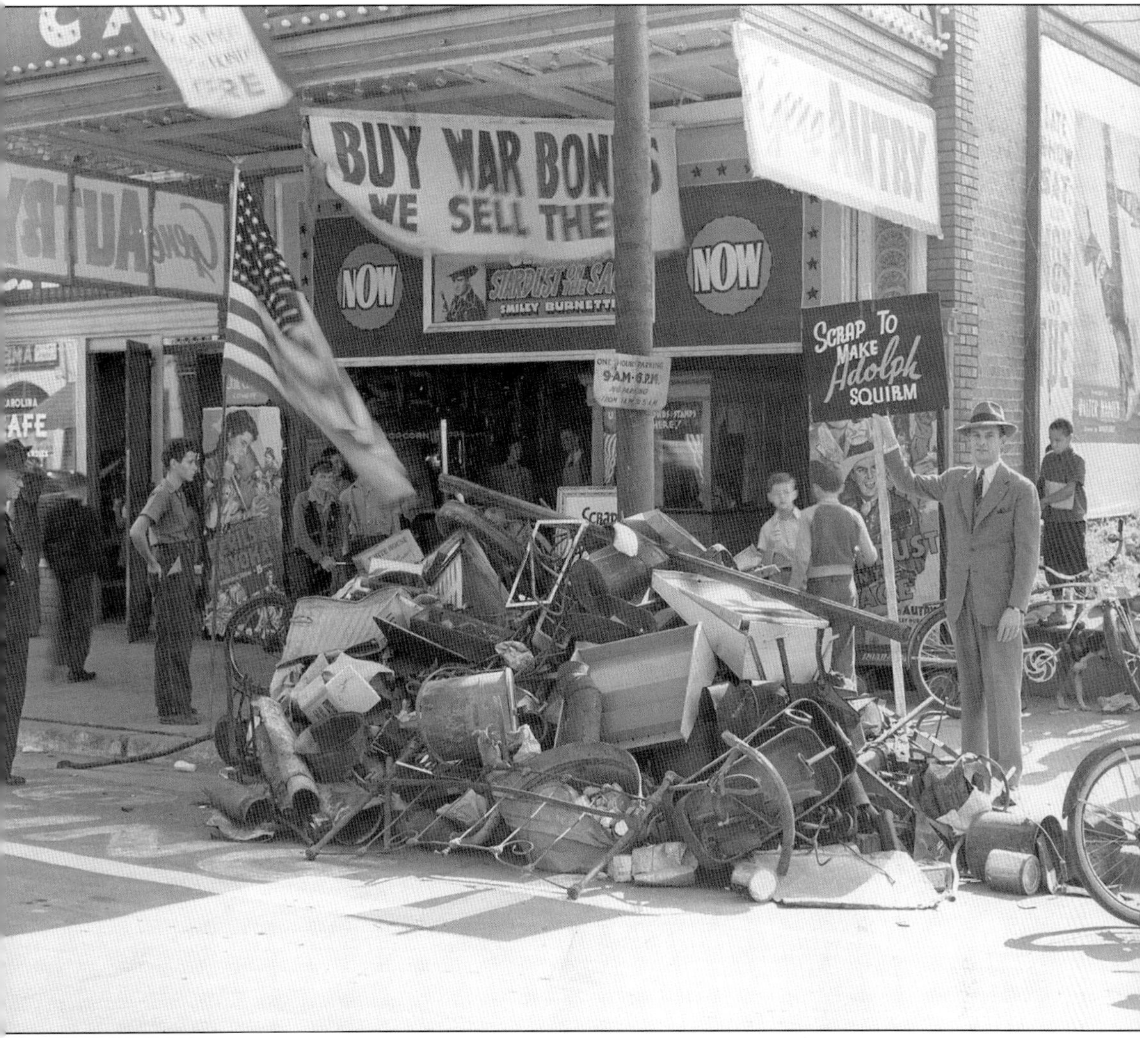

After World War II began, the good people of Davidson County joined in the war effort. This was a scrap metal drive in front of the Carolina Theater in Lexington. People also gave to the Red Cross relief effort and purchased war bonds.

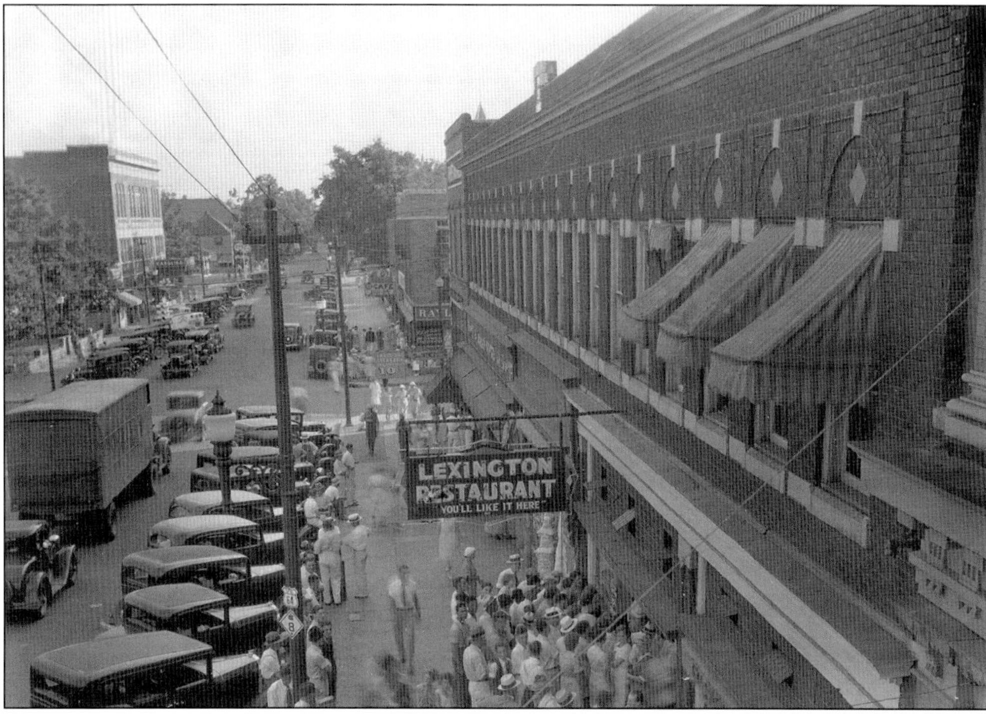

Downtown Lexington was a busy place to be in the late 1920s. You can tell a good place to eat by the crowd out front.

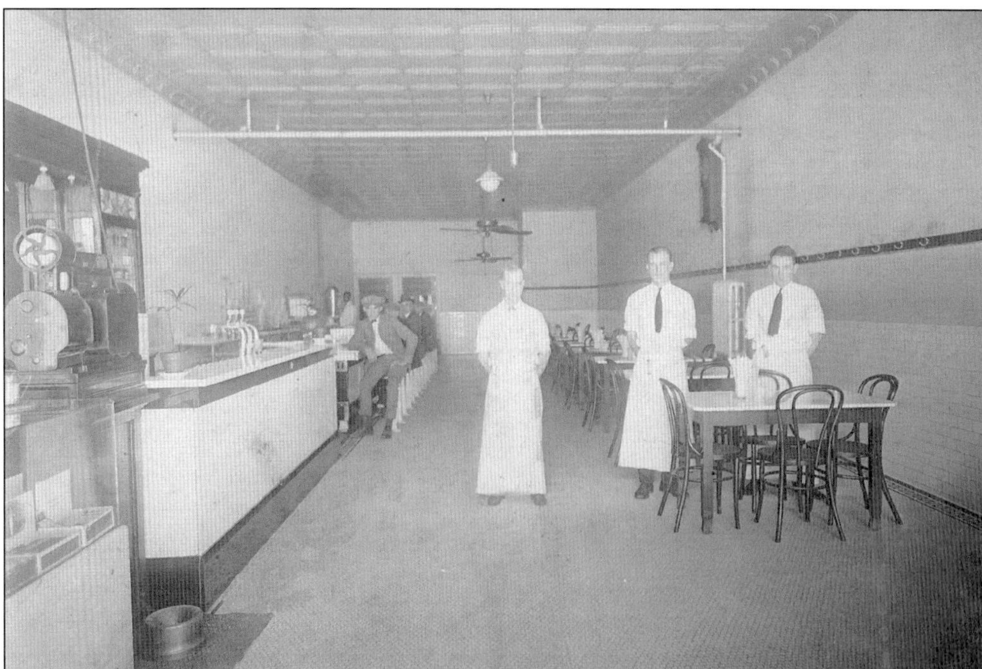

Jim Leonard's Café was a popular Lexington lunchroom in the 1920s. It was located on South Main Street, down from the March Hotel. Standing from left to right in this c. 1921 picture are Sidney Grady Underwood, Red Stout, and Gray Sowers.

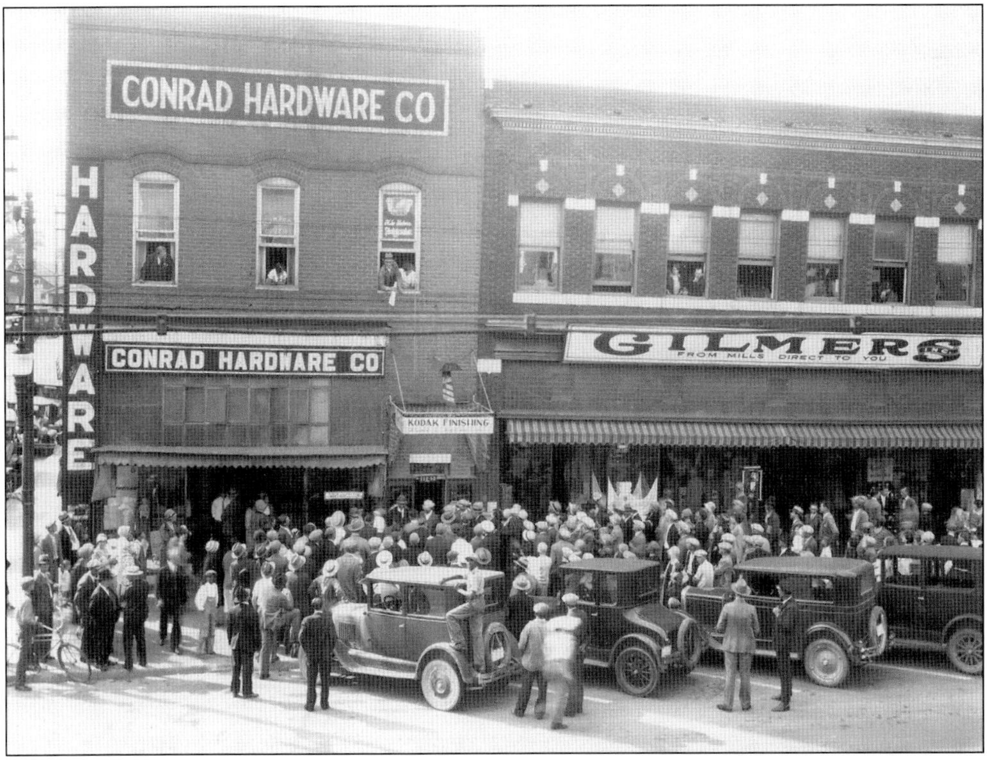

Something exciting seems to be happening near the H.L. Waters Studio, located between the Conrad Hardware Company and Gilmers. Waters was a well-known photographer who maintained his downtown location for over 65 years. His studio portraits, movies, school pictures, and commercial work touched many lives in Davidson County and the surrounding area and represent an amazing record of the 20th century. Many of his privately held photographs have been preserved by the Davidson County Historical Museum.

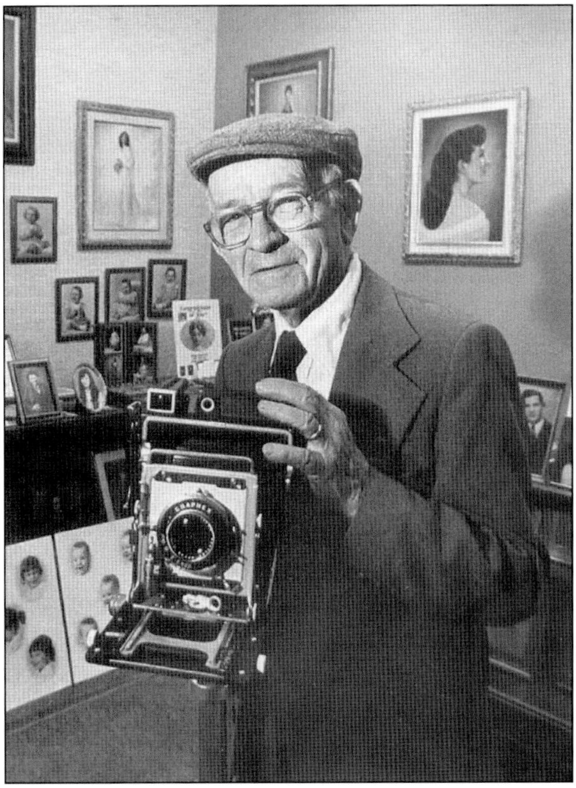

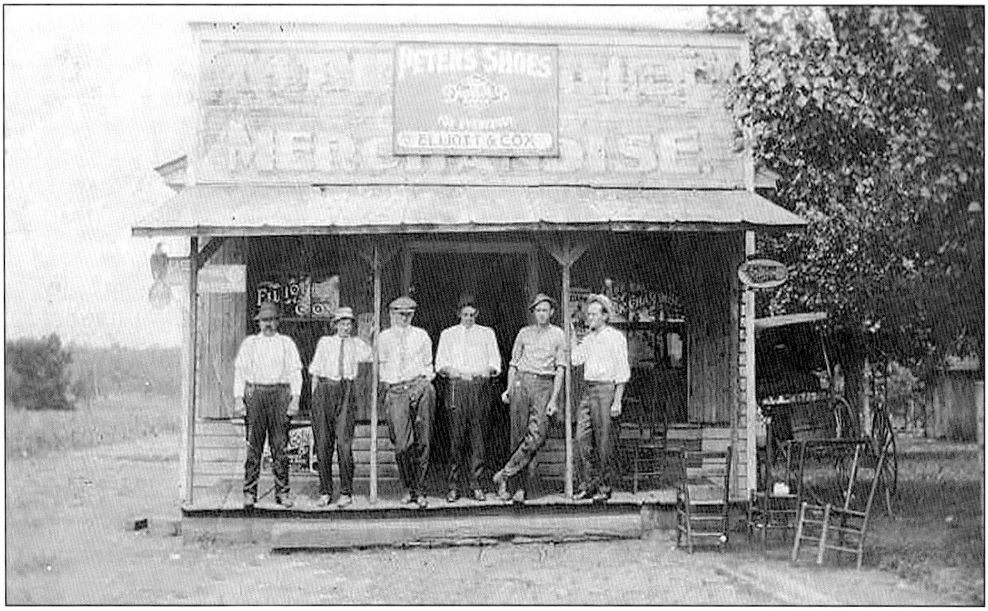

Not everyone lived in town, so country stores were also popular places to gather for country folks. Here, six fellows pose for the camera at the Elliott and Cox Store in Linwood. Although the date of the photograph may be in question, the chairs beside the porch seem to indicate that customers often visited a while when making a purchase.

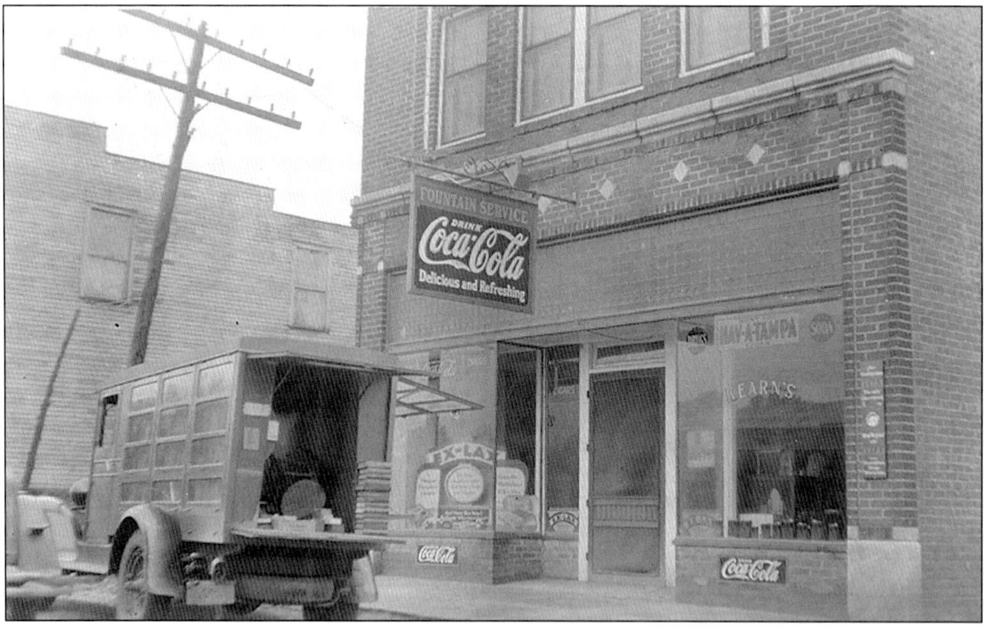

This storefront in Denton was one of the stops the public library's bookmobile made around the county.

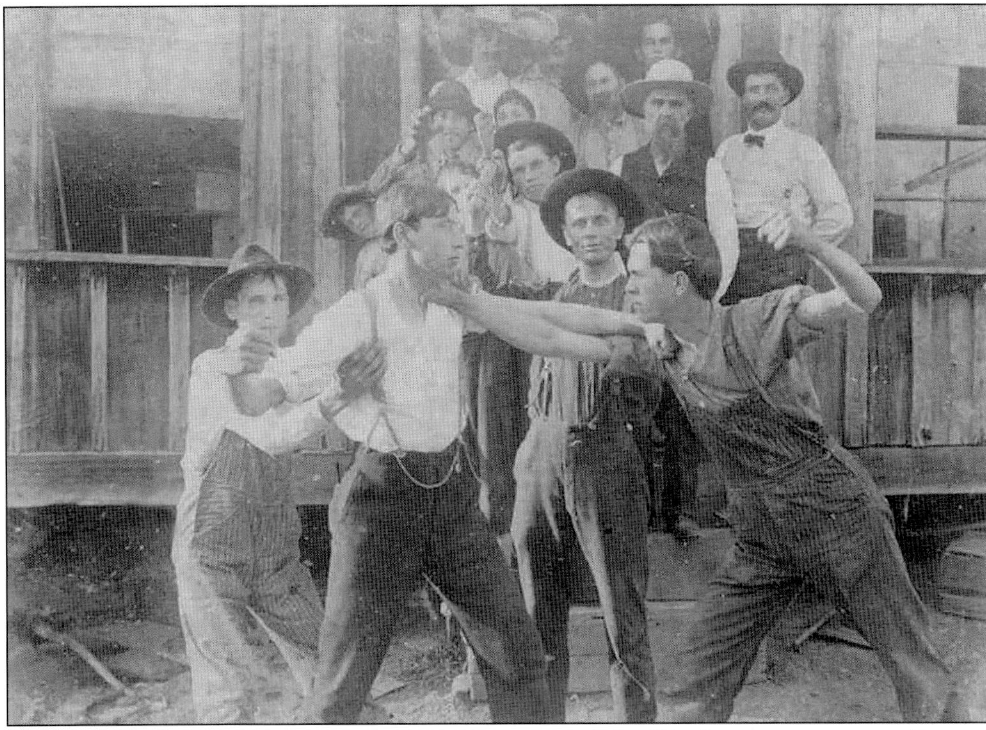

Between 1889 and 1922, the Major Morris Store served the Handy community near Denton. Located at Handy Road and Highway 109, the store was a favorite gathering place for young people on Sunday afternoons. Here, Jim Morris tries to stop the "fight" as Whit Morris and Jimmy Skeen prepare to "duke it out." Others in the background include Elkanah Lanier, Frank Stout, William Morris, Joe Scarboro, James Harrison, and Walter Loflin. W.A. Frank, in the bow tie and white shirt, was operating the store for Major Morris when this photo was taken. The picture below shows the store W.A. Frank later owned in Handy.

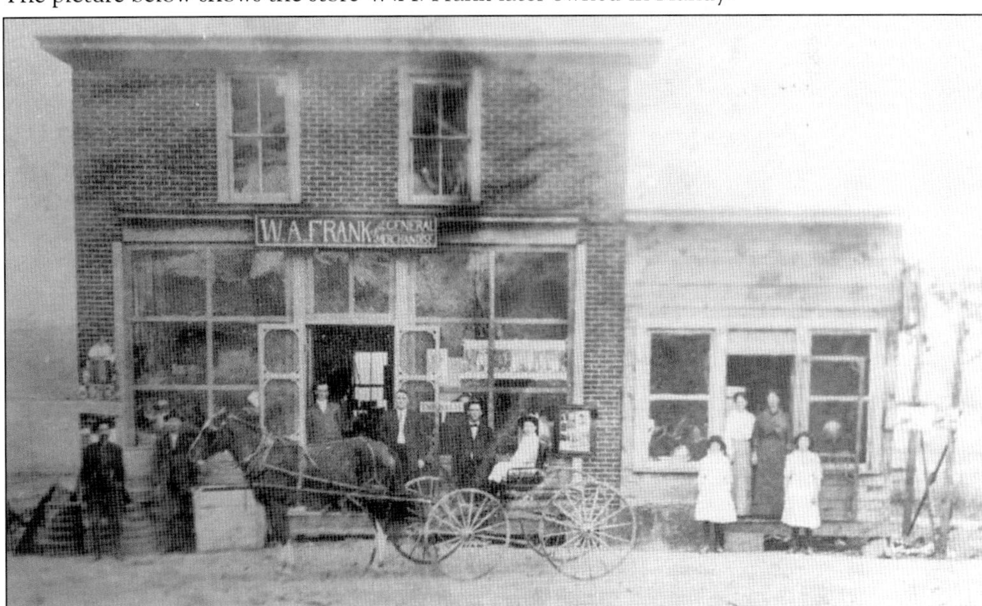

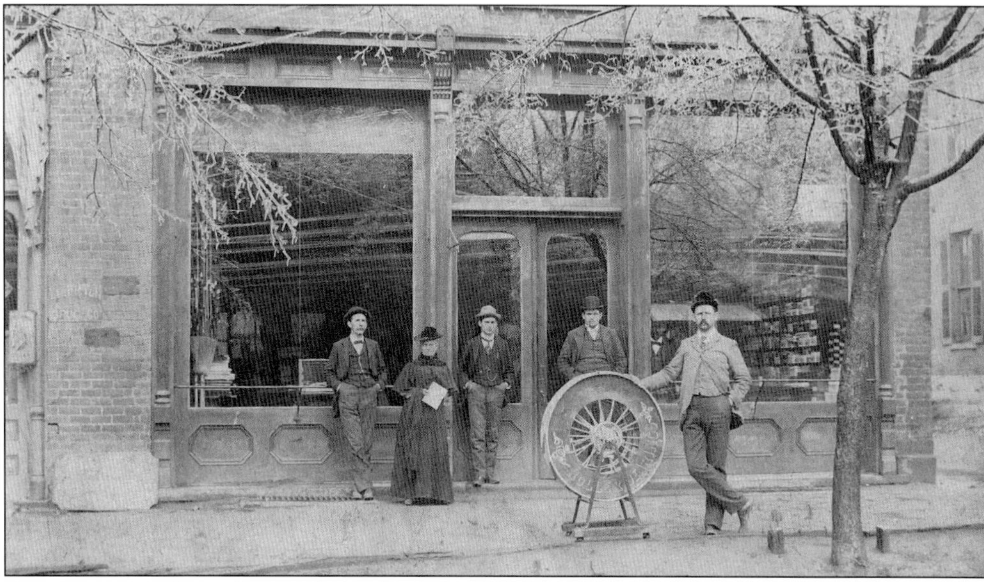

A camera was a novelty in the early days of the 20th century when this picture was taken in front of Clement & Hargrave Store on South Main Street in Lexington. Posing for the picture from left to right are J.L. Clement, Florence Hanes, W.G. Hinkle, R.S. Hargrave, and C.C. Hargrave standing by a wheel advertising ball bearings.

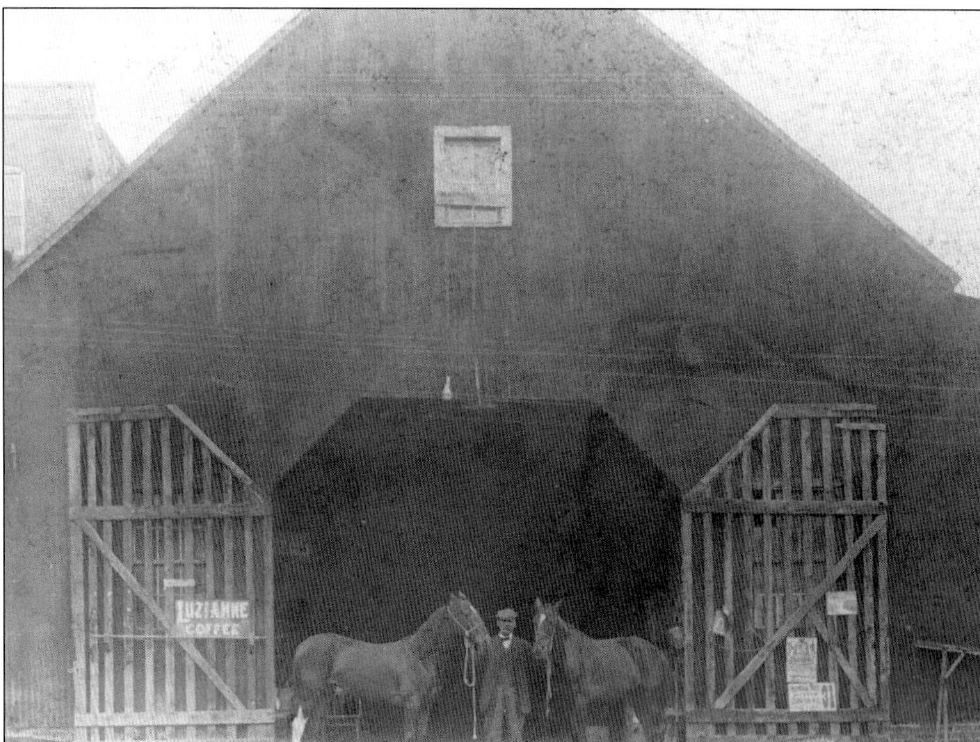

The A.L. Smith Livery Stable was located on Second Avenue in Lexington, approximately where Frazier's Bookstore is today. When the fire department purchased their first horse, "Old Brack," in 1911, they rented a stall from Mr. Smith for $15 per month.

Three

DAVIDSON COUNTY AT WORK

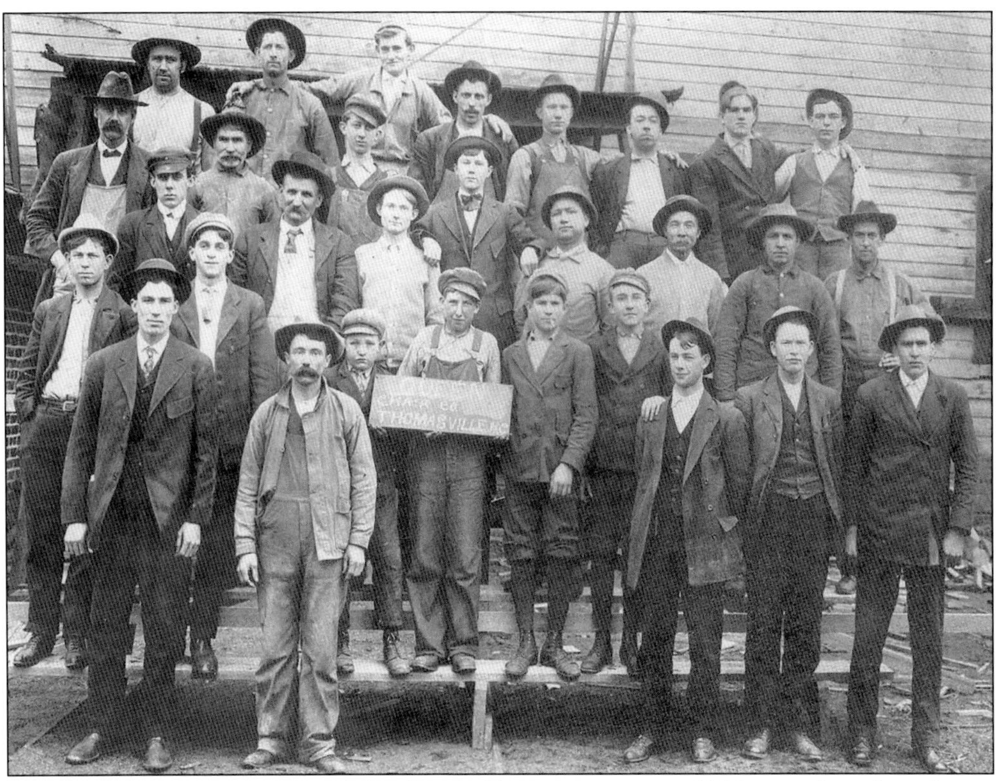

C.M. and G.M. Hoover opened the Queen Chair Company in 1903 to replace their former woodworking plant. Here are the employees in front of the business on West Guilford Street in Thomasville. The plant burned in 1918, and the Hoover brothers decided to purchase the old American Furniture Company in Lexington, rather than rebuild. Later named the Hoover Chair Company, it remained in operation until 1967.

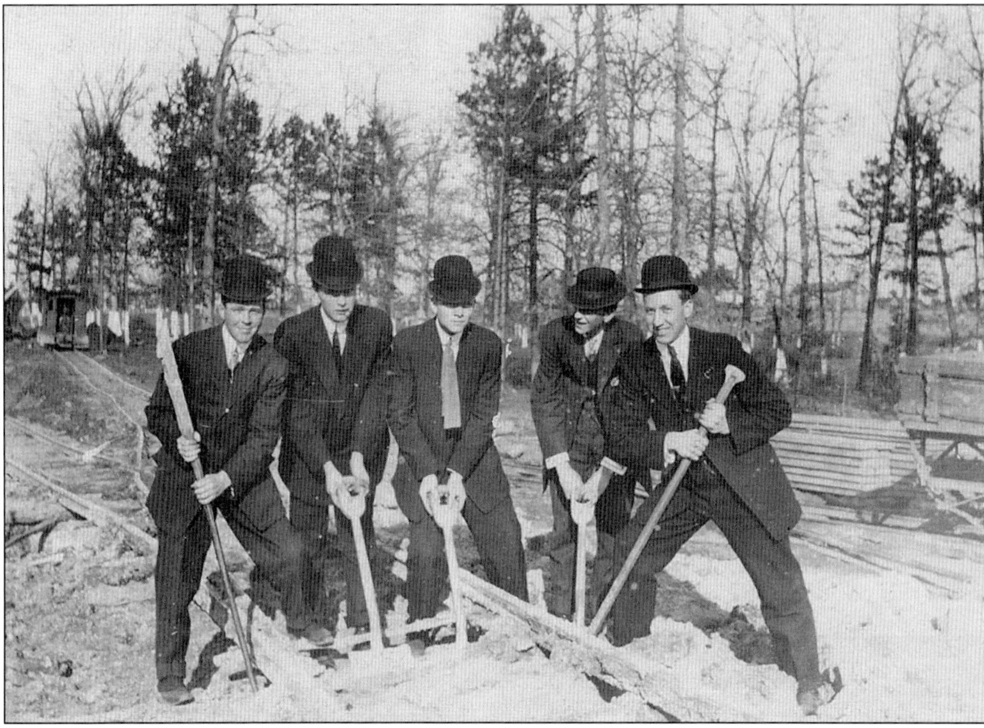

A second rail line came to Lexington in 1911. The Winston-Salem Southbound Railway ran through Midway, Welcome, Lexington, and Southmont—continuing on to Wadesboro, NC. Capt. F.C. Robbins was the attorney for the railroad, assisted by Wade H. Phillips. These young entrepreneurs seem eager to help with the construction of the track near Lexington in this photo from 1910.

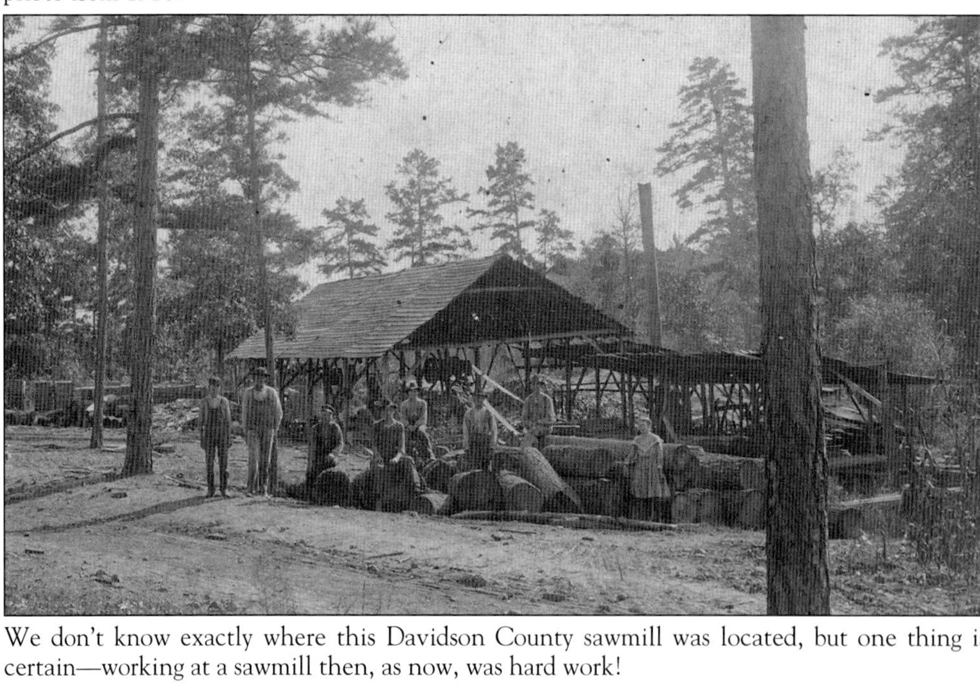

We don't know exactly where this Davidson County sawmill was located, but one thing is certain—working at a sawmill then, as now, was hard work!

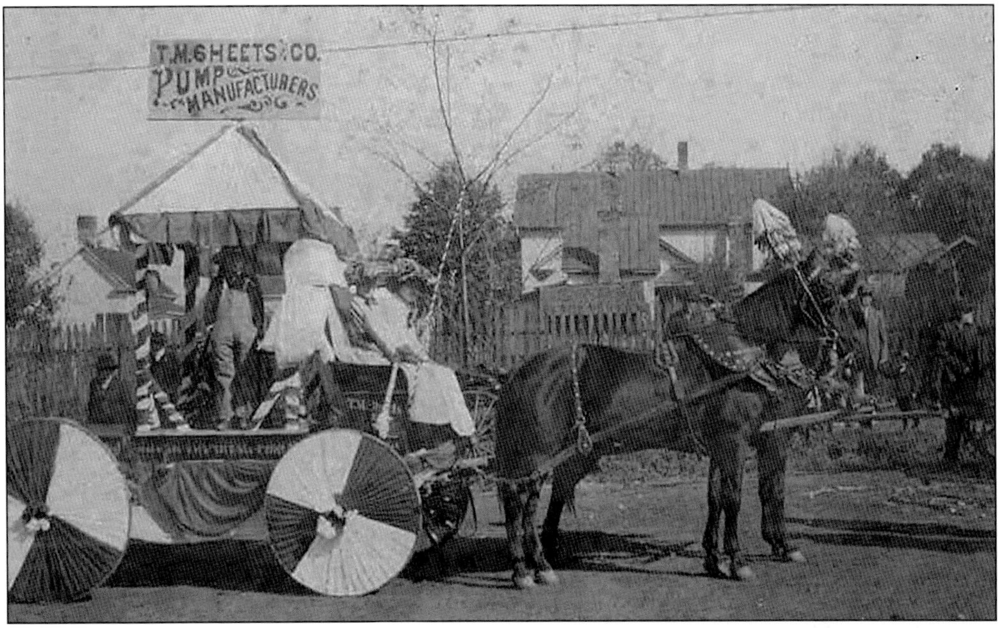

T.M. Sheets was an inventor who traveled around the area selling his goods. He developed a new type of well pump distinguished by a unique handle and proudly advertised the product in a way sure to catch the eye of prospective customers.

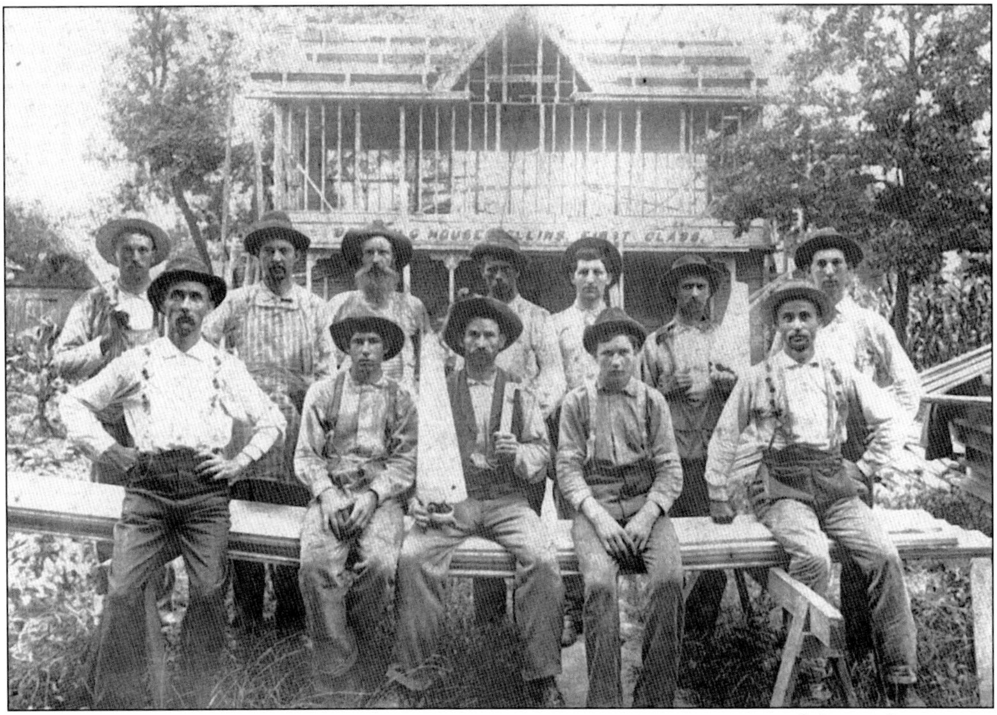

Emmett Emanual Sink was a Davidson County builder in the beginning of the 20th century. We don't know exactly where this house was located, but the picture was made between 1890 and 1895. Mr. Sink is pictured here with his building crew. He is on the back row, the third from the right.

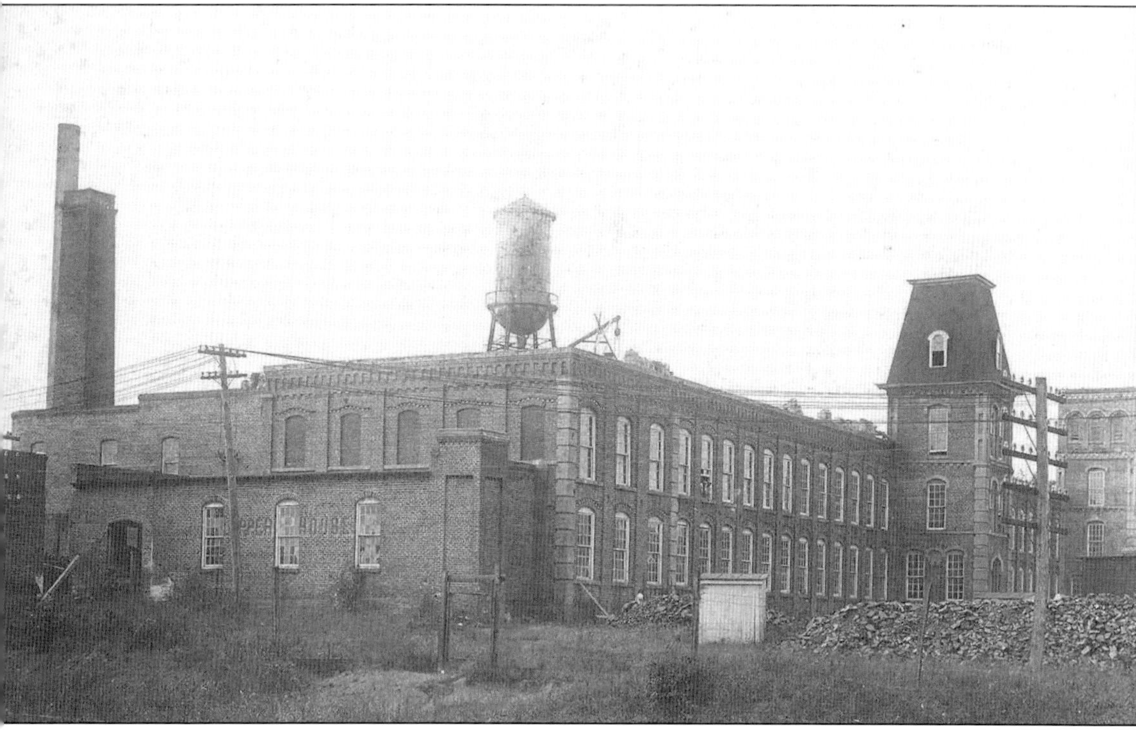

In 1908, there were 30 different manufacturing plants in Lexington. The oldest was Wennonah Cotton Mills, organized in 1887 by Mr. William E. Holt. He purchased the original 23 acres for the mill in July 1886 for $25 an acre. Mrs. Holt selected the name of the mill from Henry Wadsworth Longfellow's *Song of Hiawatha*. Wennonah Mills was the largest employer in Lexington in 1900 with 250 employees.

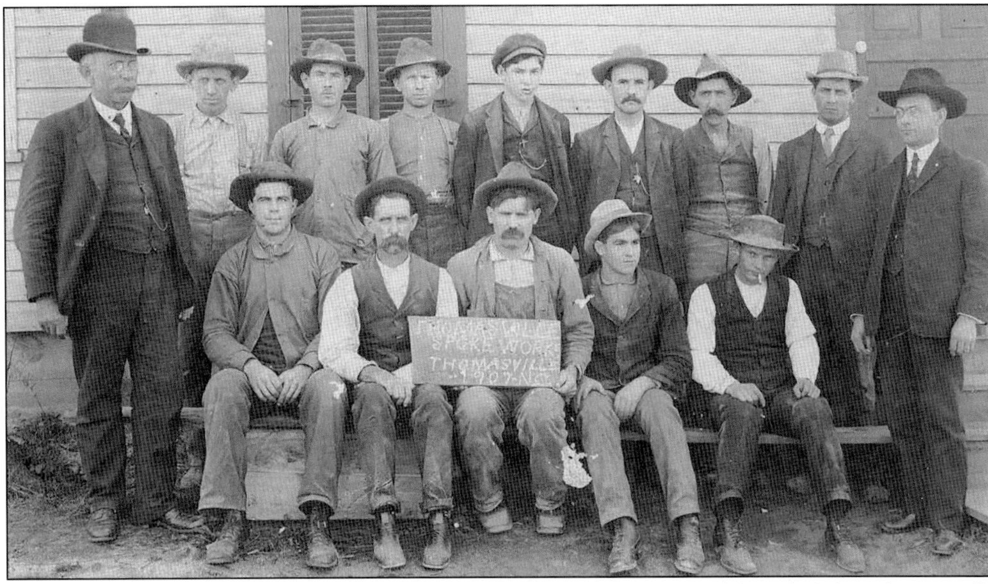

E.S. Parmalee moved to Thomasville from Connecticut in 1890 and founded the Thomasville Spoke and Handle Factory. The factory was sold in 1905 and reorganized. By 1906, the factory was turning out 1.5 million spokes and handles per year. As automobiles became more numerous, the demand for spokes decreased and later the factory was converted to a sash and door business. Here are some of the employees from 1907.

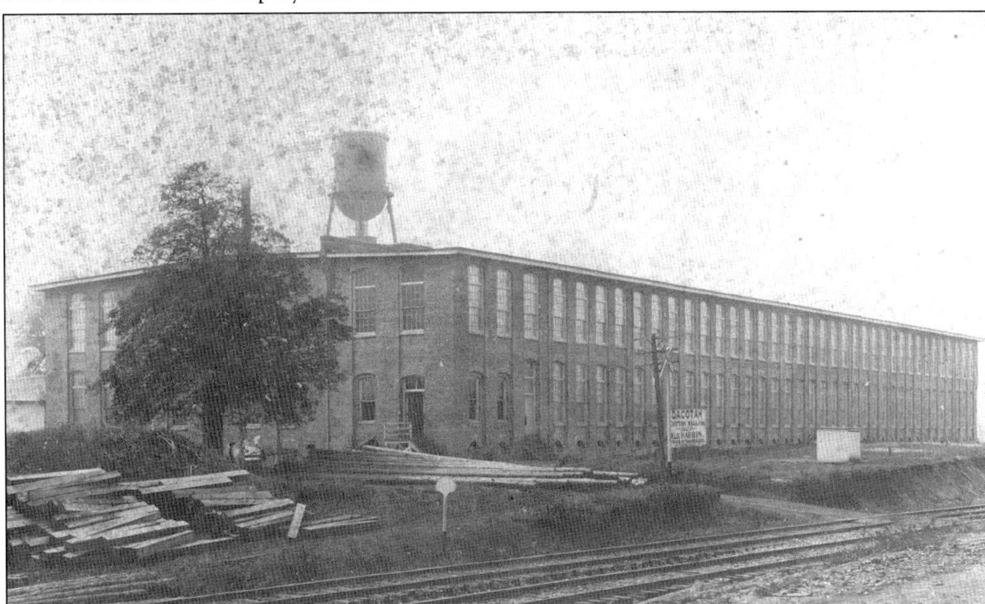

Dacotah Cotton Mills was Lexington's second oldest textile industry, organized in December 1908. Prominent local contractor T.R. Harbin built the factory. The entire factory payroll for the first year was less than $50,000. The Dacotah mill village consisted of 52 homes, which were renting in 1958 for 25¢ per room each week, the same amount established in 1910. The plant gave thousands of yards of material to the local hospital, the Junior Order Home, and other children's homes across the state.

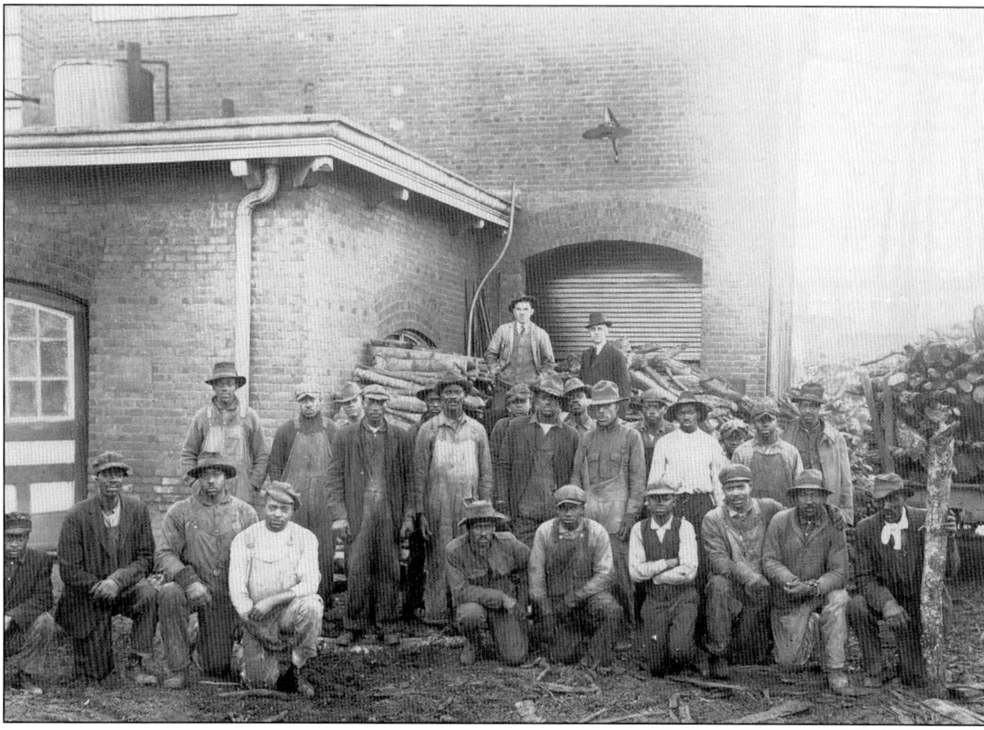

These "Day Force Firemen and Wood Passers" saved the day for Erlanger Mills in December 1919. The mill used coal for power, but a strike stopped the coal delivery. The men pictured here, a segregated work crew, cut firewood and kept the boilers going to keep the mill running.

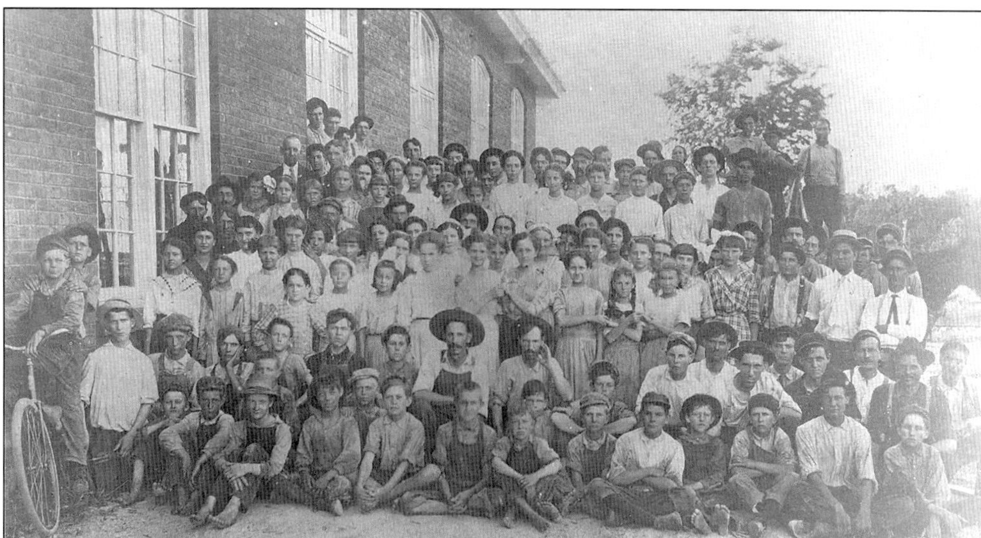

The Amazon Cotton Mills, one of the Cannon chain of mills, was incorporated on October 5, 1909, in Thomasville. The company later built a mill village with around 100 houses. This picture of the employees was taken in June 1912. Notice the young boys and girls in the first three rows. Many of the boys are not wearing shoes. The young fellow on the left brought his bicycle with him.

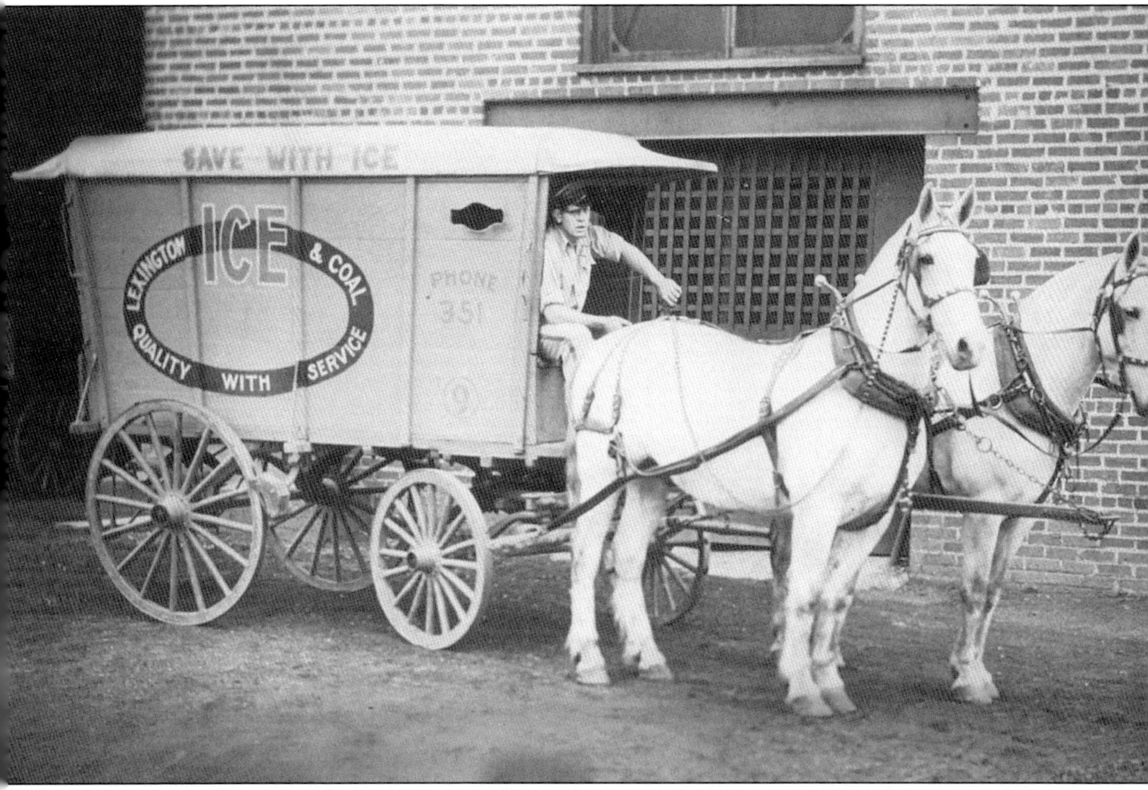

Thomas S. Eanes operated the first ice-making plant in Davidson County. In the 1920s, there were at least 14 horse-drawn wagons used in the delivery service. The business was located on North Church Street in Lexington. When you needed ice for your icebox or coal for your furnace, you simply dialed 351 and the Lexington Ice & Coal Company was at your service.

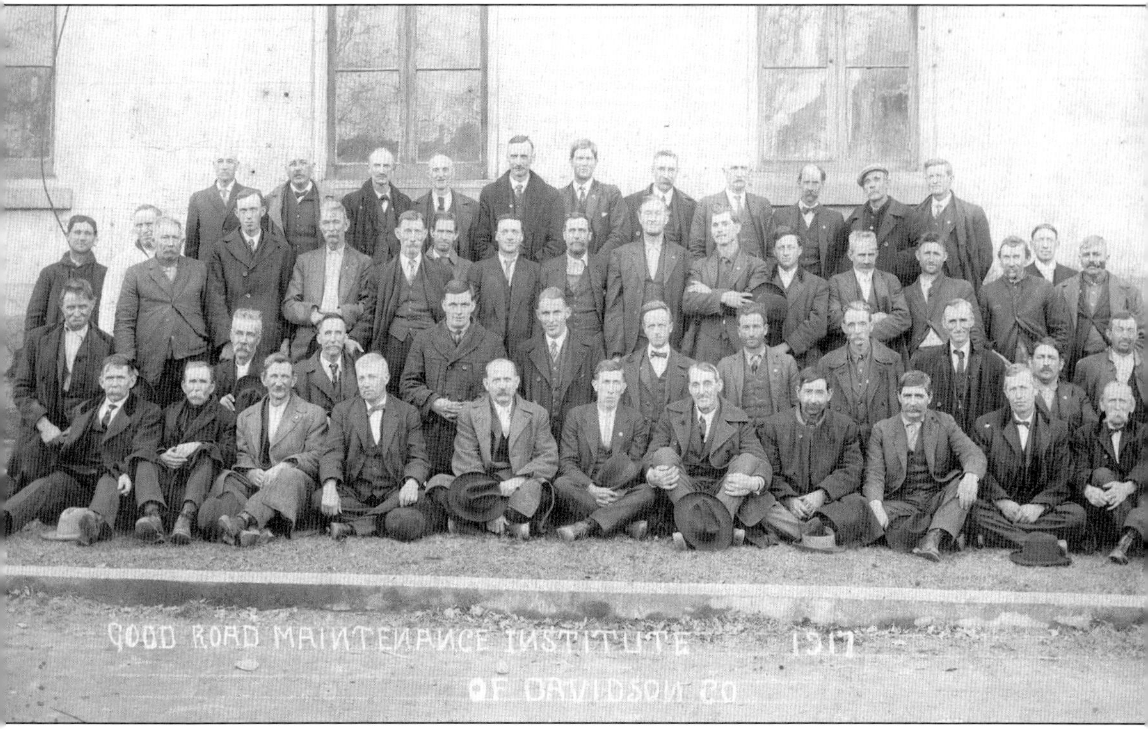

H.B. Varner, editor of the *Dispatch*, served as president of the North Carolina Good Roads Association from 1911 to 1918. The association advocated the establishment of a state highway commission to work with counties in road building. This was a "Good Roads Institute" held in Lexington in 1917. The man in the plaid coat on the second row, fourth from the left, is possibly Fred L. Everhart. Mr. Everhart did indeed start working for the county roads department in 1917, when horse-drawn grading equipment was still being used. By 1925, four years before the state took over the responsibility for road-building, Davidson County had 25 miles of paved roads.

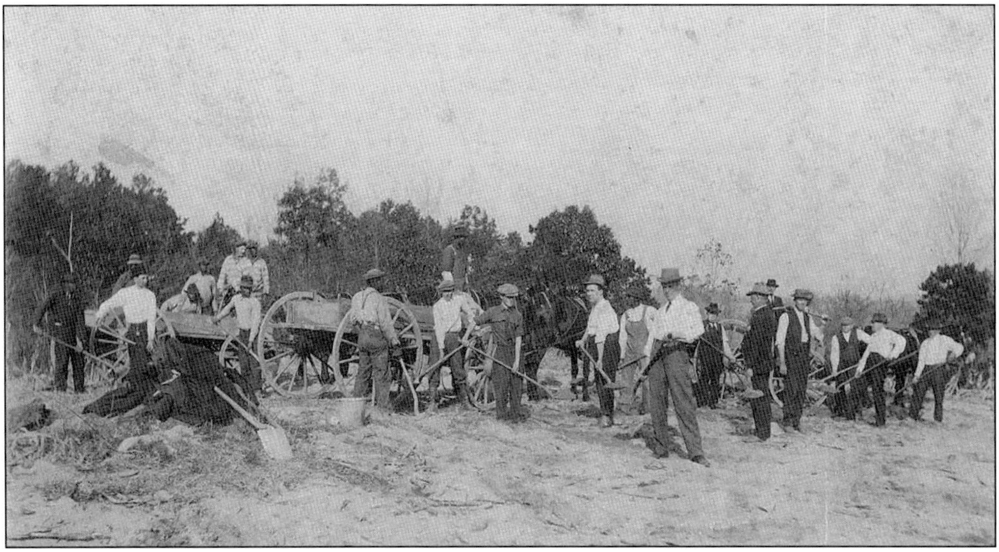

This was the ceremonial beginning of the "Good Roads" program in Davidson County in 1913. Leaders in the campaign are standing in the foreground. Wade Phillips and Sam Finch are standing in the center. Holding shovels, from left to right, are Dr. E.J. Buchanan, Police Chief Bill Thompson, Capt. C.M. Thompson (in the buggy), Charles Young, H.B. Varner, D.F. Conrad, and George W. Crouse. Most of the laborers are prisoners. This picture was taken near the old Lexington Memorial Hospital.

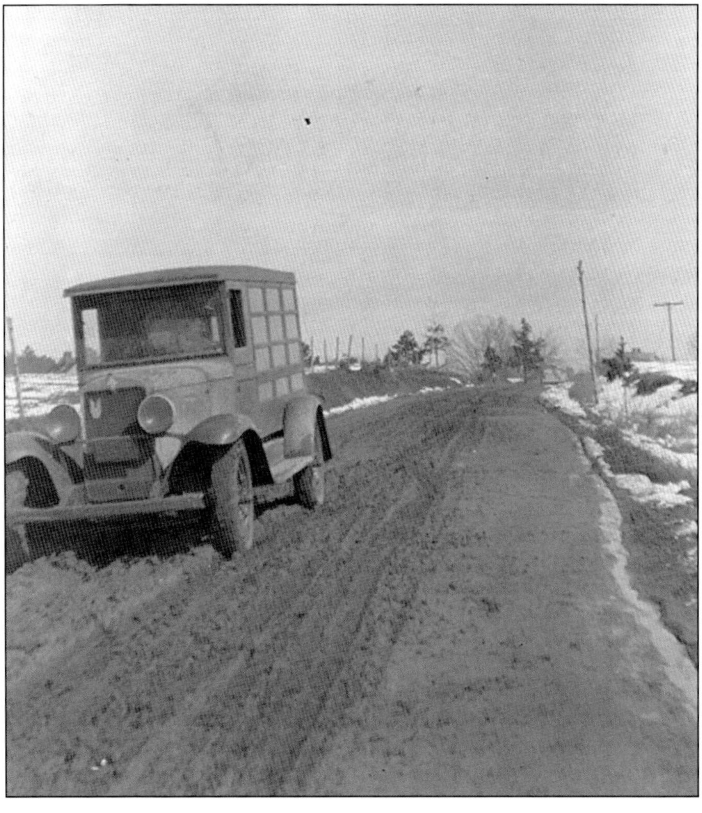

If anyone today wonders why so much emphasis was placed on "good roads" in the early 20th century, this picture of an automobile trying to navigate a muddy county road speaks for itself.

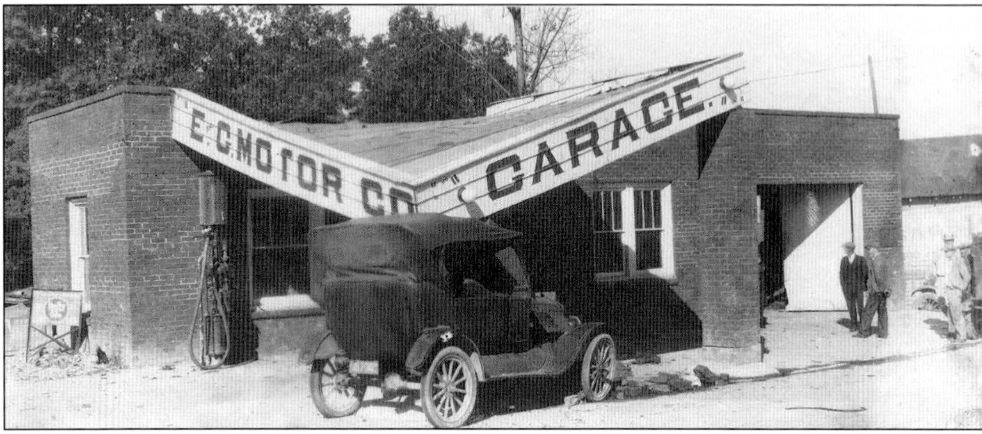

The E.G. Motor Company was located at the corner of East Main Street and State Highway No. 10, today's National Highway. State Highway 10 was called "the Main Street of North Carolina." Roy Grubb, operator of the garage, had a rude awakening when this Model T crashed into his business. Perhaps accidents like this led to the unofficial name of the intersection, "Slimey Corner."

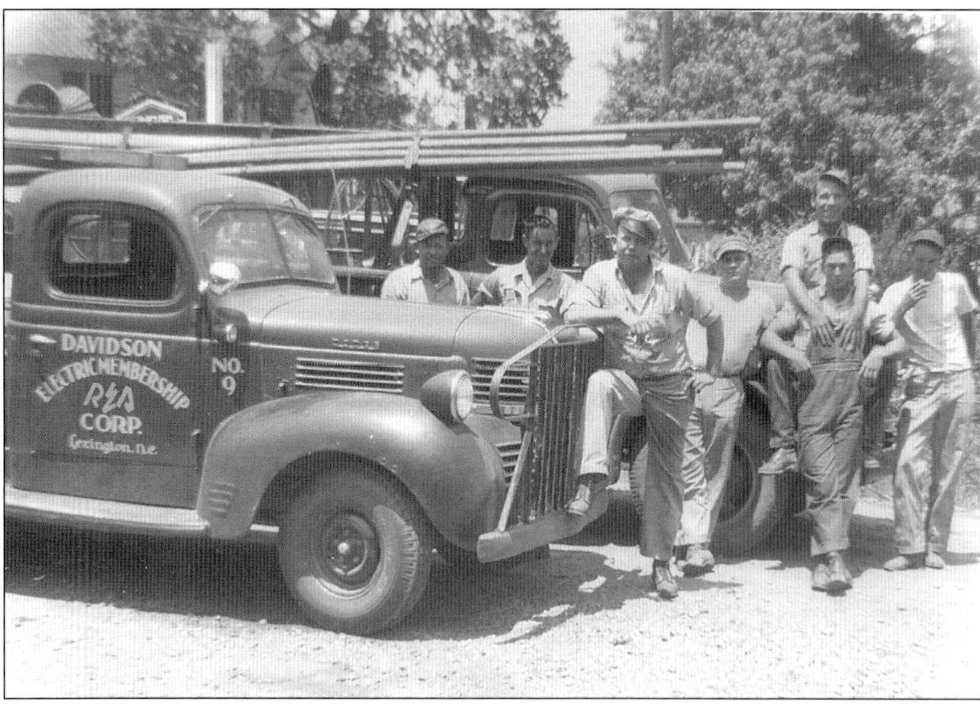

After the war was a time of prosperity and opportunity. This REA crew was working to provide electricity to new areas of the county. Soon all of Davidson County could access electrical power.

The Depression hit Davidson County in the early 1930s, but it could have been worse. Nearly all of the factories and the mills remained opened. The Depression did force wages to be cut. In December 1932, the average wage for a Davidson County mill worker was 19 to 32¢ per hour. Most of the cotton mills in the South were paying only 10¢ per hour. When the mills ran out of money, they used script, which was accepted by merchants all over town. When the mills recovered following the Depression, the script was converted to cash.

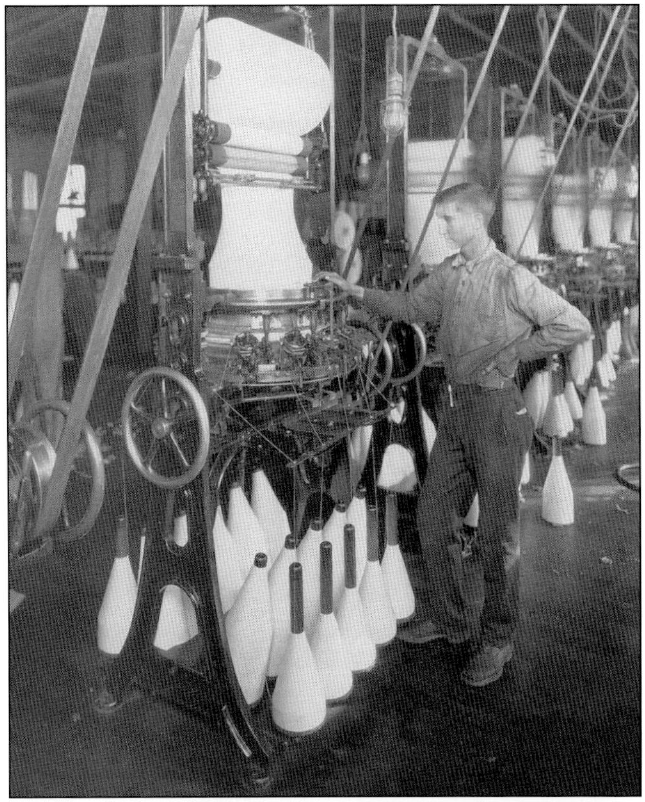

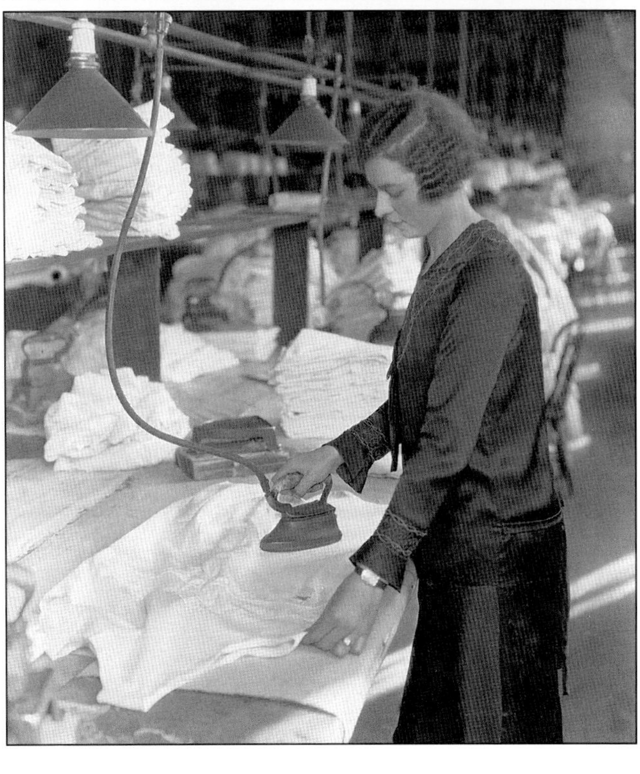

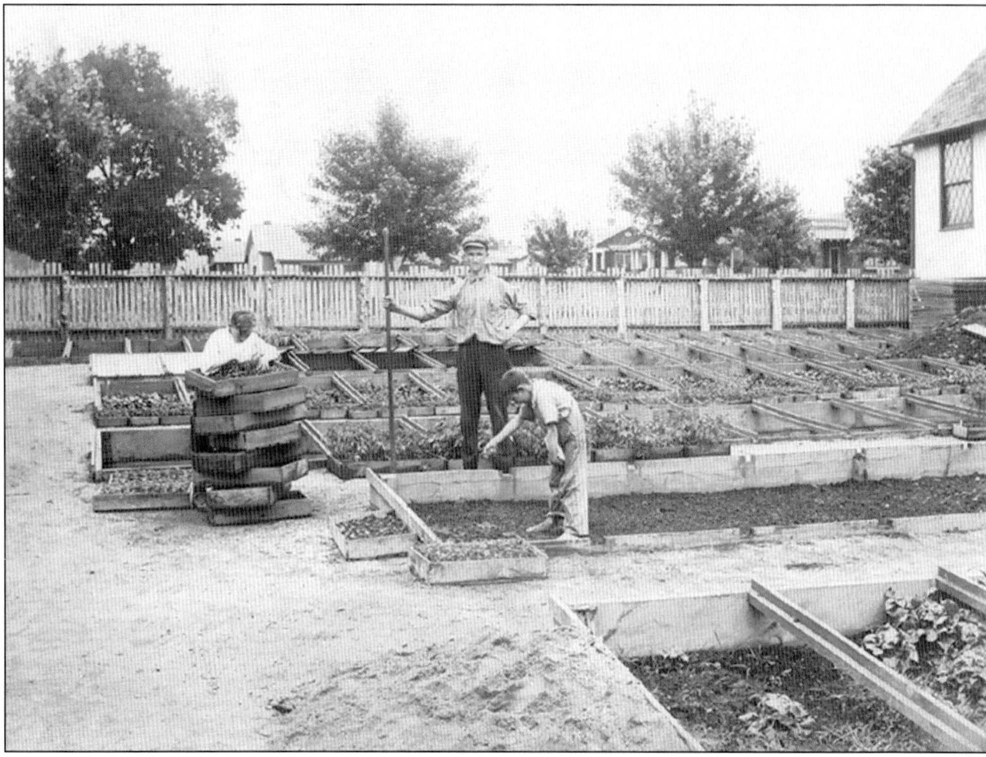

Many of the homes in Erlanger Village had their own gardens. These folks found a unique way to maximize the small amount of land available.

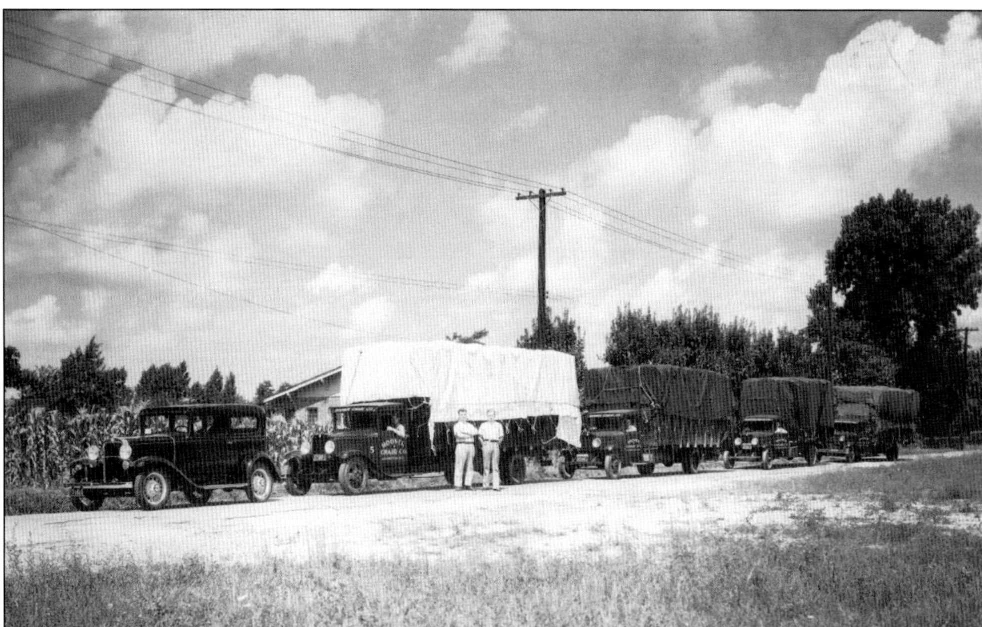

Davidson County has become synonymous with quality furniture. These trucks belonged to the Hoover Chair Company, which manufactured chairs and dining room furniture. Charles and James Hoover operated the company until it closed in 1967.

D. Wyatt Cope served as district supervisor for the Davidson County Soil Conservation office in the early 1960s. He is pictured here in a field of one of Davidson County's primary crops—corn. Mr. Cope ran Davidson Supply for many years and later managed the Farmer's Exchange in Lexington.

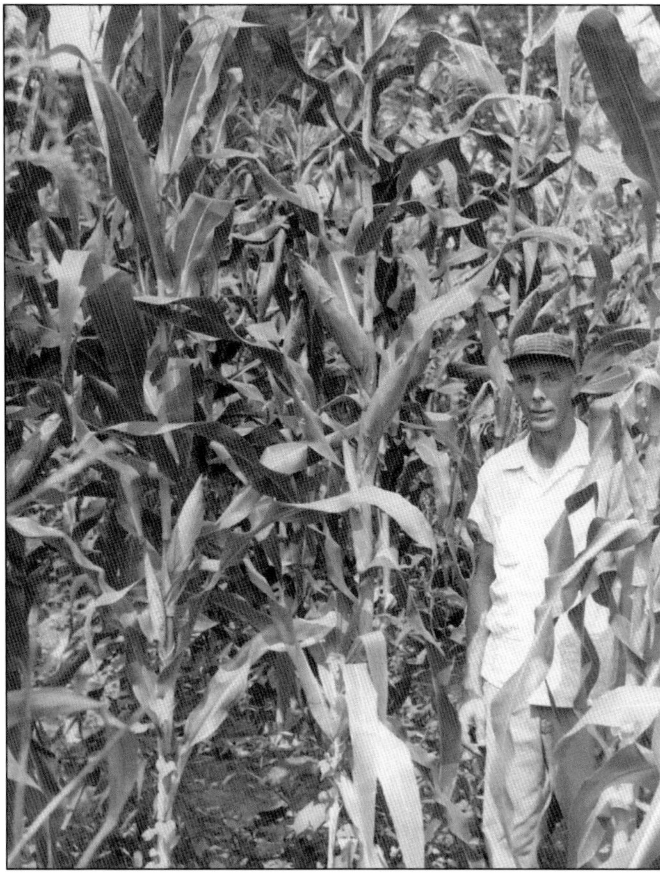

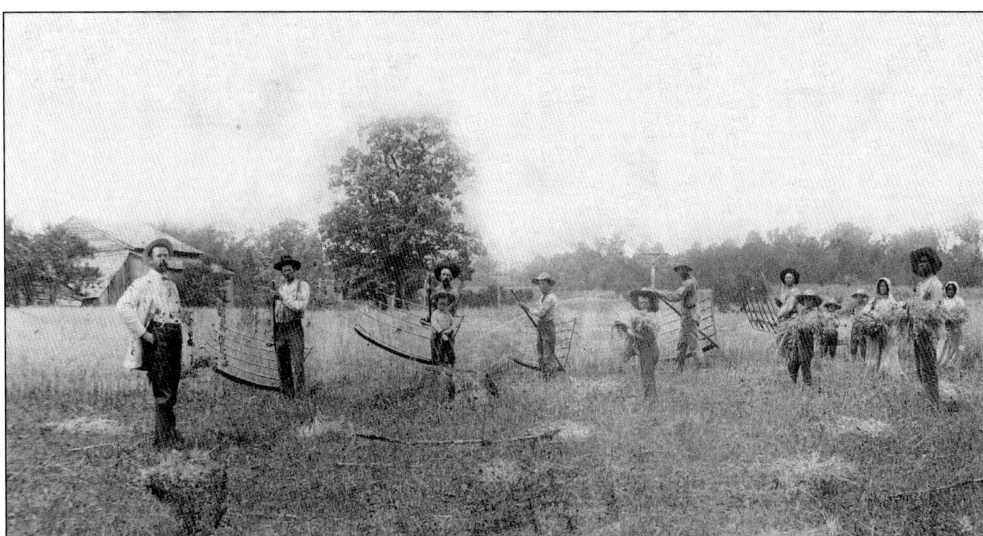

Here is a c. 1905 wheat harvest on the Hargrave farm near what is now the Sapona Country Club near Linwood. Note the state-of-the-art farm machinery for the early 20th century.

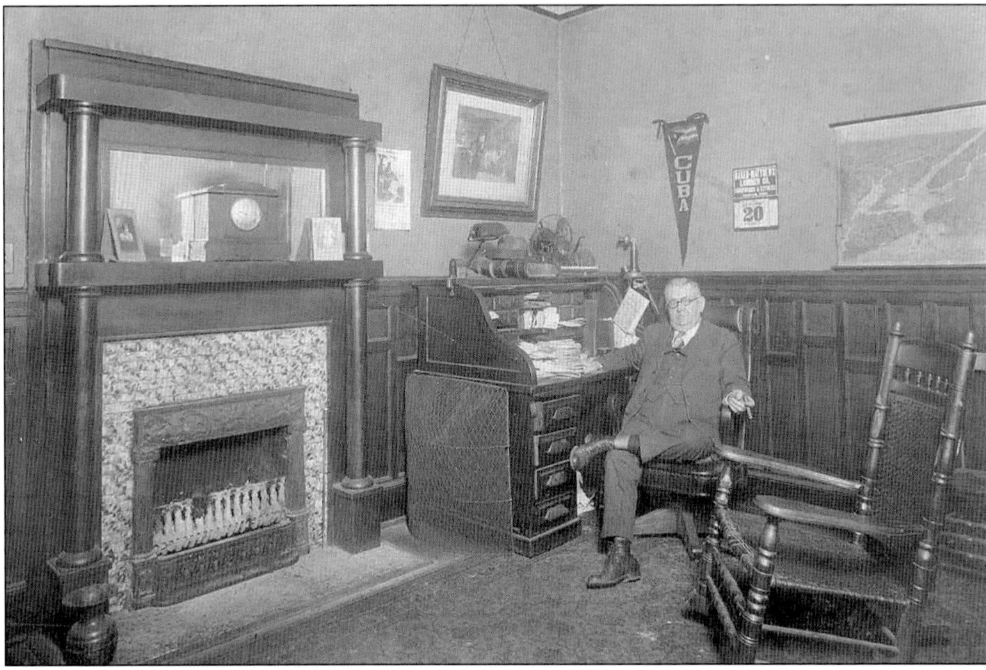

Dr. E.J. Buchanan was a prominent Lexington physician, banker, and manufacturer. Pictured here in his office on Main Street, Dr. Buchanan was the local surgeon for the Southern Railroad. He was one of the founders and the first president of Dixie Furniture, a founder and director of the Commercial & Savings Bank, and the owner of the Lexington Theater (today's Smith Civic Center). He was one of the original members of the Lexington School Board, serving for 26 years and a faithful member and elder of the First Presbyterian Church.

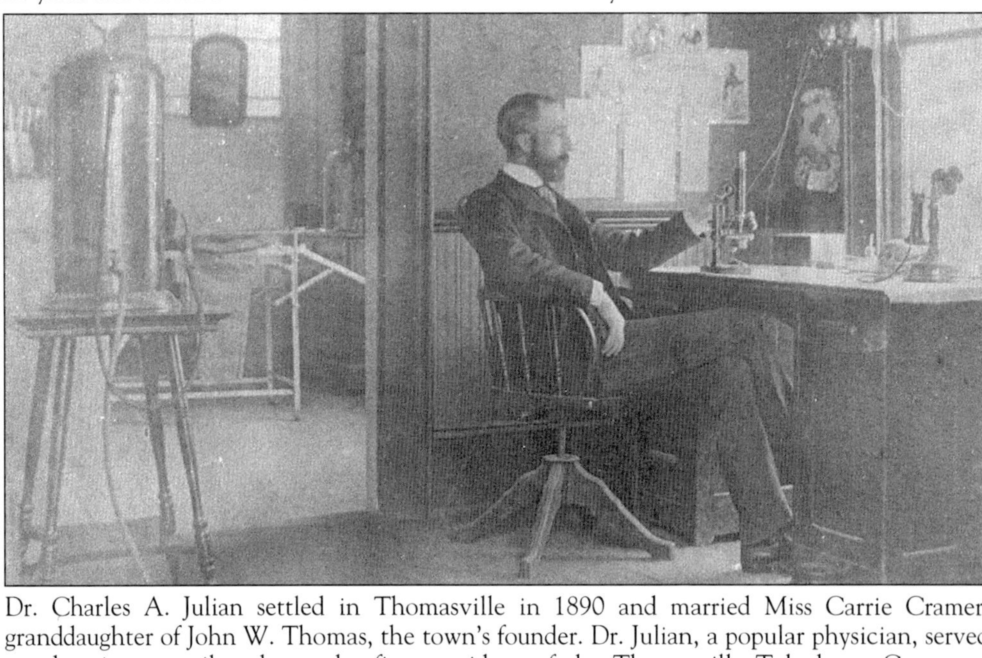

Dr. Charles A. Julian settled in Thomasville in 1890 and married Miss Carrie Cramer, granddaughter of John W. Thomas, the town's founder. Dr. Julian, a popular physician, served on the city council and was the first president of the Thomasville Telephone Company, organized in 1898.

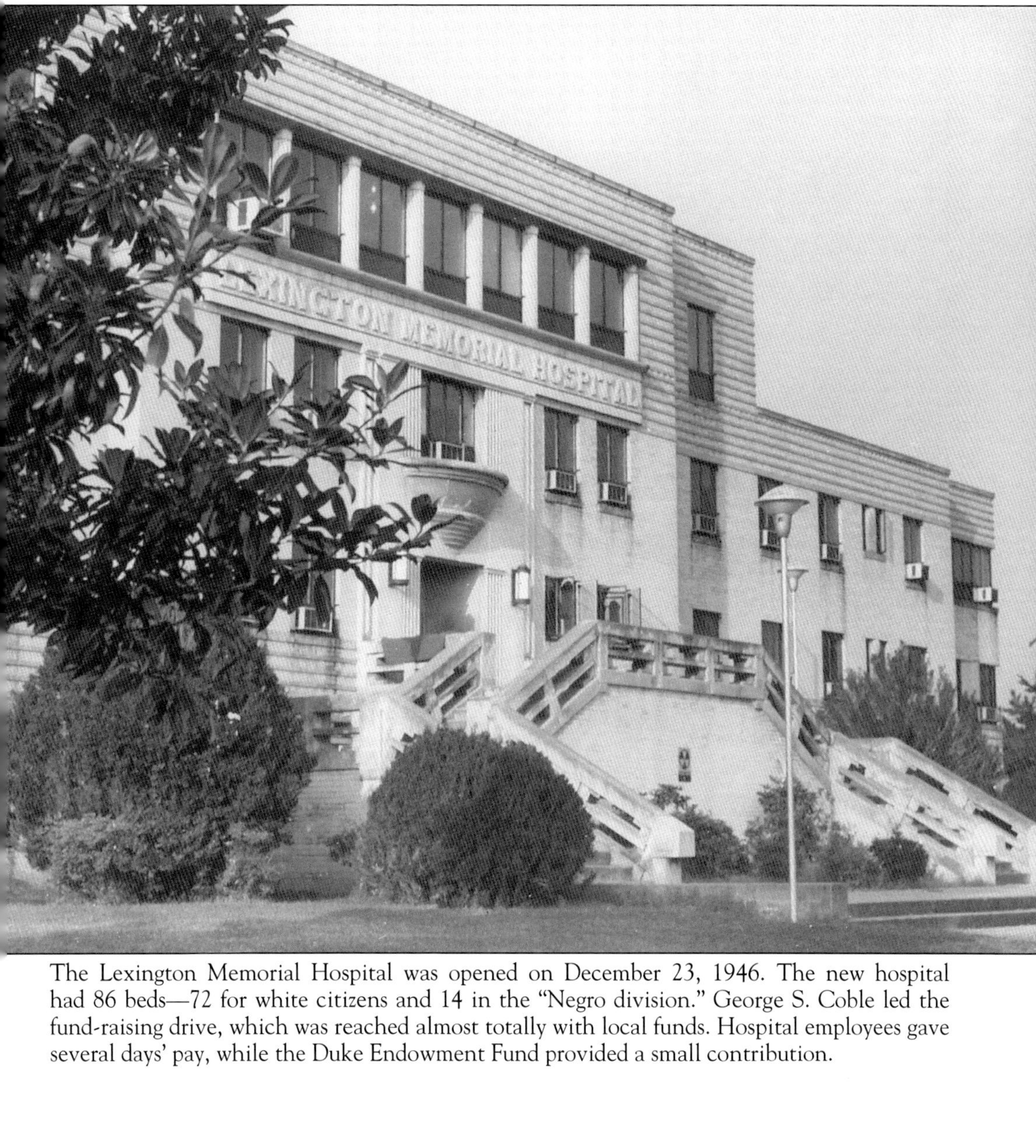

The Lexington Memorial Hospital was opened on December 23, 1946. The new hospital had 86 beds—72 for white citizens and 14 in the "Negro division." George S. Coble led the fund-raising drive, which was reached almost totally with local funds. Hospital employees gave several days' pay, while the Duke Endowment Fund provided a small contribution.

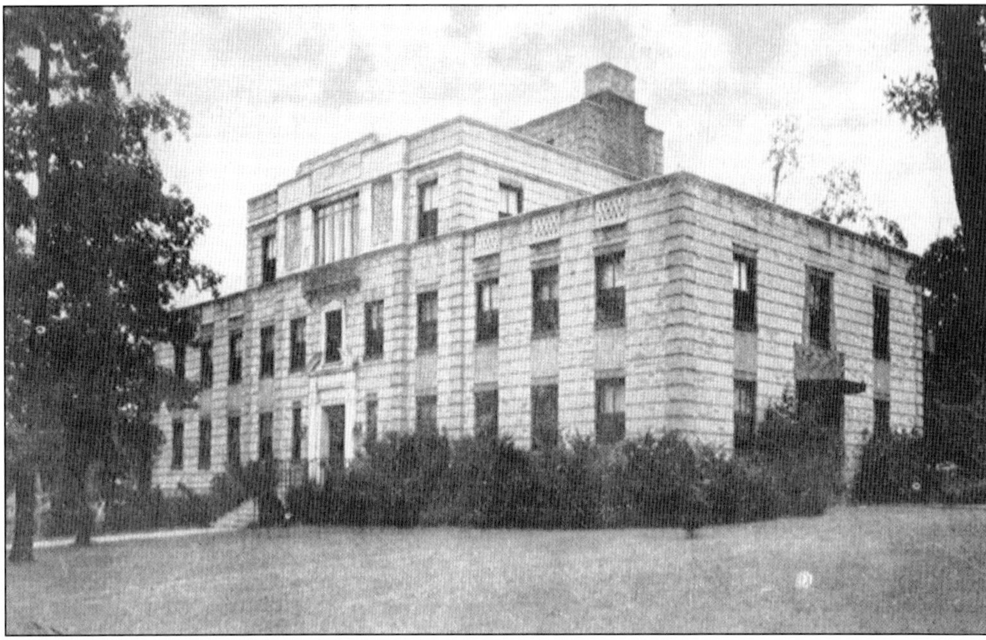

The City Memorial Hospital in Thomasville was opened in 1930 on Pine Street with 31 beds. T.A. Finch, James E. Lambeth, C.H. Phillips, Doak Finch, and A.H. Ragan were instrumental in its organization. The old hospital served Thomasville until 1971.

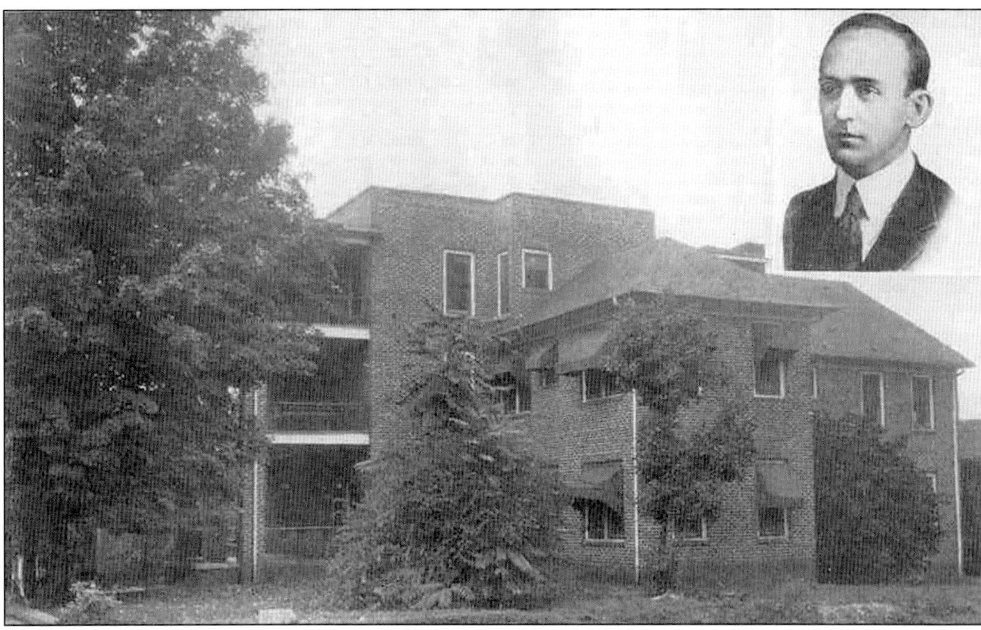

The first hospital in Davidson County was opened in July 1924 at the corner of North Main Street and Sixth Street in Lexington. The modern building opened with the latest in medical equipment and technology and had a capacity for 30 patients. Dr. J.A. Smith (inset), a prominent physician, businessman, and civic leader, owned and operated the hospital.

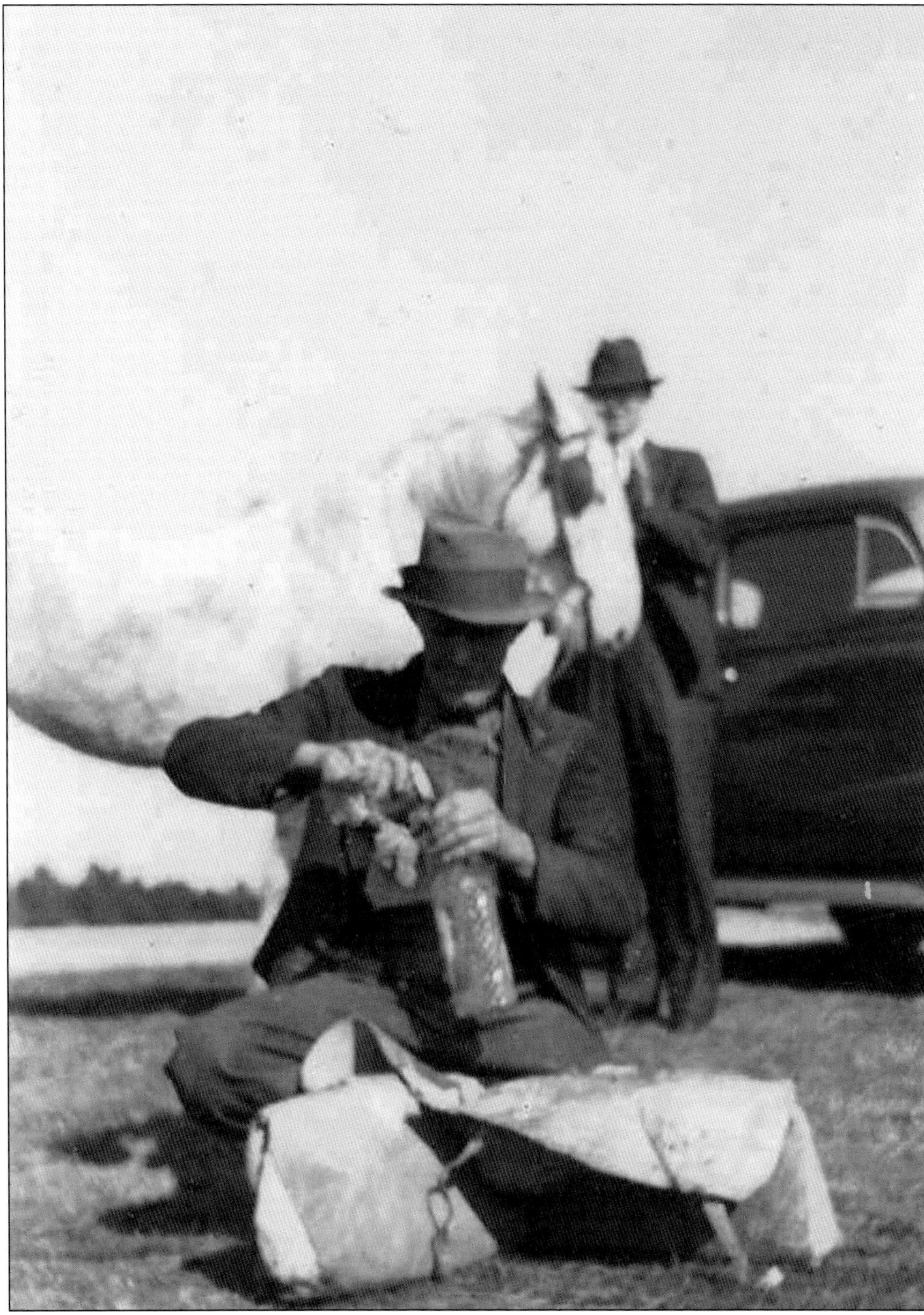

Julius Baxter Cope, a country animal doctor, started his practice in the 1920s in the Reeds community. He never drove a car, requiring the owner of the sick animal to provide his transportation. It was said the only animal he ever lost was after a frightening experience in which the car he was riding lost a wheel and threw both him and the driver out onto the road. Supposedly, he administered the wrong medicine because he was so "shook up."

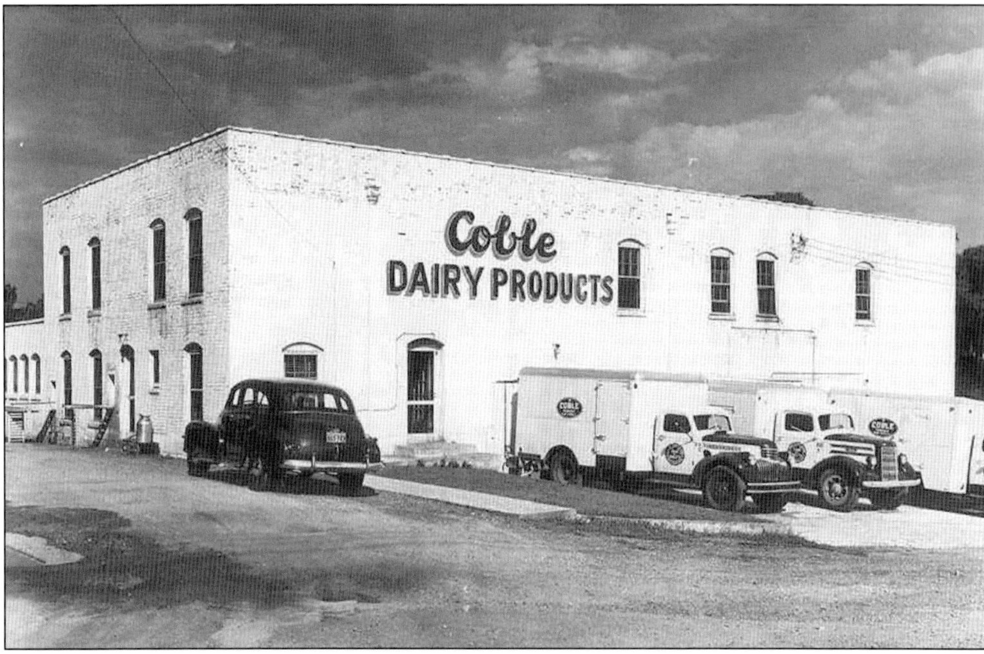

Coble Dairy Products in the last 1950s was the largest dairy cooperative in the Southeast and one of the largest in the nation. Coble distributed its products in five Southern states to over one million people every day.

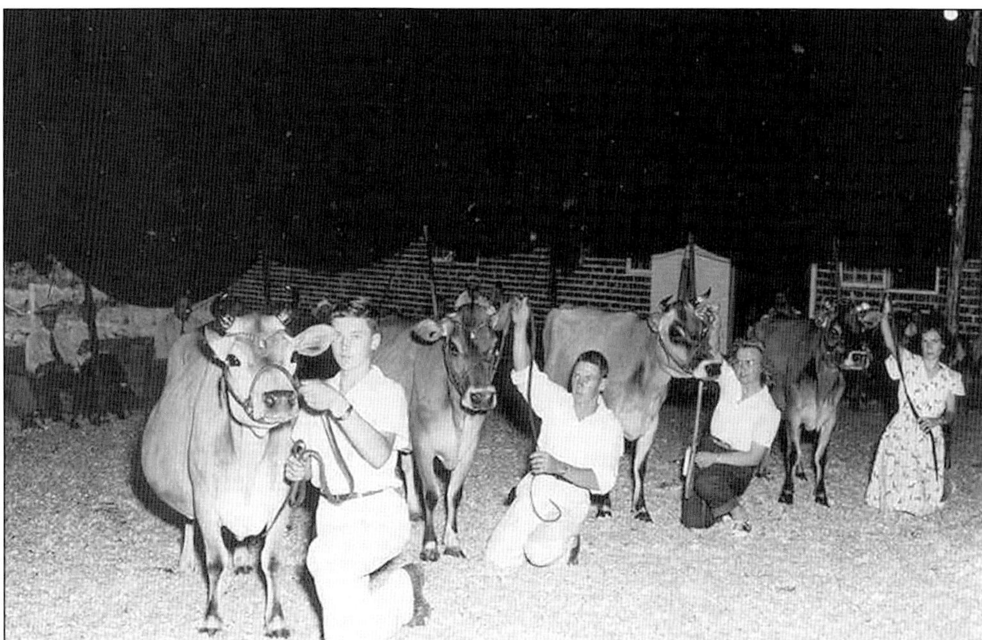

Davidson County farmers supplied over 10 million gallons of milk each year to Coble Dairy. Developing good stock to meet future demands was important to this cooperative, which produced "Golden Guernsey" milk. Coble sponsored "cow judgings" at Maegeo Farms on Old Salisbury Highway; the farm's name came from a combination of the owners' names—George and Mae Coble.

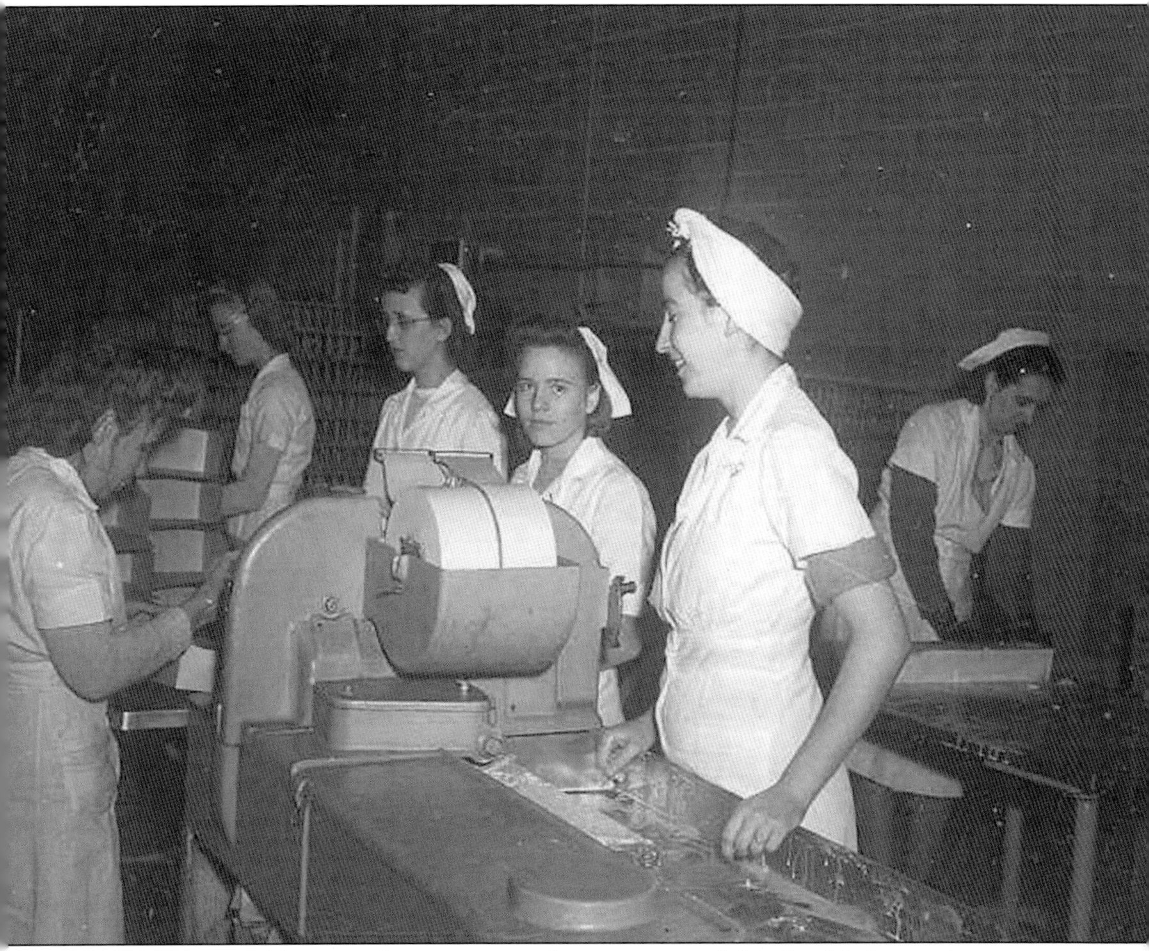

Ice cream anyone? For years, Lexington was home to one of the South's largest ice cream plants at Coble Dairy. All ice cream was produced at the Lexington plant by workers in the ice cream room. The plant even offered curb service for local residents. Remember those great milkshakes?

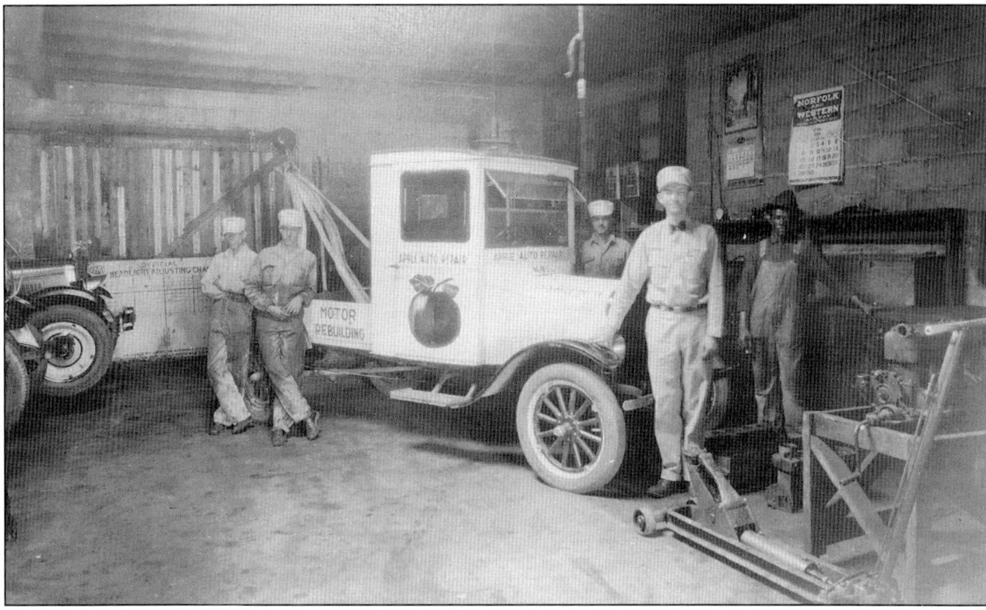

L.W. Apple ran an auto repair garage on West First Street in Lexington. Mr. Apple was also a dealer for Willys-Knight Overland automobiles. In April 1928, he proudly posed for a picture with his wrecker, the first in Lexington. The apple painted on the vehicle's door also appeared on the sign in front of the garage.

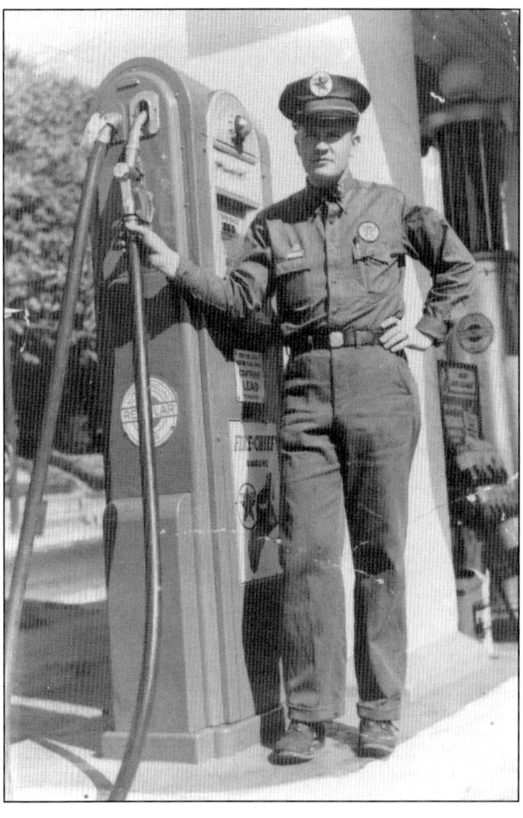

Bruce Evans Berrier is the "man who wears the star." He is pictured here in 1939 at his Red Star Service Station, located at the corner of South Main Street and Cotton Grove Road in Lexington.

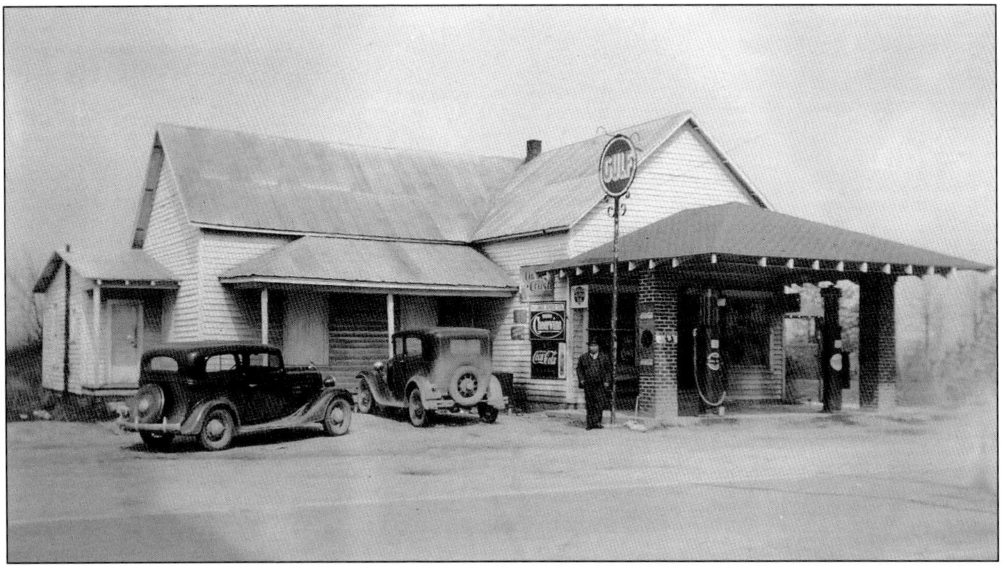

Virgil Valentine Lanier, standing in front of his store, was born on Valentine's Day, 1878. He purchased the old Ebenezer School building and converted it into this service station and store, which became a favorite gathering place. Mr. Lanier, who was blind, also sold and tuned pianos and manufactured mattresses. In 1937, while walking to his store, he received fatal injuries when a car struck him. The curve in front of his home where the accident occurred became known as "Blind Man's Curve."

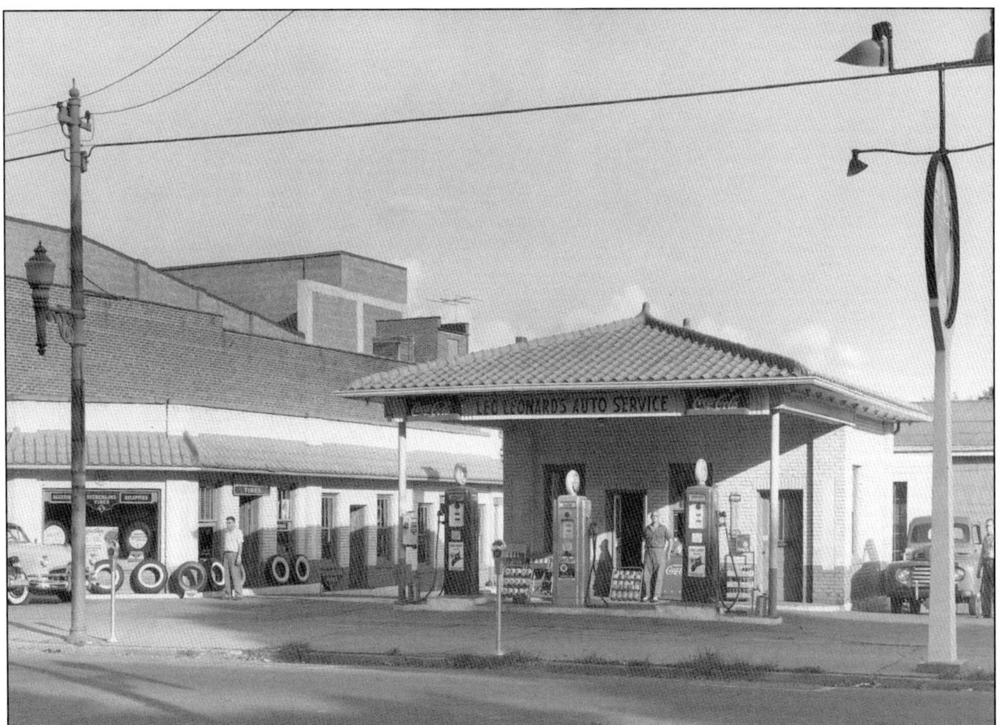

Leo Leonard's service station was a fixture on the corner of Main Street and Third Avenue in Lexington.

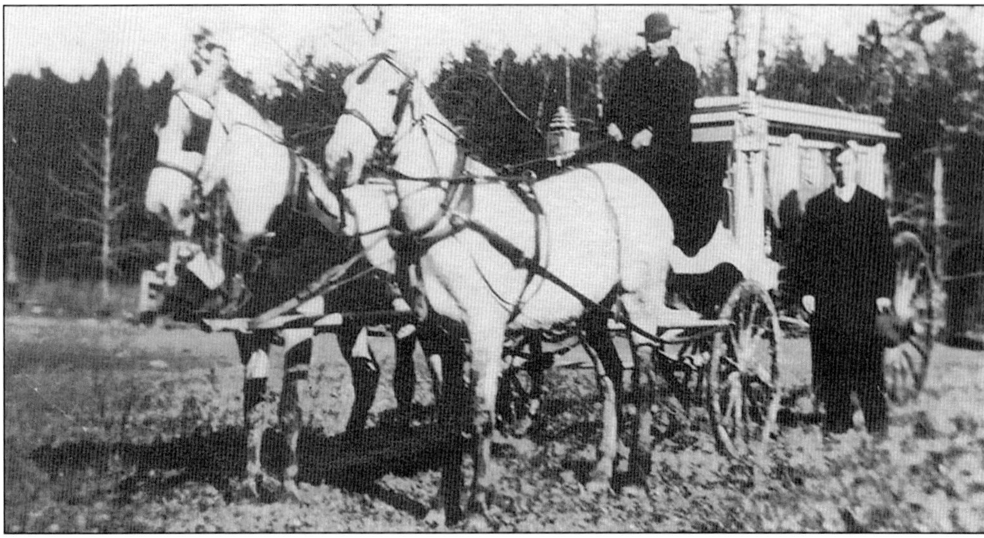

On January 16, 1916, R.O. Kirkman Sr. directed this funeral at Jerusalem Church using a horse-drawn hearse. Mr. Kirkman, one of the first licensed embalmers in the piedmont section of North Carolina, entered the funeral business with John W. McCrary, who had operated an undertaking and furniture establishment since 1865. James Greer is the driver of the hearse and Mr. Kirkman is standing.

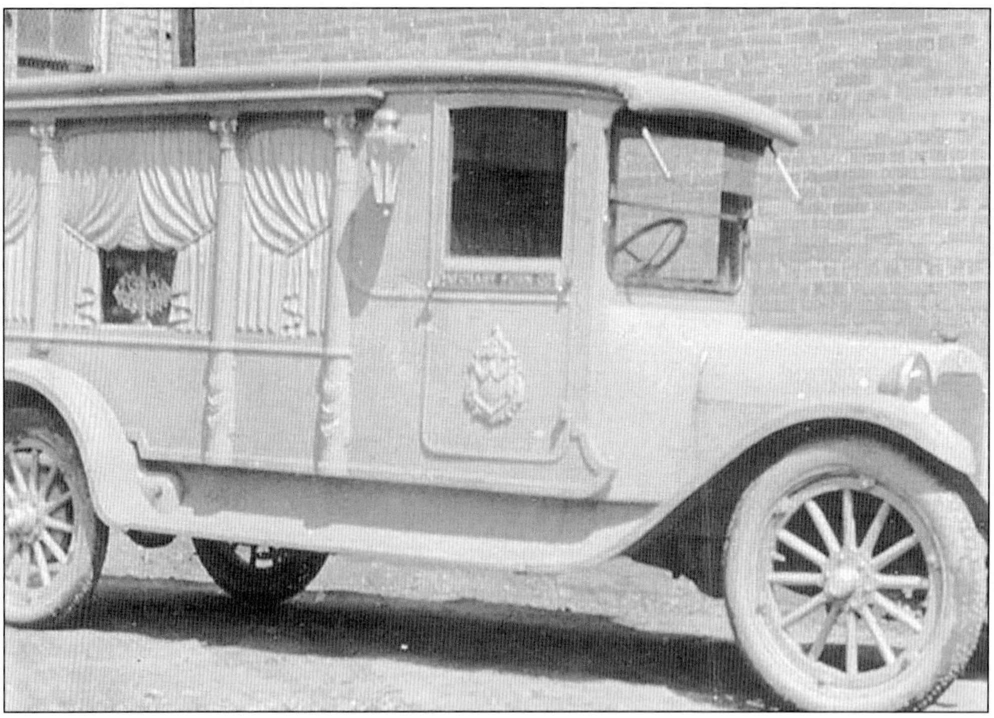

This is the first motorized hearse in Davidson County, owned by R.O. Kirkman Sr. The body of the hearse was built on the chassis of a 1915 Reo truck. Mr. Kirkman did all of the woodcarving, while Lewis Rothrock, a blacksmith, and Hammett Hedrick, a carpenter, helped with the project. The hearse was first used for the funeral of Mrs. O.L. Shemwell of Tyro, who died on February 21, 1916.

Four

Davidson County at Play

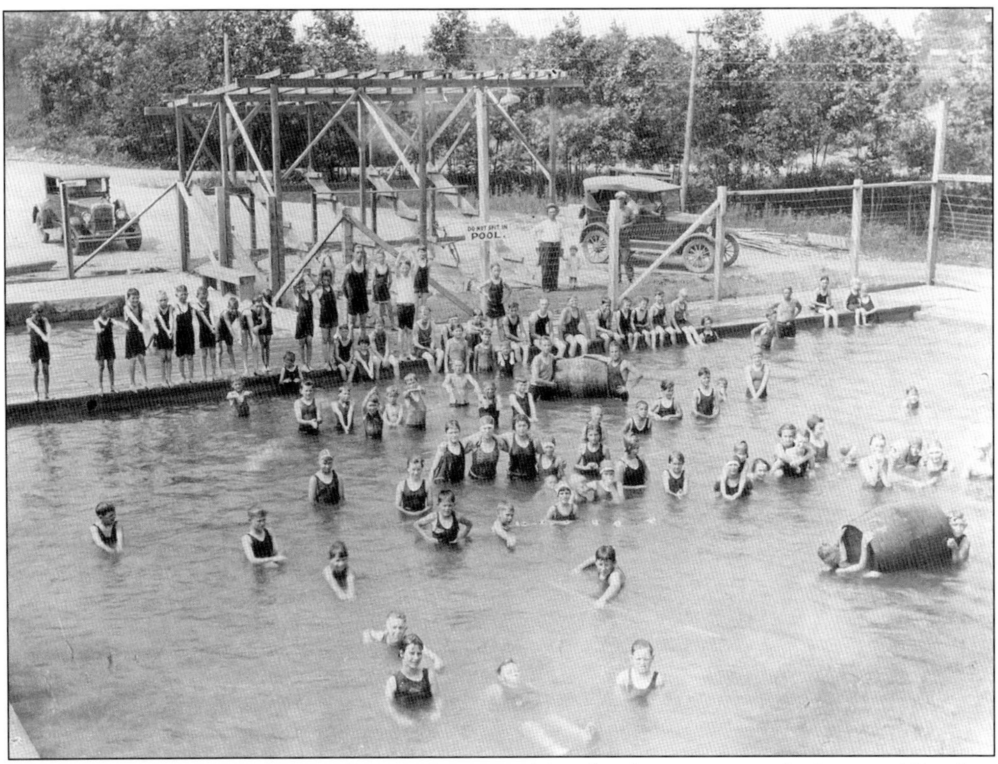

Holton's Swimming Pool opened in 1925. Located 2 miles from town on the Linwood Road, it was billed as "Lexington's greatest summer recreational center." In 1930, a miniature golf course known as "Shady Pine" was opened next to the pool. A bus would transport the children to the pool from downtown Lexington. As you can see from the sign prohibiting spitting—proper decorum was expected of all swimmers!

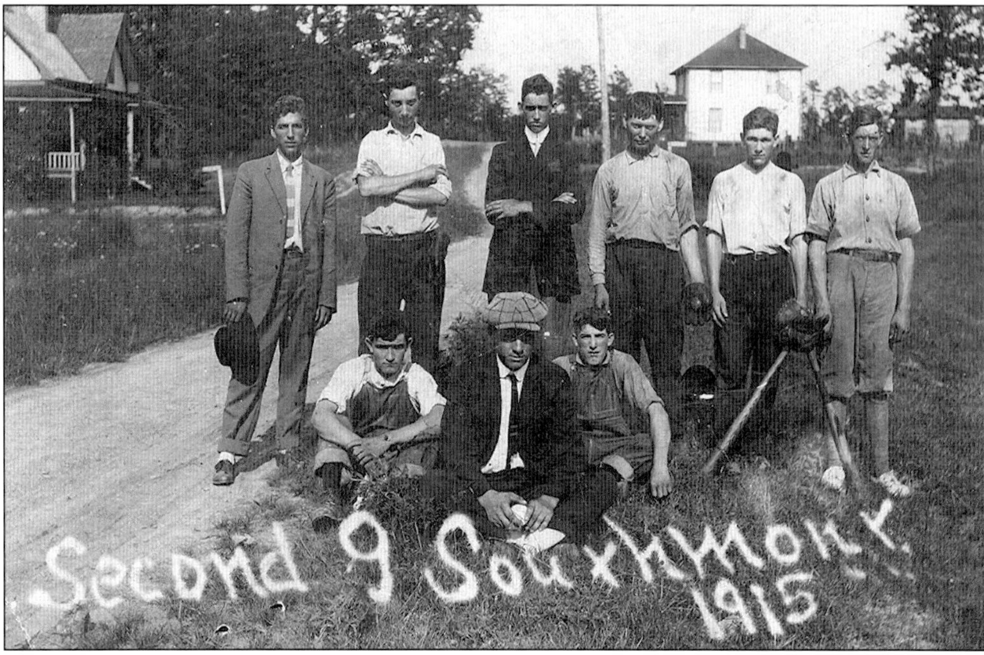

This Southmont baseball team in 1915 was not dressed to play ball—but just right to have a picture taken!

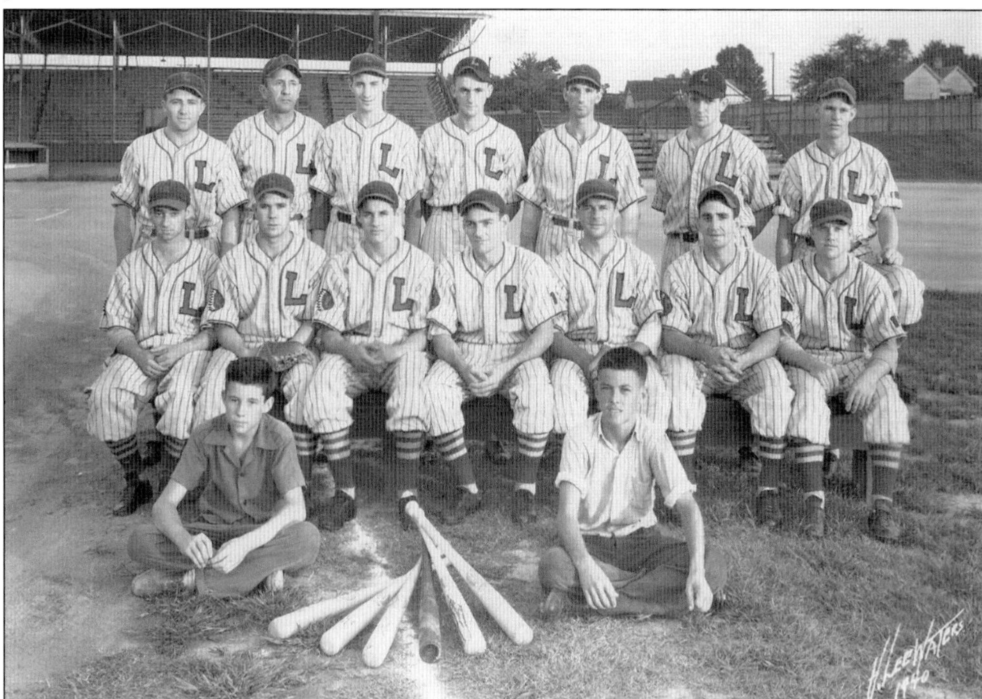

The Lexington Indians were part of the old North State League. The league was Class D professional baseball and the Indians had a working agreement with the Williamsport, PA, Class A team, an affiliate of the Philadelphia Athletics. This 1940 team finished third in the league standings but won the championship in the playoffs. "Pop" Fite was the team president.

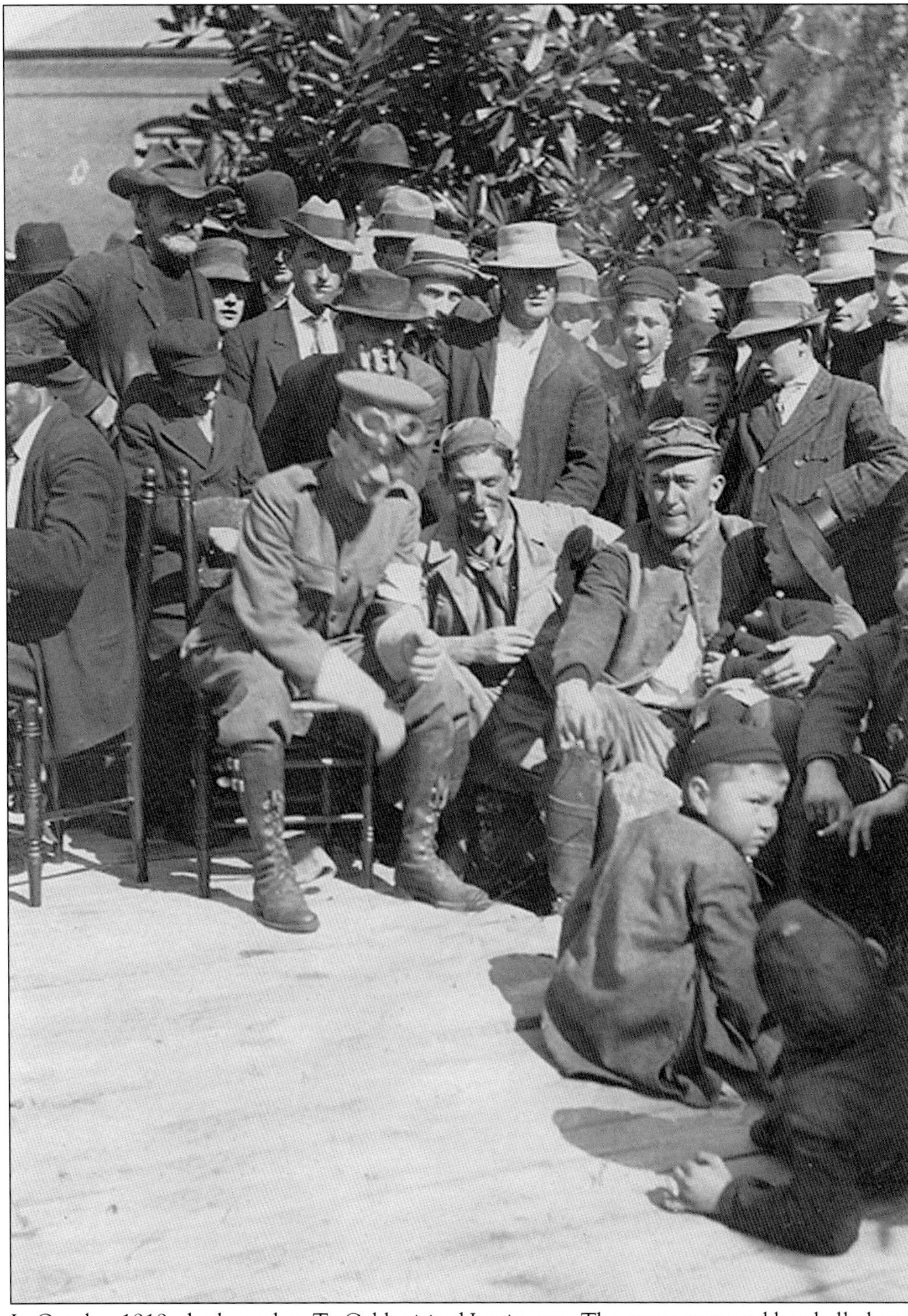

In October 1919, the legendary Ty Cobb visited Lexington. The temperamental baseball player received a warm welcome from local fans of America's national pastime. Based on this rare photograph, there was no controversy in Davidson County when one of baseball's greatest players came to town.

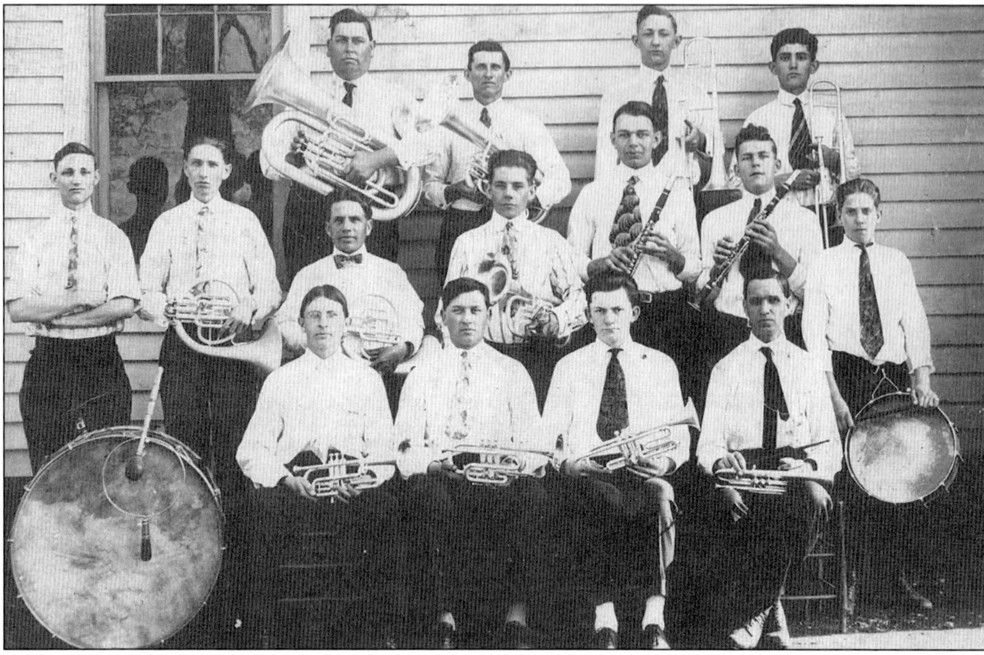

The South Lexington Band is pictured here around 1915. The band included the following members: (front row) Jesse Winfield Yarbrough, Clyde Gobble, and Cary Pickard; (middle row) John Miller, Odell Gibson, Kearney Parker, Oscar Richardson, Lee Myers, and Johnnie Parker; (back row) Carl Gibson, Charlie Shular, Arch Miller, and Marvin Smith.

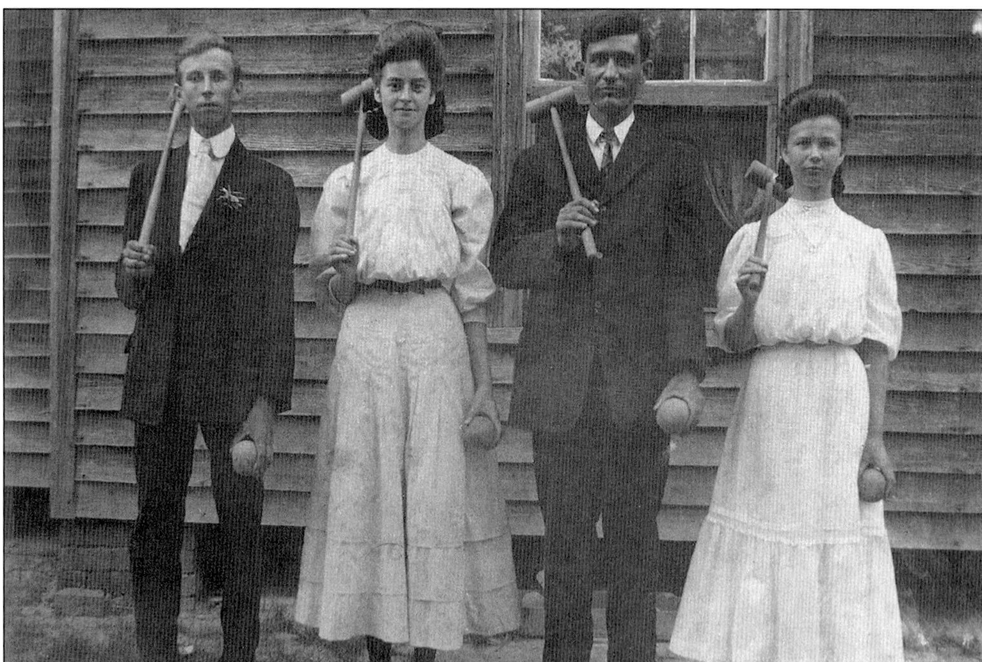

This *c.* 1910 group is an original "croquet quartet" at the John Eddinger home in the Rich Fork community near Thomasville. From left to right are George Eddinger, Nova Kennedy Royal, Samuel Eddinger, and Florence Eddinger.

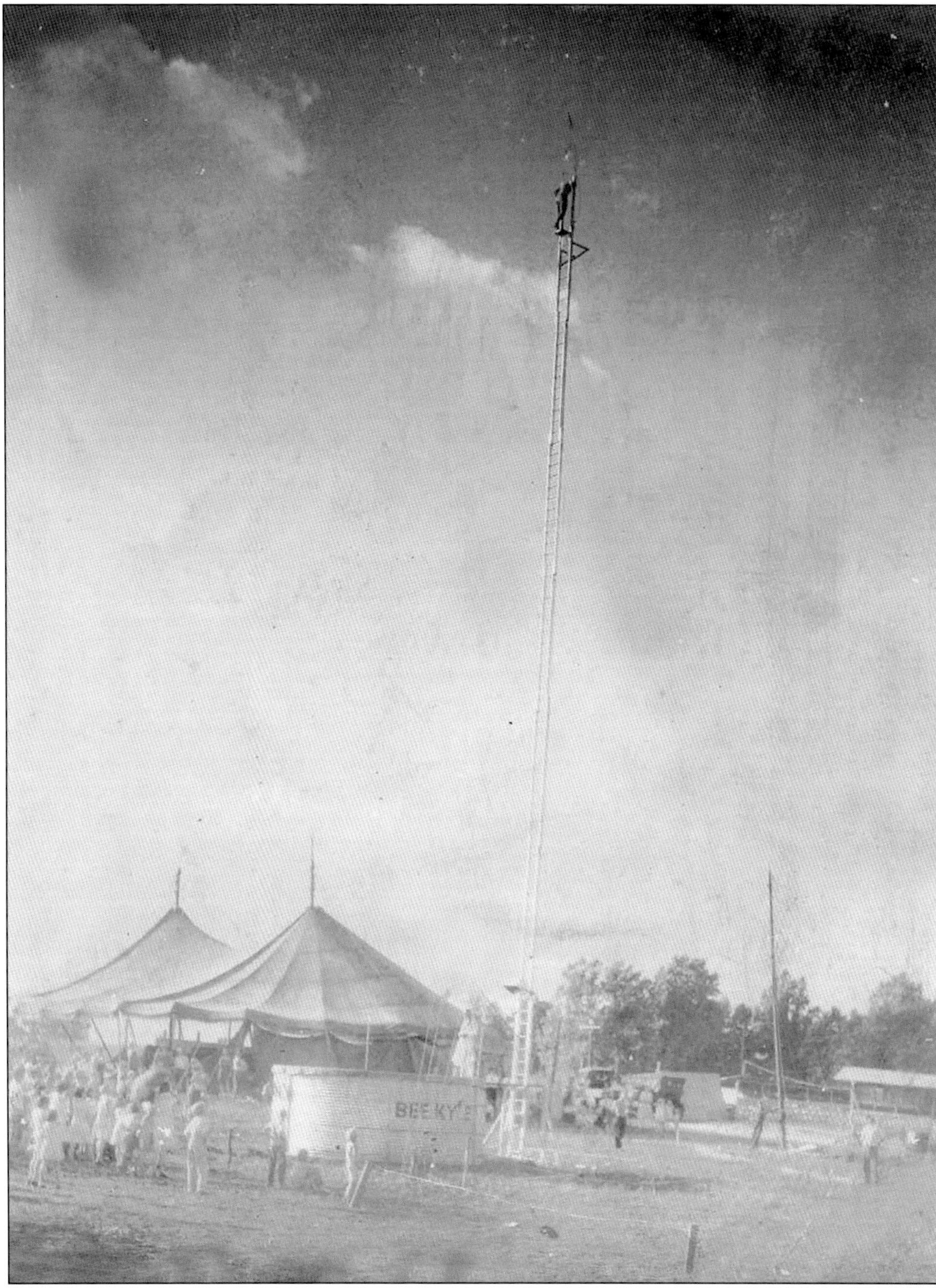

The Lexington Kiwanis Club started the Davidson County Agricultural Fair in 1946 to fund the Kiddie Kamp. Not much is known about this early photograph of a high-rise diver, but as entertainment it was breathtaking! As far as is known, the diver made it.

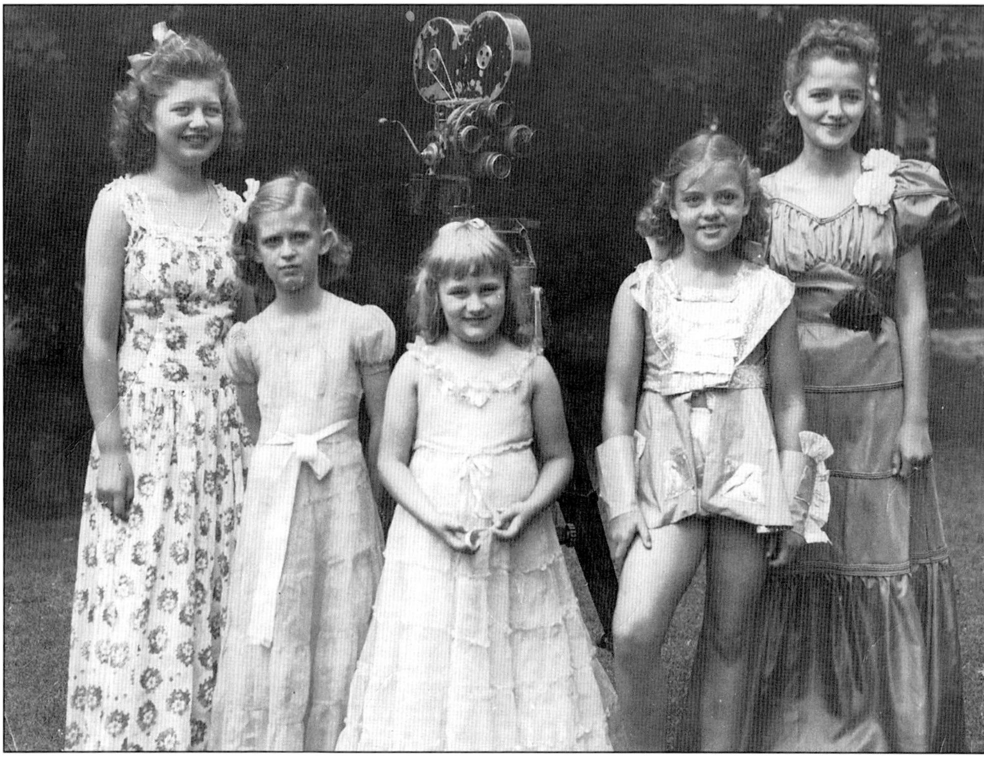

Hollywood came to Lexington in 1941! A California production company filmed a short movie about the kidnapping and rescue of a small child. Joan Kearns Clodfelter was the young heroine. The local children in the movie were, from left to right, Elizabeth Zimmerman Sink, Joan Everhart Zimmerman, Joan Kearns Clodfelter, Roxanne Disher, and an unknown girl.

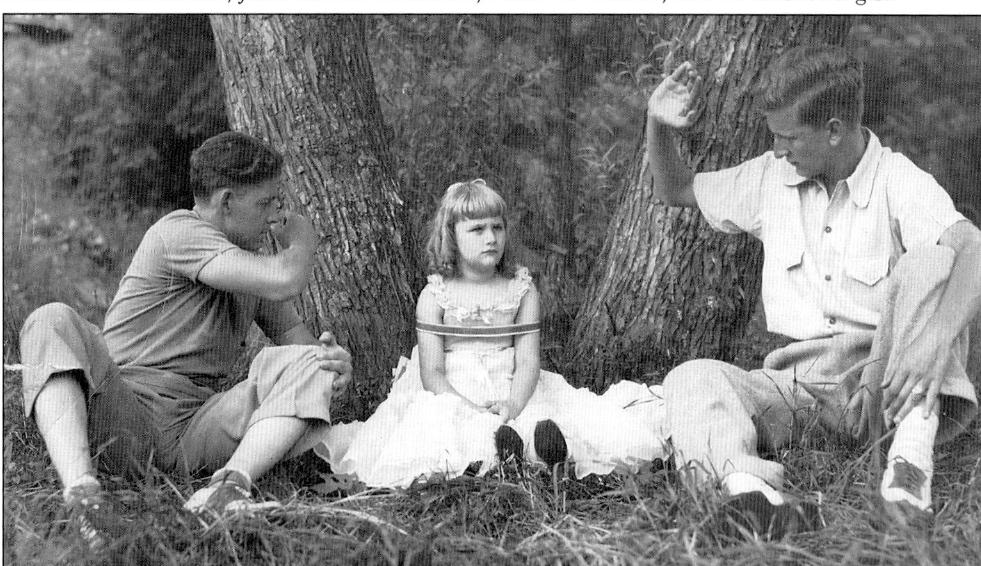

Heroine Joan Clodfelter is shown with her two captors deep in the "woods," actually the behind present-day First Baptist Church. The heroine's "house" was the Wall home on West Third Avenue. The only known copy of this movie was lost when the Carolina Theatre burned.

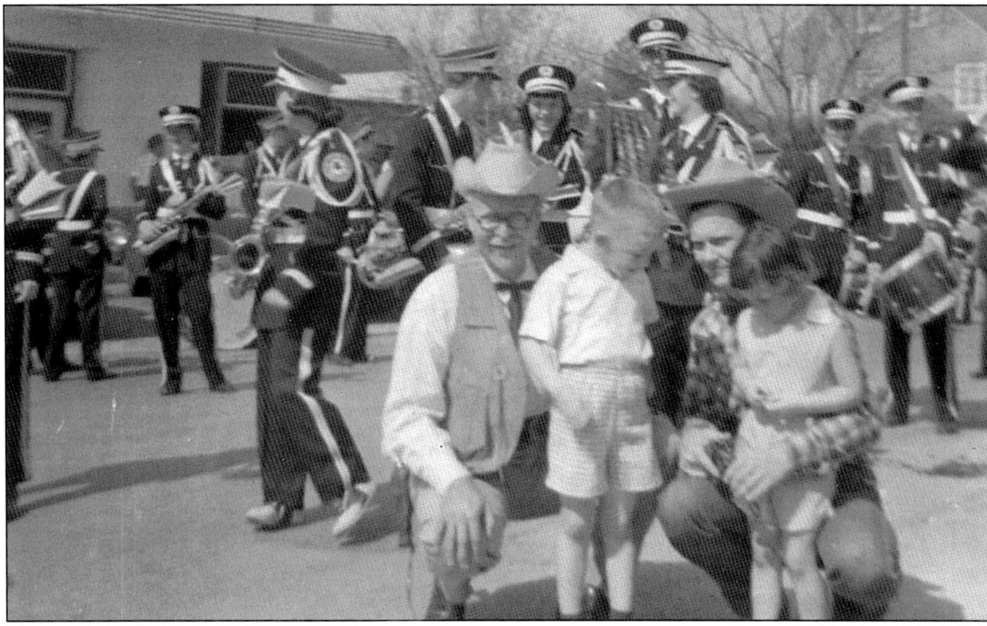

Two young fans pose with "Old Rebel," a local television celebrity, while the North Davidson High School Marching Band is in the background for this 1959 parade.

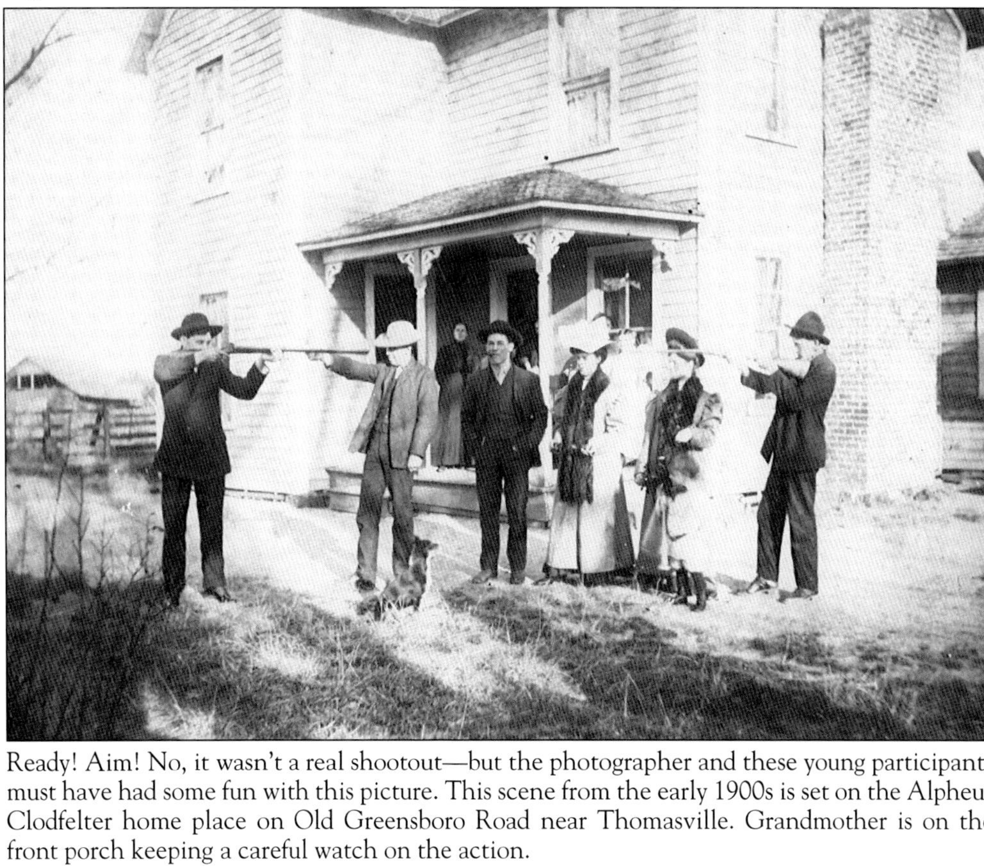

Ready! Aim! No, it wasn't a real shootout—but the photographer and these young participants must have had some fun with this picture. This scene from the early 1900s is set on the Alpheus Clodfelter home place on Old Greensboro Road near Thomasville. Grandmother is on the front porch keeping a careful watch on the action.

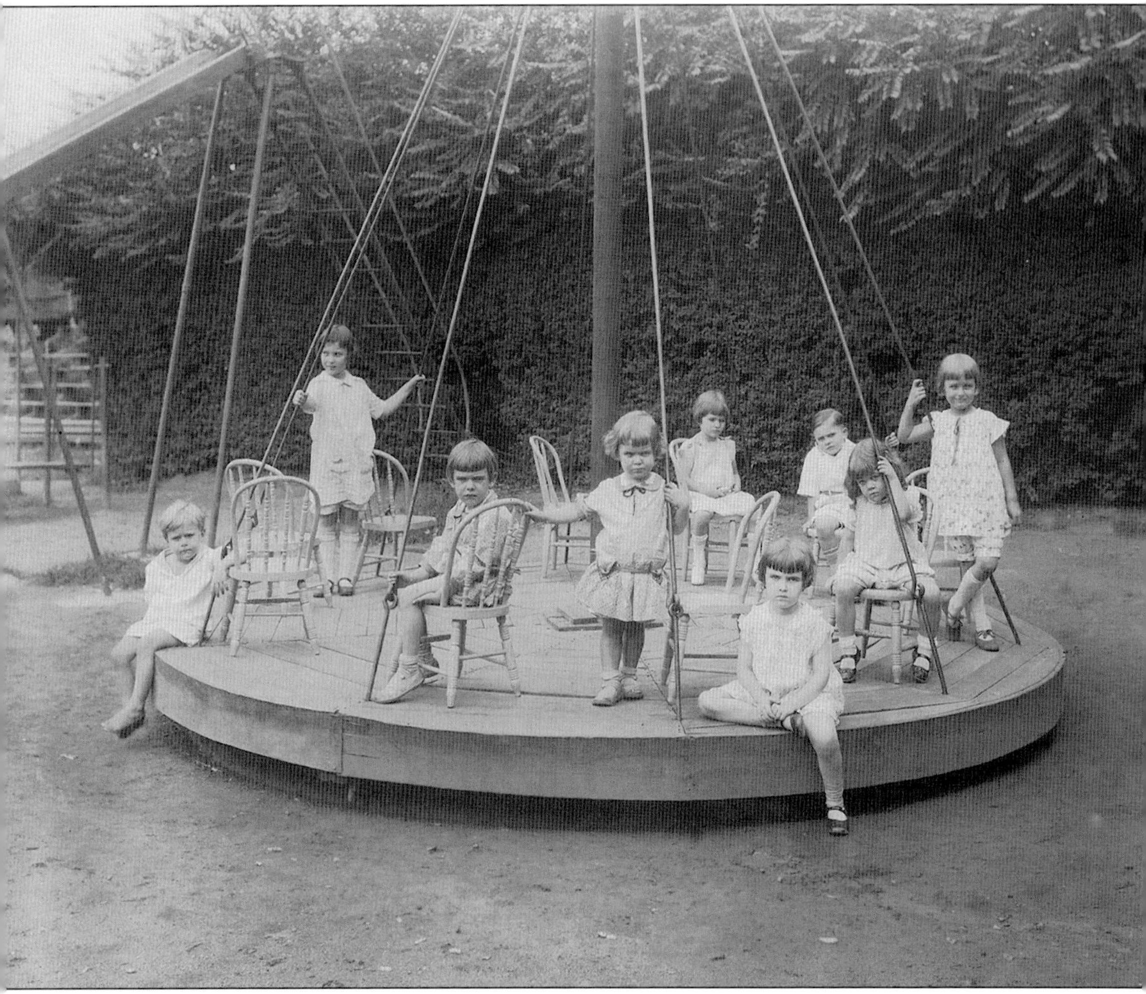

Why are these children not smiling? Because they were called in from play and made to take a bath and dress up for this picture. The somber children include Jessie Gordon Wright, Virginia Hartzog, and Margaret Wallace.

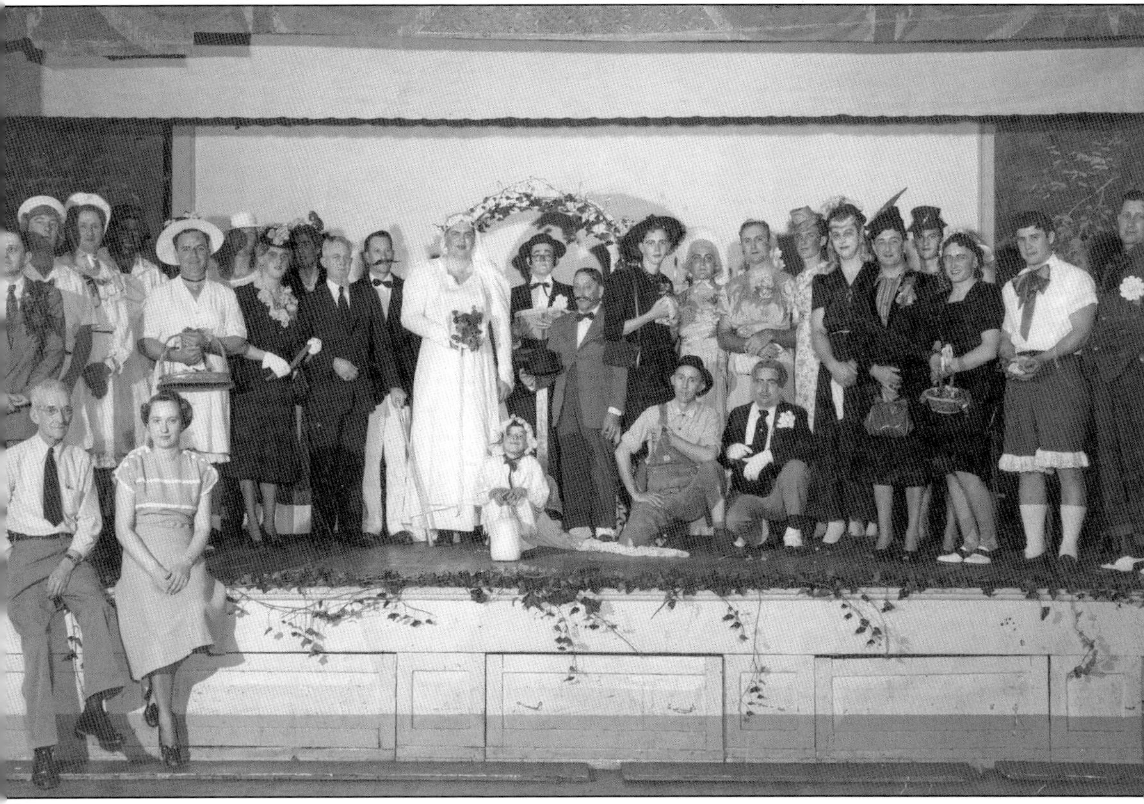

The Erlanger community was the center of social activity as evidenced by this "Womanless Wedding." It was a Saturday night filled with fun and laughter in April 1947. The only real woman in this picture is Sarah Hedrick Coppley. Behind her, dressed as a flower girl, stands her husband, Mock Hedrick.

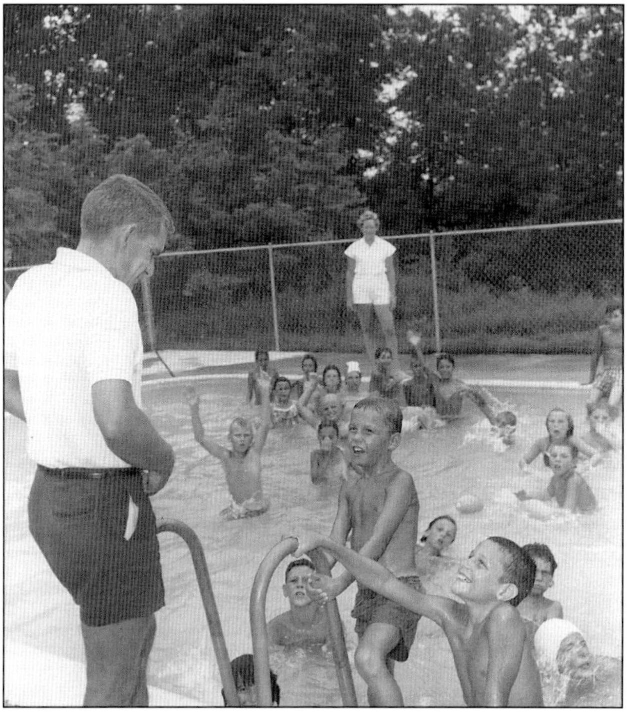

These happy children were 1961 campers at the Kiwanis Kiddie Kamp. The first Kiddie Kamp was held in 1928 on the Woodrow McKay farm off of Arnold Road. The goal of the early camps was to prevent tuberculosis in at-risk children and the results were amazing. Over the first 12 years, there were 360 underprivileged campers with an average weight gain of 10 pounds per child!

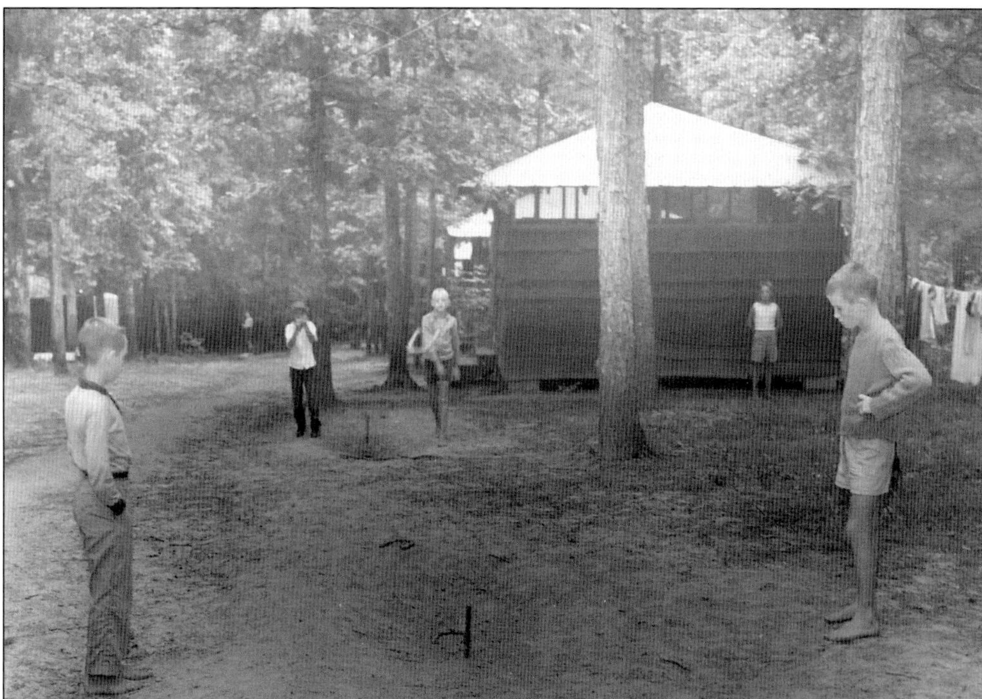

In 1953, the Lexington Kiwanis Club purchased land and developed the present Kiddie Kamp off of Ridge Road. The club invested around $45,000 in the land and buildings. The Kiddie Kamp, now called Kamp Kiwanis, continues to operate every summer serving around 200 children selected by the Department of Social Services.

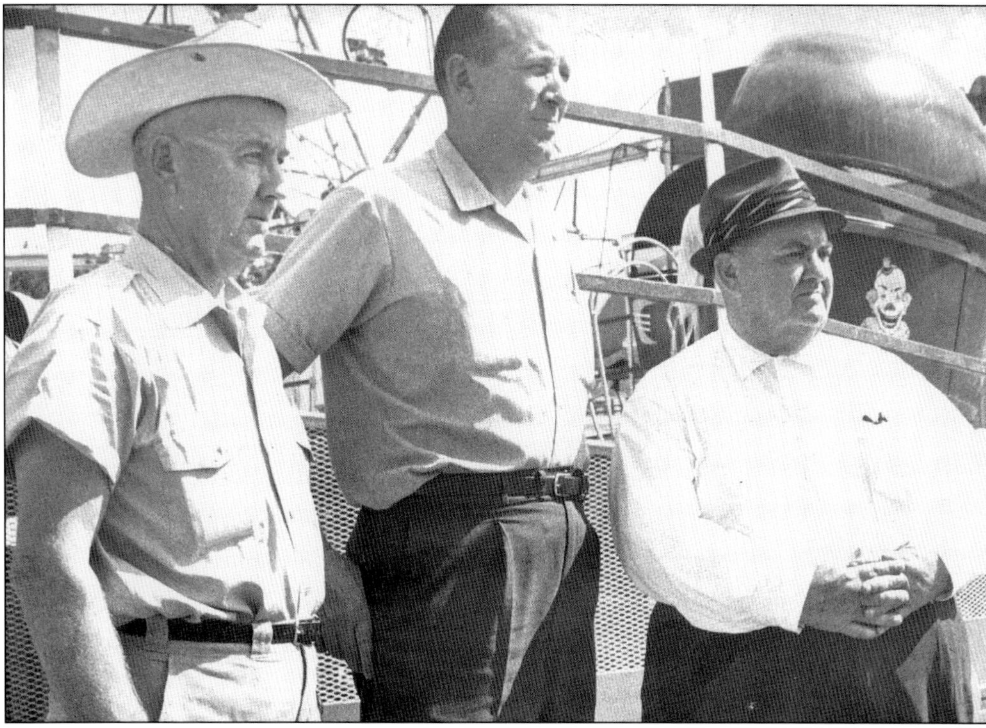

Longtime fair president Archie Sink is pictured here in 1967 with vice-president Carl Bernhardt on his right and Lloyd Thomas, owner of the midway rides, on his left. The Miss Davidson County beauty pageant is an annual event at the fair each September.

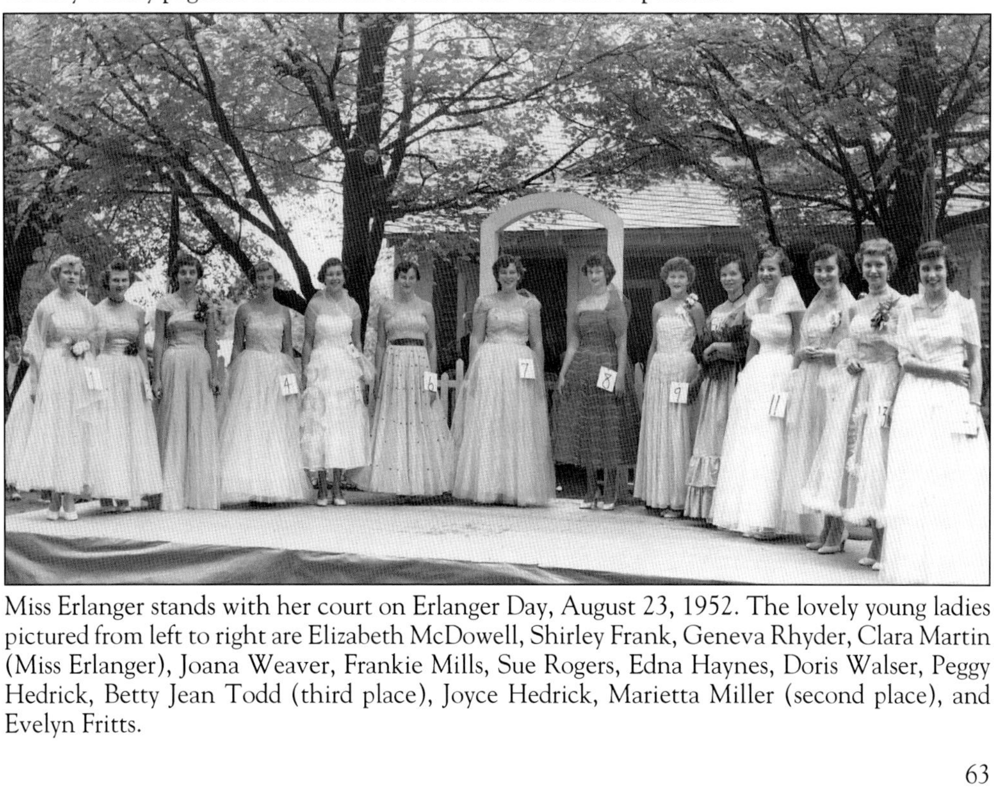

Miss Erlanger stands with her court on Erlanger Day, August 23, 1952. The lovely young ladies pictured from left to right are Elizabeth McDowell, Shirley Frank, Geneva Rhyder, Clara Martin (Miss Erlanger), Joana Weaver, Frankie Mills, Sue Rogers, Edna Haynes, Doris Walser, Peggy Hedrick, Betty Jean Todd (third place), Joyce Hedrick, Marietta Miller (second place), and Evelyn Fritts.

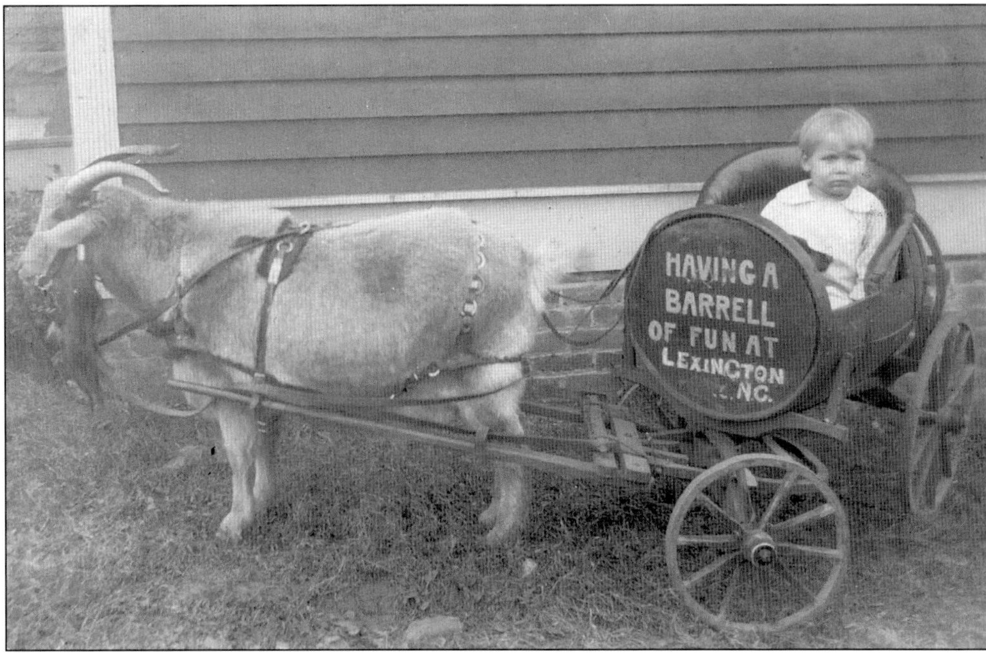

Many children had their pictures made in the goat cart during the 1920s. A traveling photographer came ready with the goat, cart, and customized sign. In this picture taken about 1922, Vernon Morris isn't quite sure if he is having a "barrel of fun" or not!

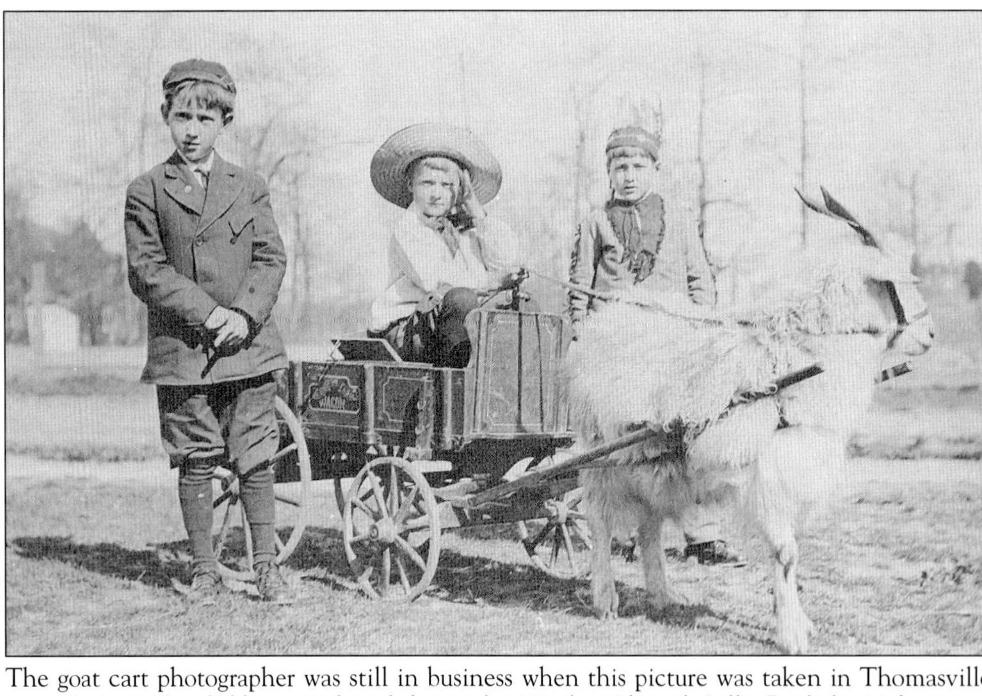

The goat cart photographer was still in business when this picture was taken in Thomasville around 1929. The children are, from left to right, Waylon Clinard, Sallie Rutledge Nifong, and Carlos Clinard.

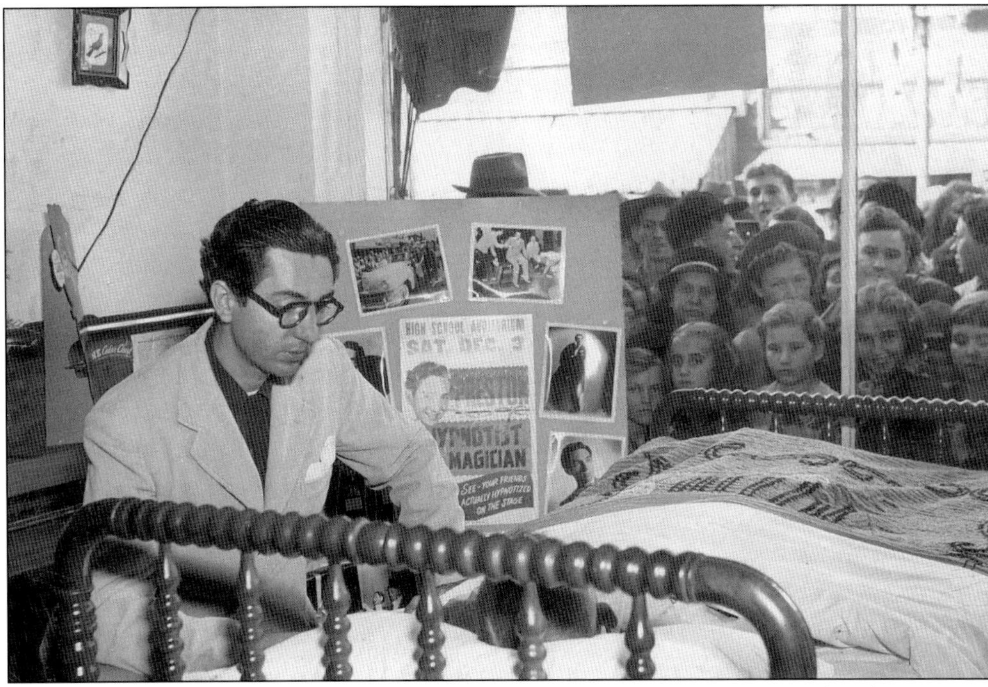

A young crowd presses against a storefront window to watch "Preston" as he demonstrates hypnosis. Downtown stores used a variety of displays and events to attract business and this one proved simply "magical."

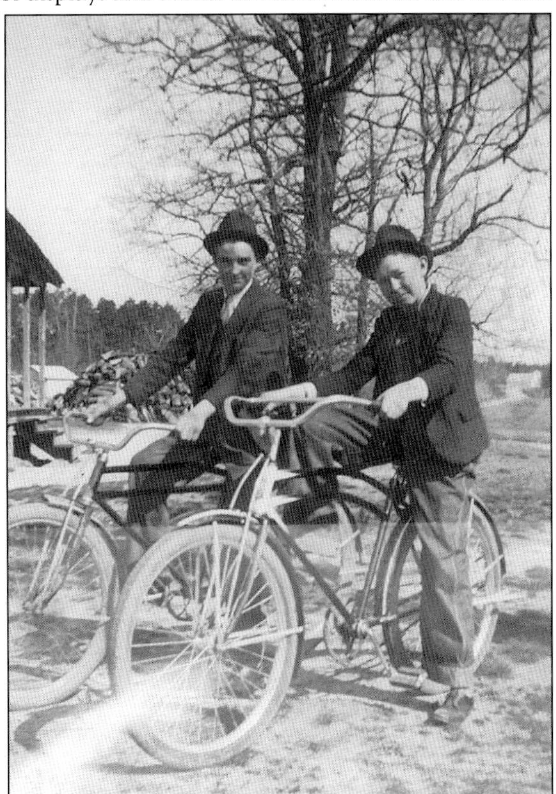

Grady Shoaf and John L. DeLapp enjoy a bicycle ride in the Reedy Creek community. This early 1930s picture was taken at Grady Shoaf's home at the corner of Perryman Road and Highway 150.

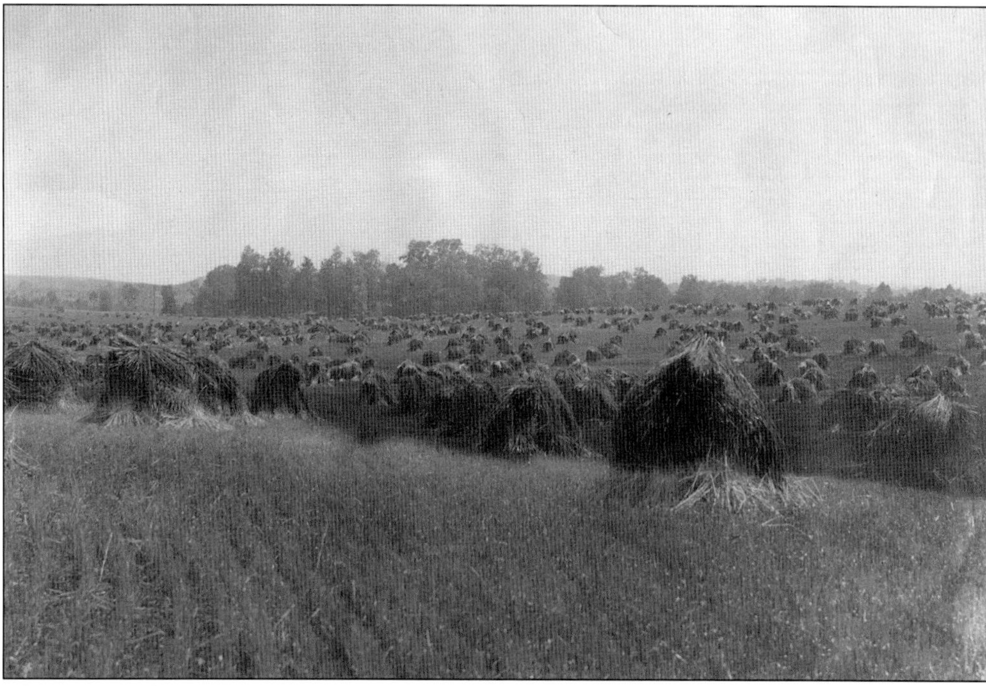

These pastoral scenes are from the old Hargrave farm in Linwood. Adelaide Hargrave Gordon saved a newspaper clipping of a memorable hayride and moonlight picnic here in 1916. Gen. Zebulon Vance Walser was the chaperone for the evening. The Linwood hosts provided a picnic spread on the lawn with a wagonload of watermelons. The young people played "the old-timey games of leap frog, dropping the handkerchief, and King William." It was reported that General Walser was "the king bee in all the merry making." The wagons returned to Lexington at 1 a.m.!

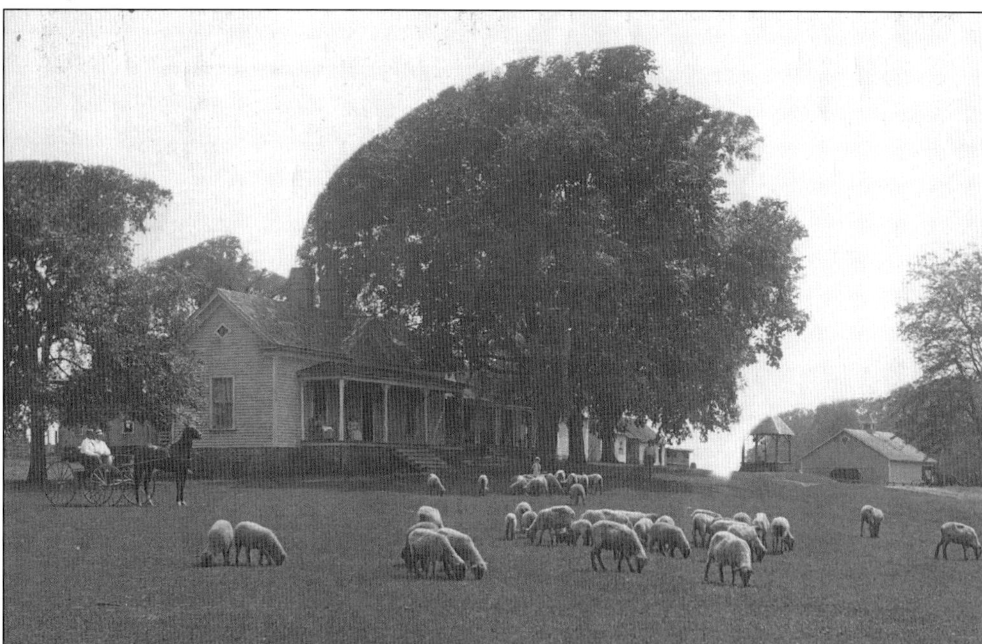

Five

Schools and Children's Homes

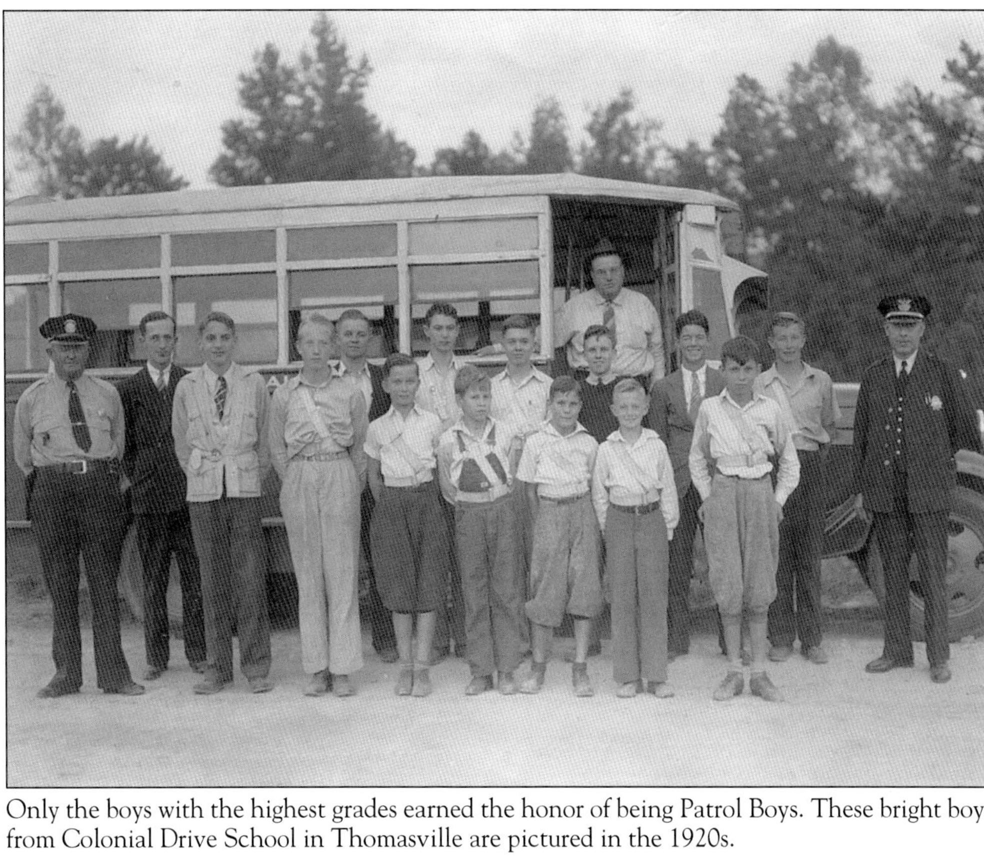

Only the boys with the highest grades earned the honor of being Patrol Boys. These bright boys from Colonial Drive School in Thomasville are pictured in the 1920s.

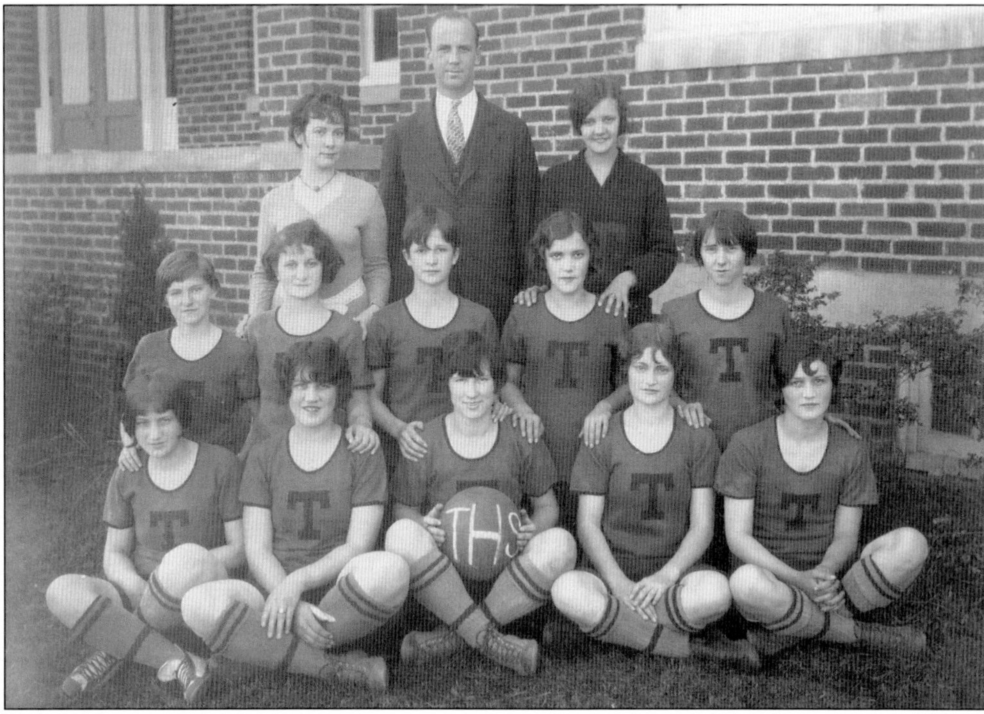

These 10 young ladies made up the girls' basketball team at Thomasville High School during the 1920s.

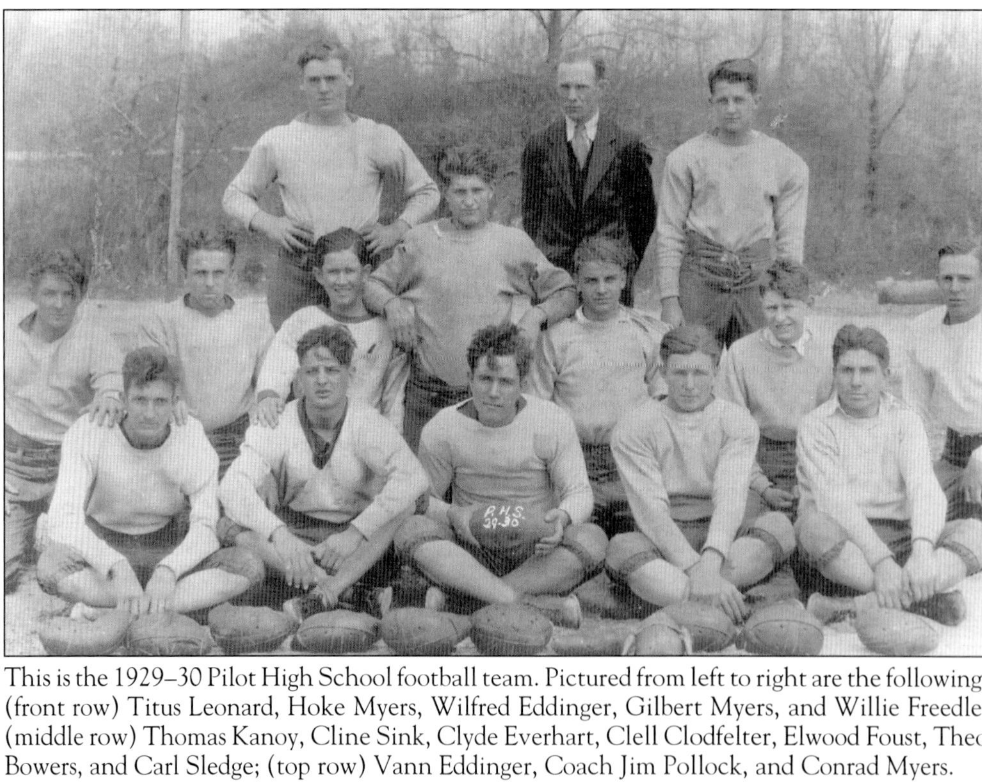

This is the 1929–30 Pilot High School football team. Pictured from left to right are the following: (front row) Titus Leonard, Hoke Myers, Wilfred Eddinger, Gilbert Myers, and Willie Freedle; (middle row) Thomas Kanoy, Cline Sink, Clyde Everhart, Clell Clodfelter, Elwood Foust, Theo Bowers, and Carl Sledge; (top row) Vann Eddinger, Coach Jim Pollock, and Conrad Myers.

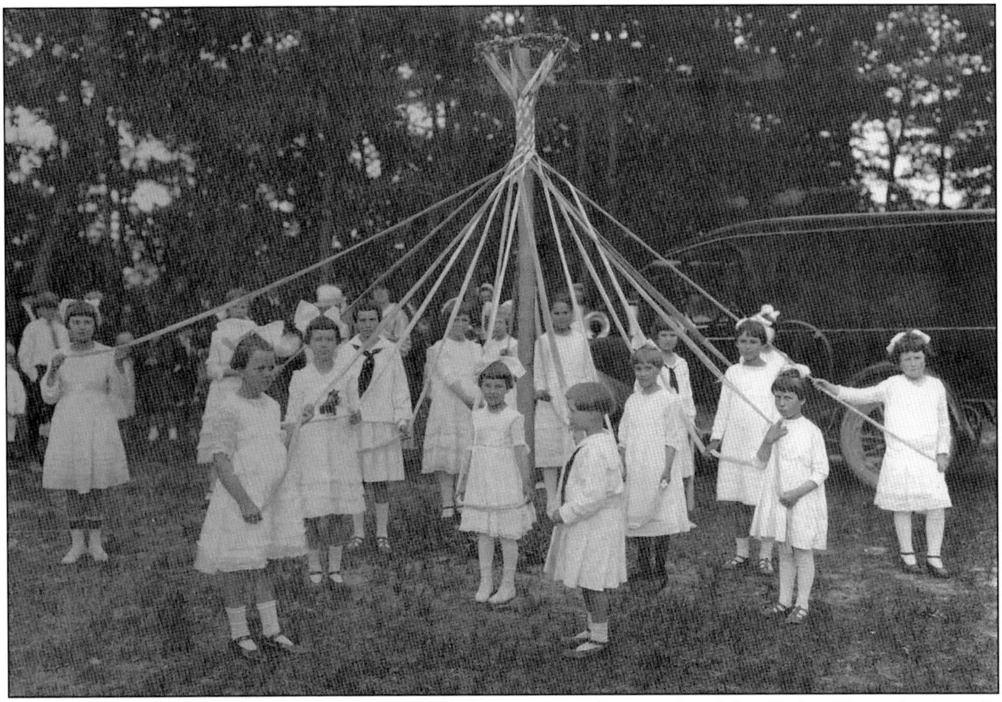

May Day was once quite an occasion for children, complete with a May Pole. These little girls came to share in May Day festivities at Reeds High School in 1922. Children around the May Pole include Elayne Snyder Beeker, Kathleen Mock Craver, Adelaide Craver Farabee, Arlene Leonard Hill, Vada Snider McMahan, Geneva Hunt Leonard, and Virginia Hunt Blaylock.

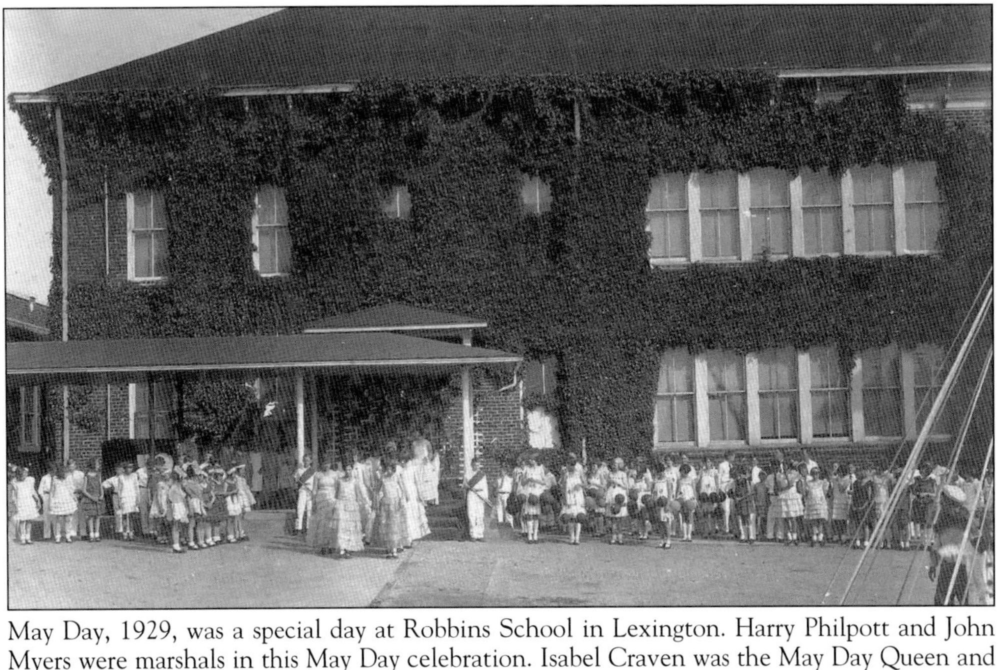

May Day, 1929, was a special day at Robbins School in Lexington. Harry Philpott and John Myers were marshals in this May Day celebration. Isabel Craven was the May Day Queen and Joe Miller was the crown bearer. Robbins School was named for Capt. Frank C. Robbins, a member of Lexington's first school board, who donated the land for the school.

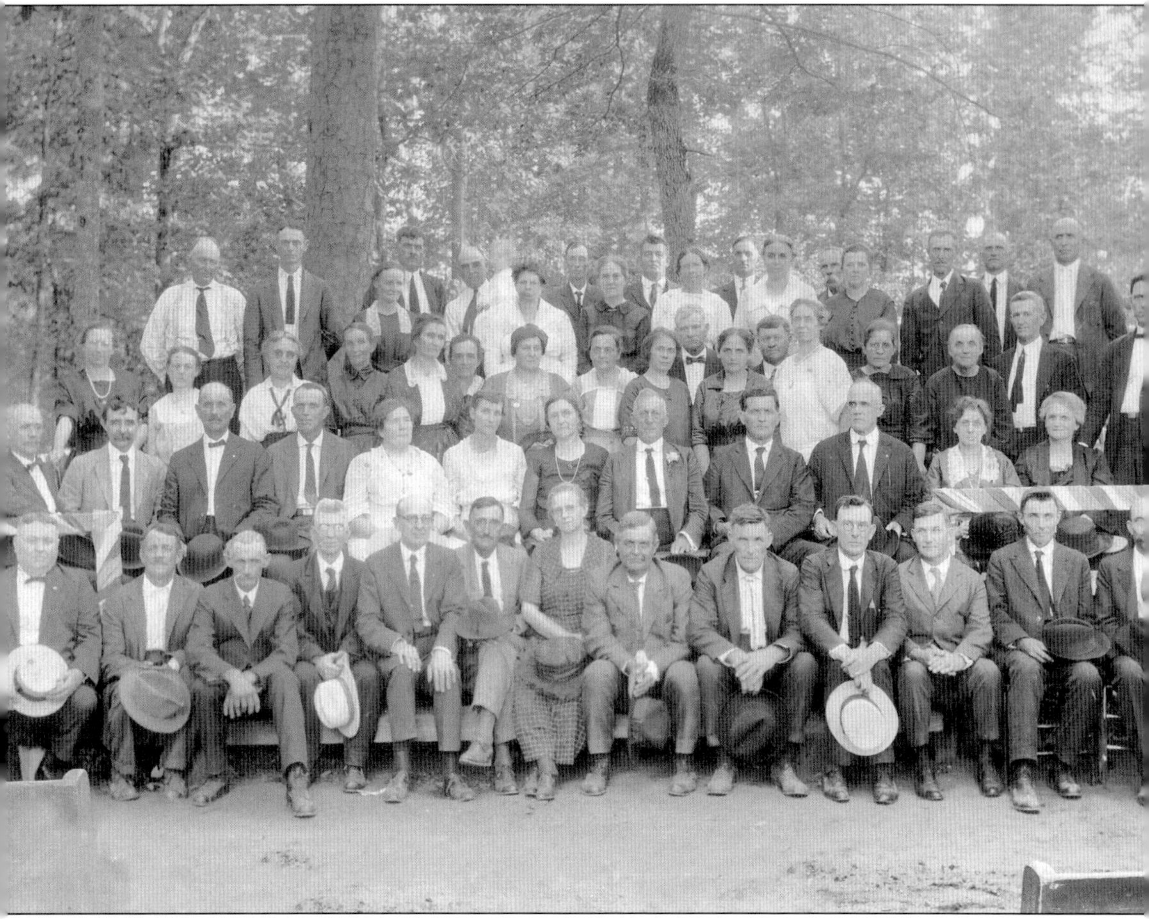

The Reverend W.P. Cline established Holly Grove Academy in January 1886. The two-story school building was truly a community effort, with all but $500 of the cost of labor and materials donated. Later, a large two-story house was built for boarding students. There have been three different buildings in the history of Holly Grove Academy, which operated until the opening of Davis-Townsend School in 1930. This is one of the early classes, pictured here on August 30, 1922, at a class reunion. Reverend Cline later became one of the founders of Lenoir-Rhyne College in Hickory.

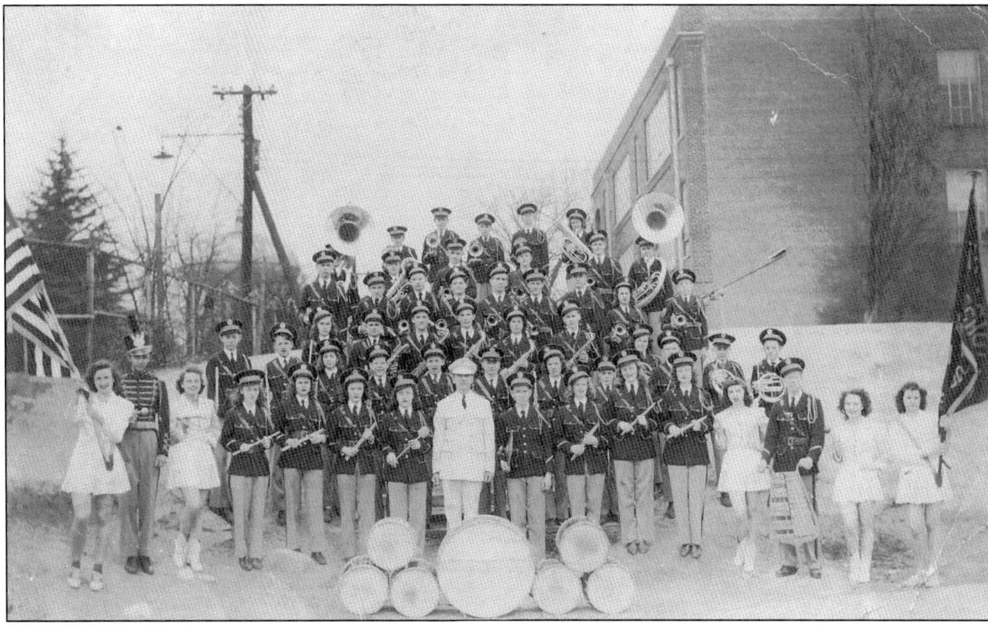

The marching band from Thomasville High School poses for a picture during the 1946–47 school year.

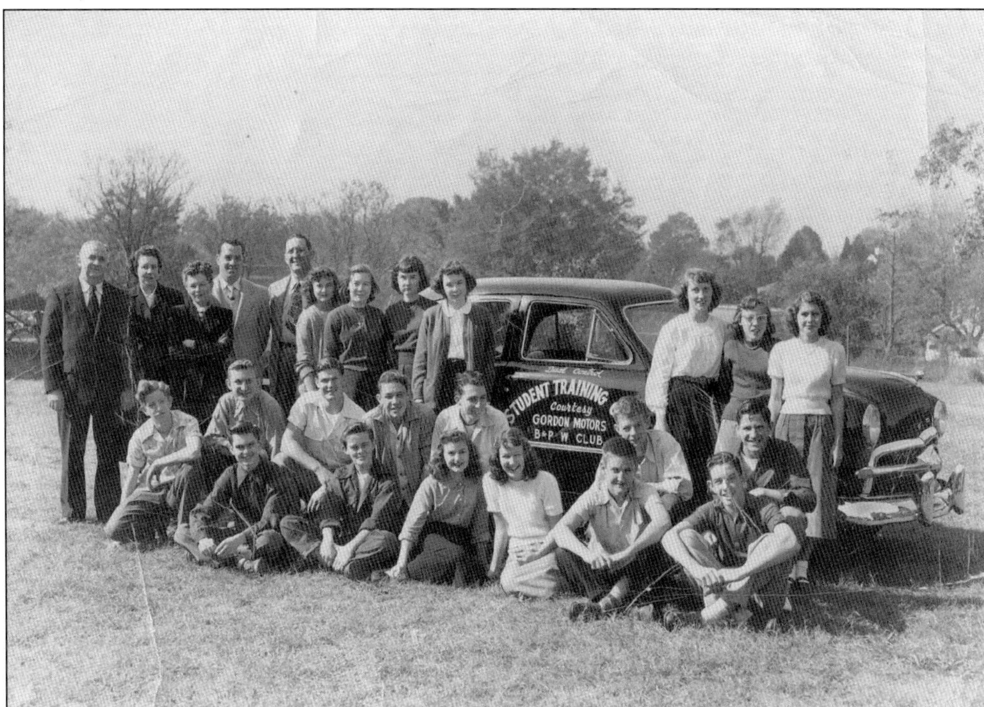

The year was 1949, and the first driver's education class was offered at Lexington High School. The five adults on the left rear, from left to right, are school superintendent L.E. Andrews, M.S. Trice, unknown, driver education instructor Harold Bowen, and A.E. Gordon, the Ford dealer who supplied the car.

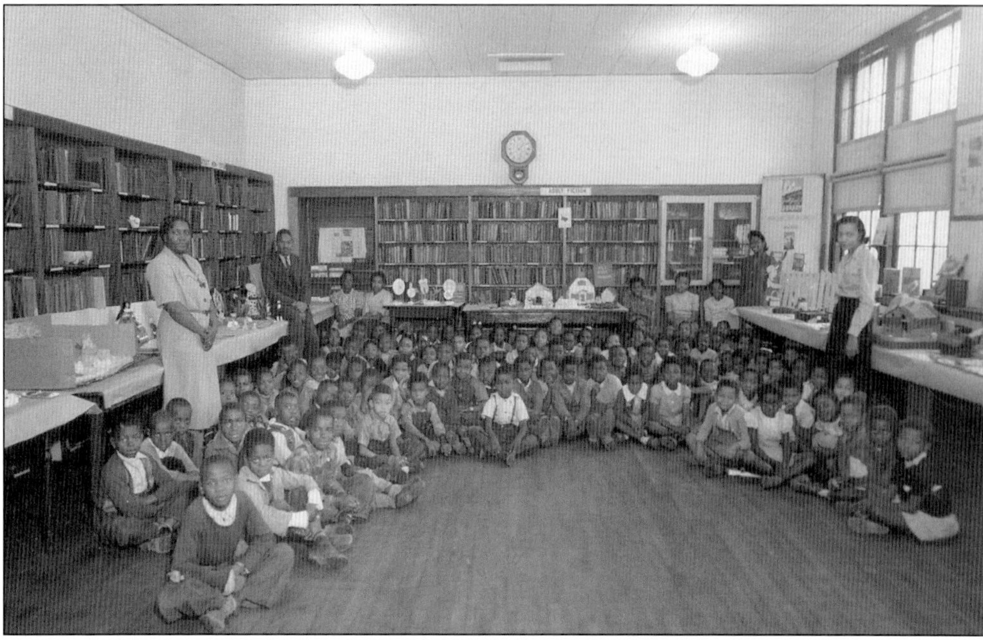

It was time for a story at Dunbar School in Lexington. Faculty members and children are assembled in the school's library in the fall of 1944. Notice all the school projects on the tables.

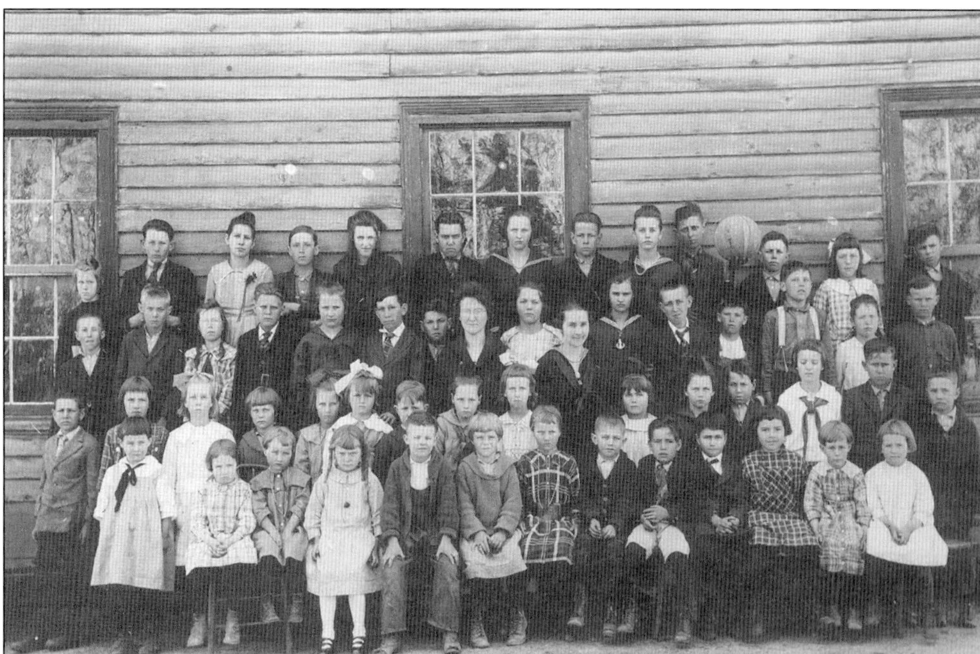

Ebenezer School was located just south of Welcome, where new Highway 52 intersects with old Highway 52. This school picture was taken in 1916 or 1917. A Miss Surratt is the teacher on the left and Mr. Harvey Shoaf is the teacher on the right. This photograph was labeled "W.F. Jackson & Co., Traveling Photographer."

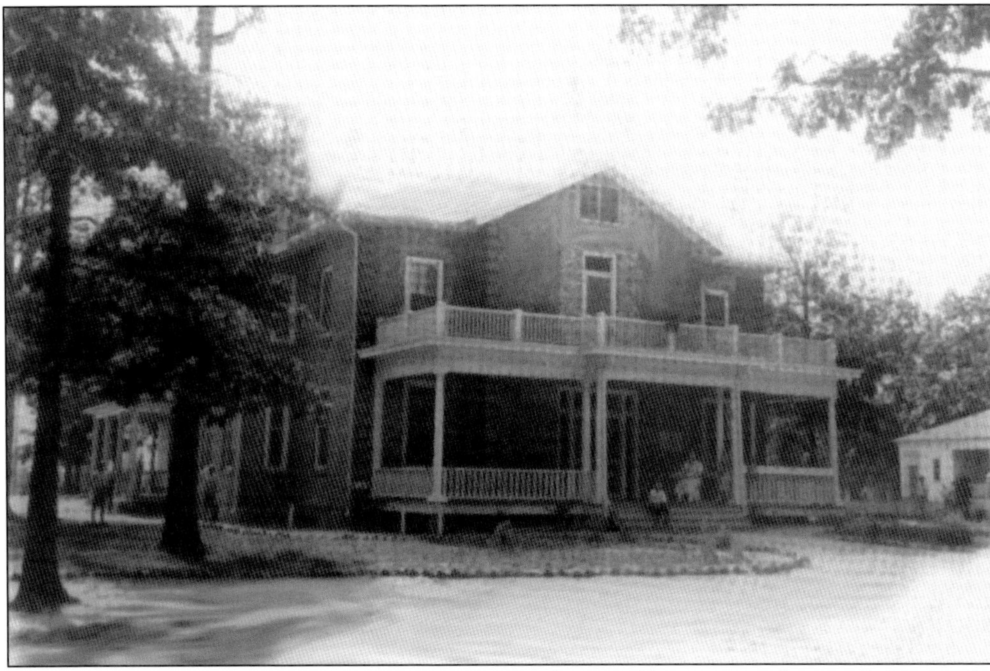

John H. Mills founded the Baptist Orphanage in Thomasville in November 1885. This is the first residence hall for boys, the Watson House, constructed in 1888. The campus had its own school as well as an assembly hall, church, and administrative offices in the central building. A little girl named Rena Baucom requested on her deathbed that her total wealth of 25¢ be donated to the orphanage. The furnishings in the central building were in her memory.

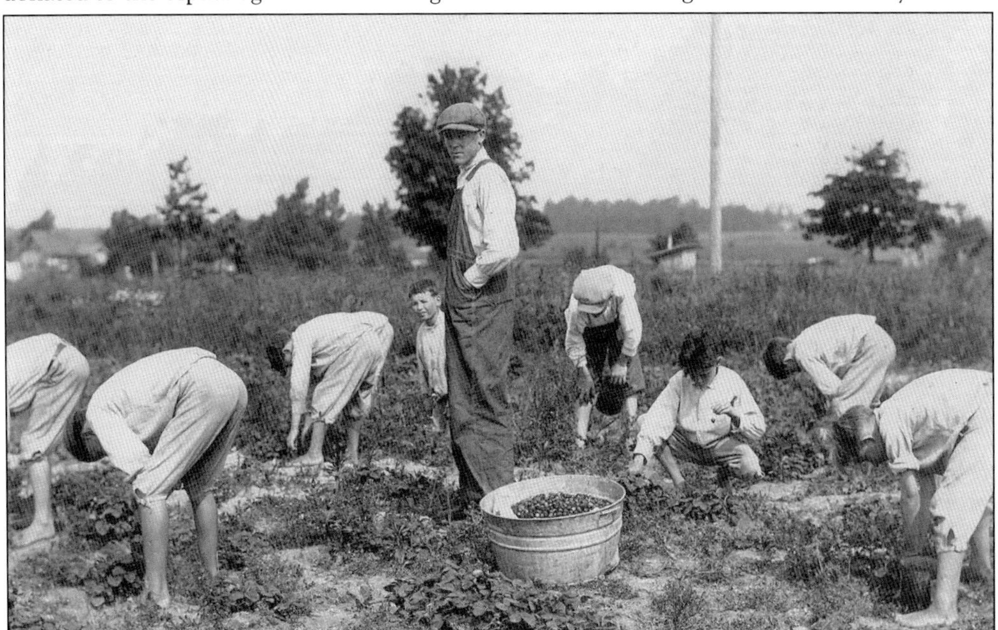

The strawberries were in season when this picture was made, and all hands, young and old, were helping with the harvest. Every child at the Baptist Orphanage was expected to work. Everyone is working here but the supervisor!

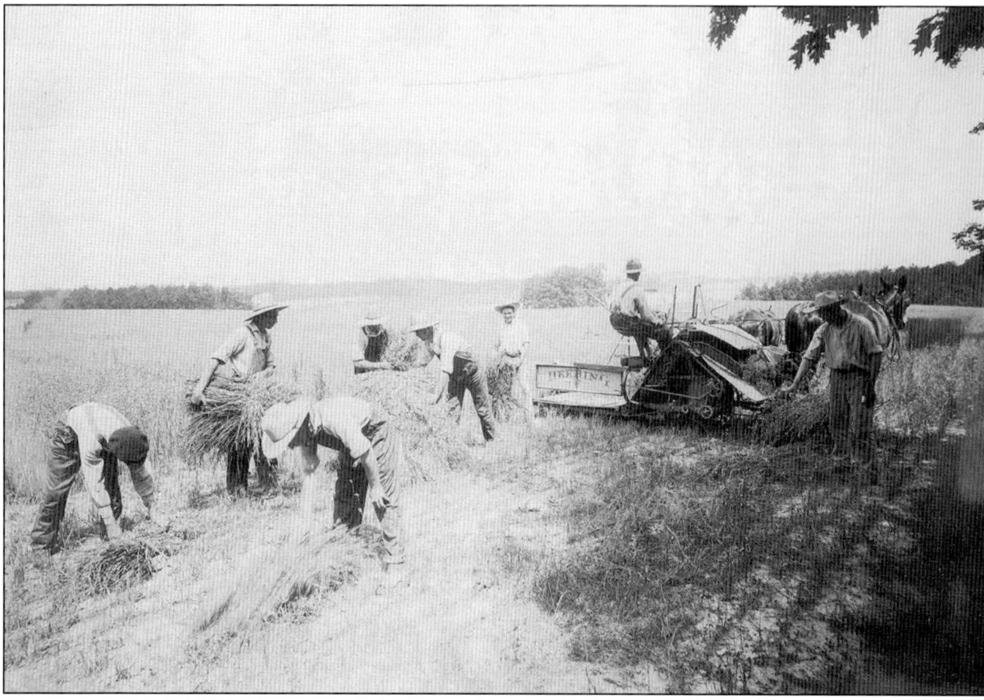

For many years, Mills Home operated its own farm with the boys of the orphanage supplying the labor. This undated picture shows some of the boys working on the farm.

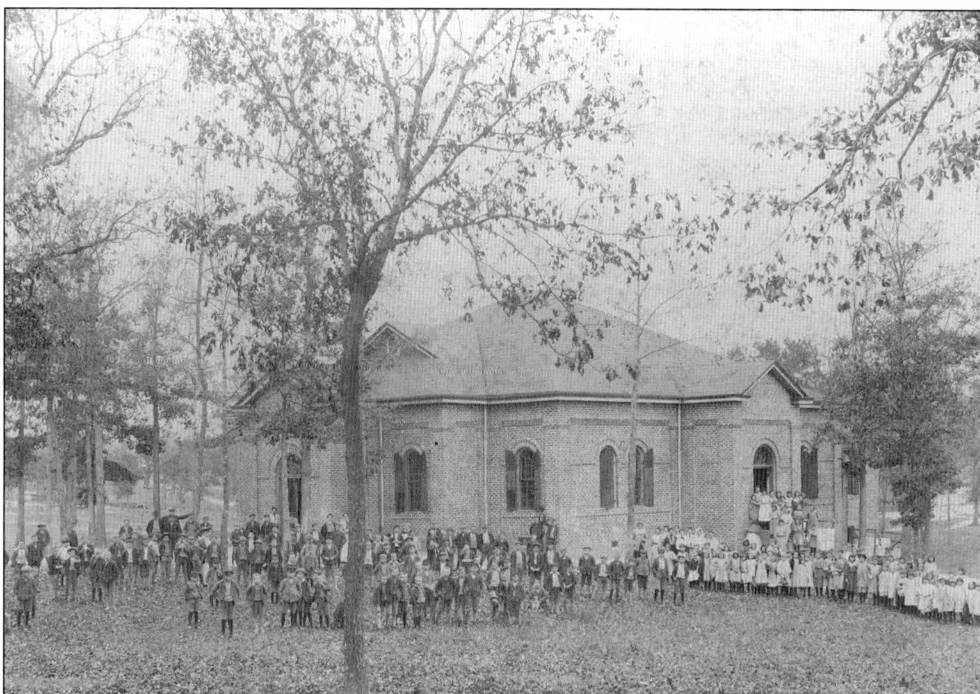

The Central Dining Hall was completed in 1905 and paid for by the estates of Chief Justice W.T. Faircloth of Goldsboro and Mr. P.W. Johnson of Wake Forest.

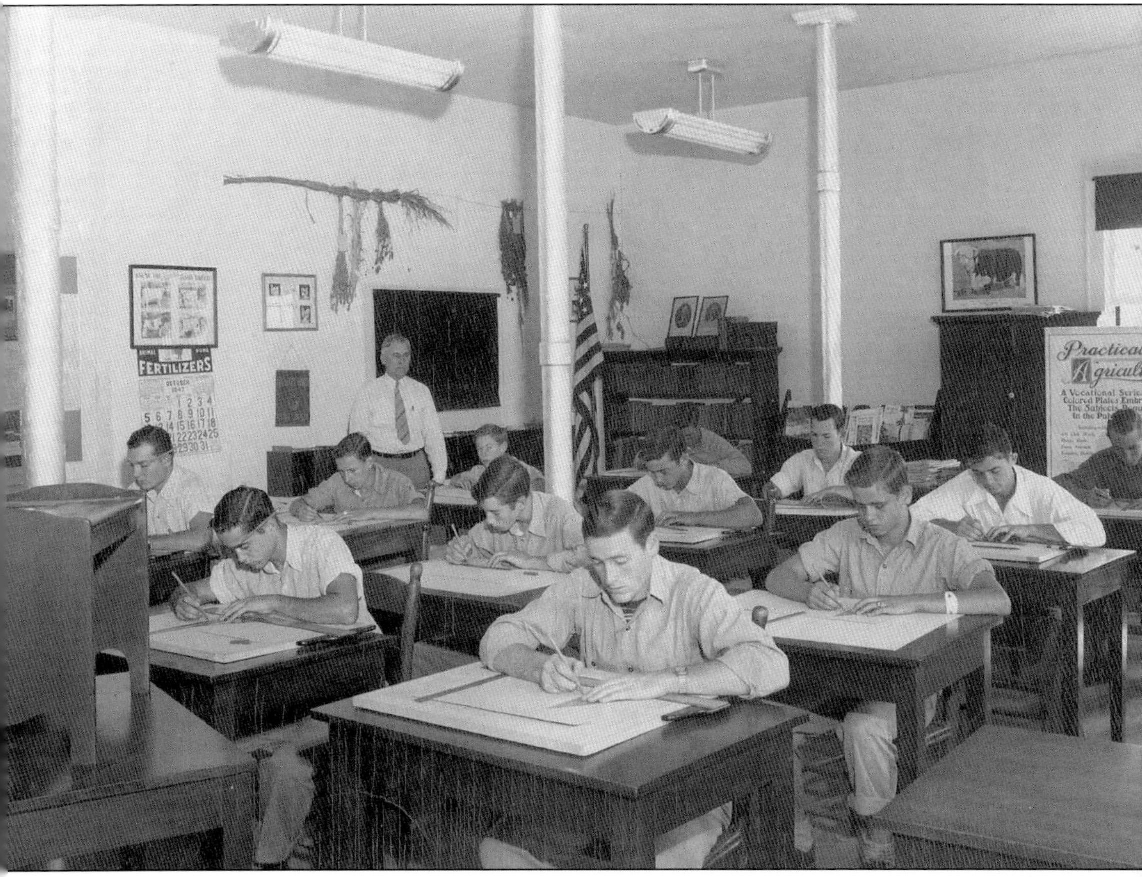

The boys not only worked on the farm, but also studied agriculture. The calendar on the wall tells us that this agriculture class was in October 1947.

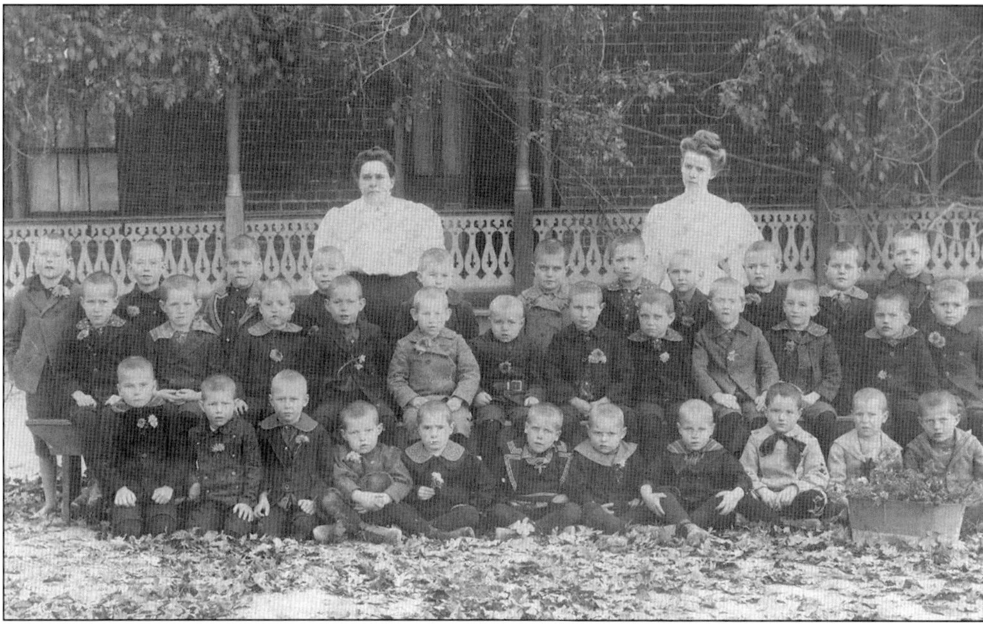

By 1905, 307 children were residents of the Thomasville Baptist Orphanage. Many of the children came when they were young and stayed until they were old enough to be on their own.

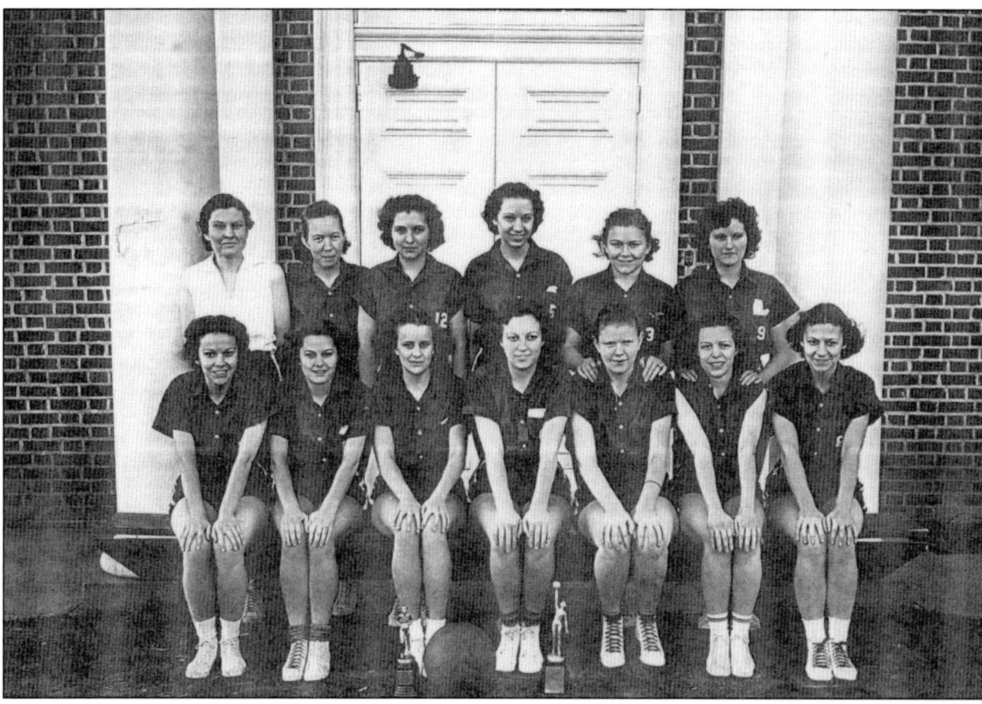

The Junior Order Home girls' basketball team posed for a group picture around 1936. Pictured from left to right are the following: (front row) Margaret Murray McCurdy, Doris Neighbors, Helen Ferguson, Golden Pence, Kara May Spencer, Bernice Carroll, and Louise Stamper; (back row) Minnie Baldwin Banks, Margie Cope, Madge Conley, Ollie Mae Hollifield, Mary Sue Sumners, and Mary Wells.

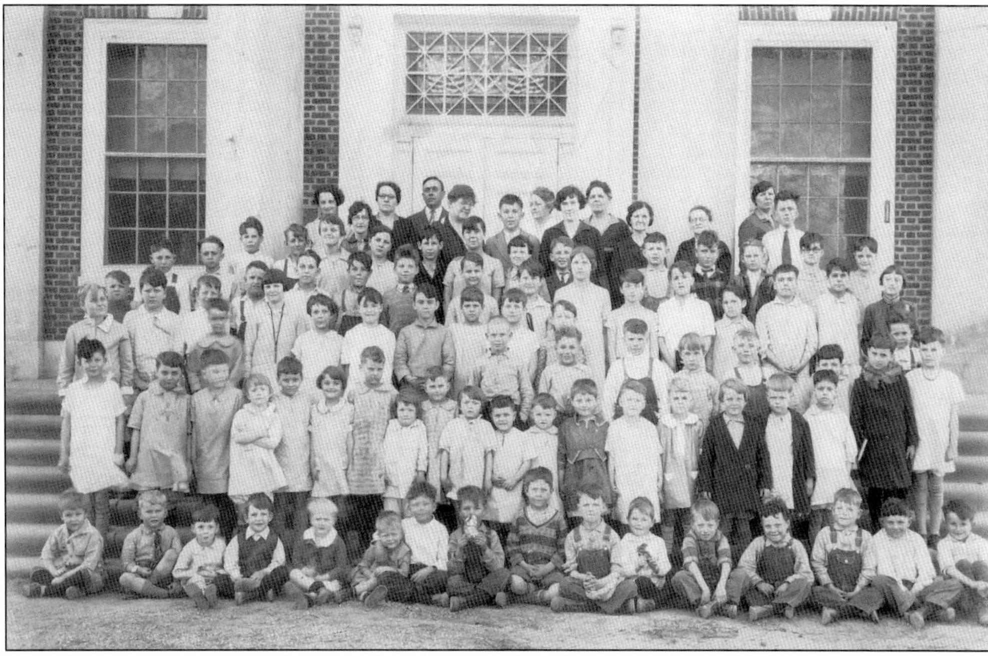

In 1928, the National Council of the Junior Order of American Mechanics opened a branch orphanage on 313 acres southeast of Lexington. Community leaders worked hard to have Lexington chosen as the site of the new home, and the citizens of Davidson County donated over $530,000 to pay for the original buildings and land. The first group of children to arrive was photographed in March 1928, along with the first superintendent, Mr. W.A. Shuford, seen with his wife just in front of the door. Other adults in the picture were teachers.

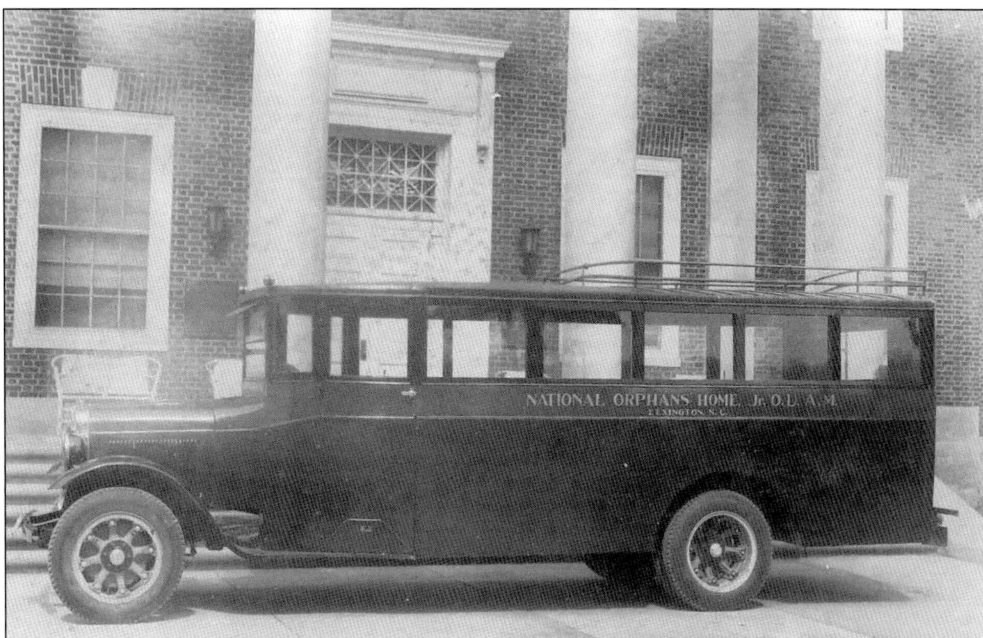

There may be some who still remember the old bus at the Junior Order Home. This bus traveled thousands of miles transporting children to activities and special events.

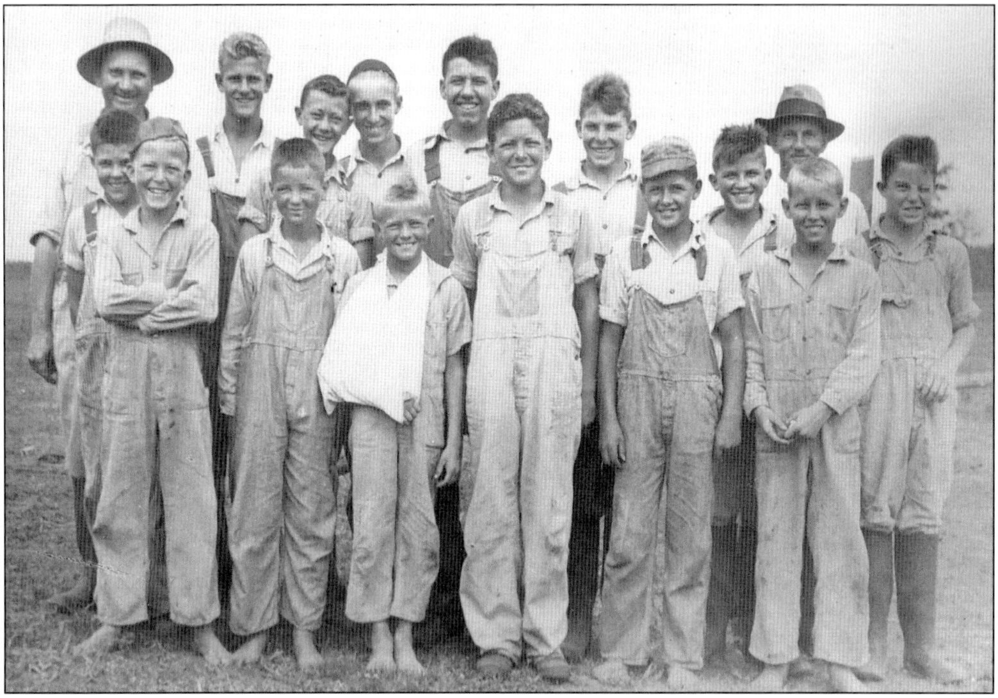

Everyone has a smile as the "milking boys" of the Junior Order Home posed for this picture in 1936. Registered Holsteins at the orphanage's farm, which maintained a leading dairy herd for many years, provided the milk. From left to right are the following: (front row) Warren Mason, Dalton Hinsley, Sammy Bright, Jessie Bright, Roy Hubbs, Ballinger Perry, and Charles Thompson; (back row) J.R. Durham, Mr. Jarrett, Jones Lumsden, Don Barlow, Eddie Smith, Kay Bailor, Skinny Ellis, Tom Jackson, and Mr. Leonard.

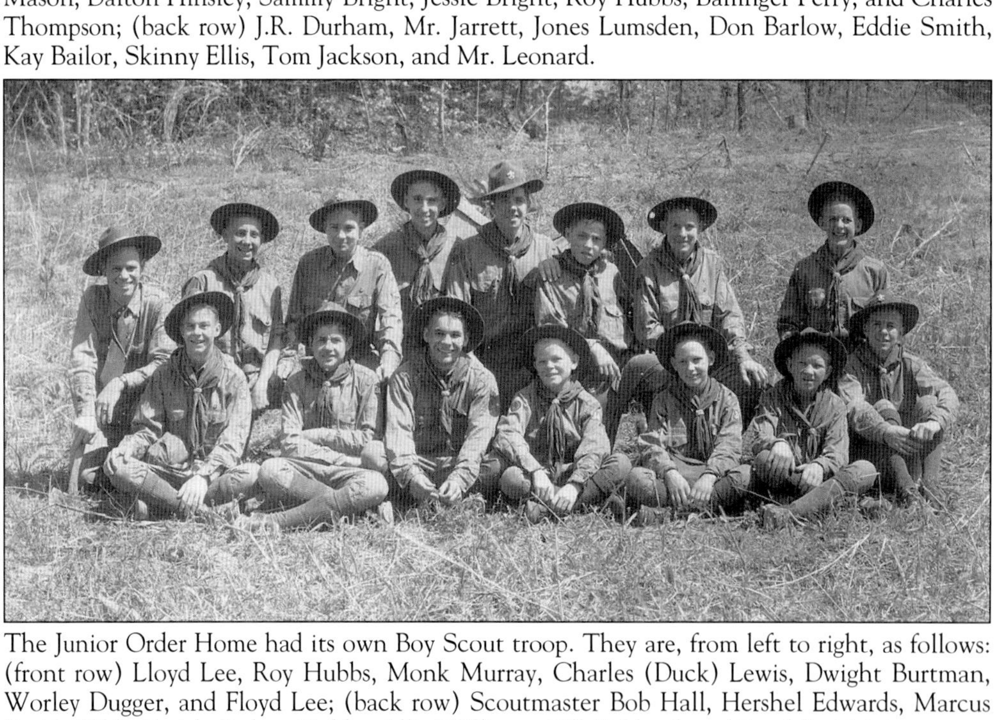

The Junior Order Home had its own Boy Scout troop. They are, from left to right, as follows: (front row) Lloyd Lee, Roy Hubbs, Monk Murray, Charles (Duck) Lewis, Dwight Burtman, Worley Dugger, and Floyd Lee; (back row) Scoutmaster Bob Hall, Hershel Edwards, Marcus Smith, Eddie Smith, Robert Hubbs, Allie Williams, Bill Gabbard, and Franklin Calvin.

In 1942, the Junior Order Home held its own scrap metal drive to support the American troops in World War II. Deanna Hubbs stands behind the collected items.

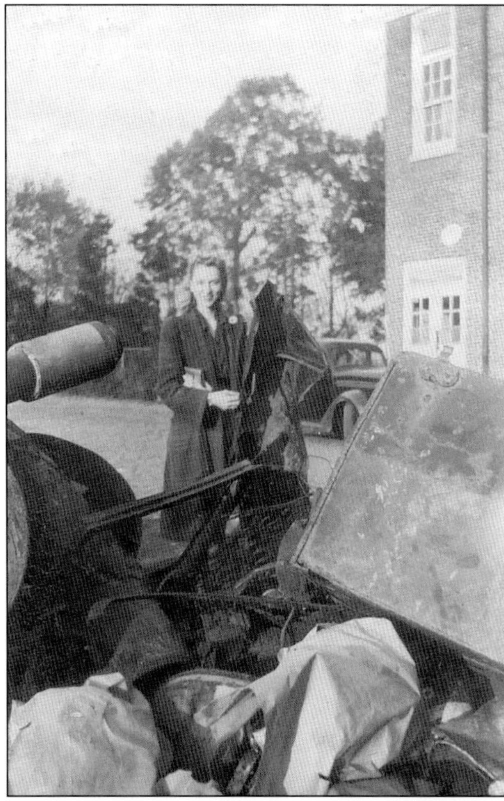

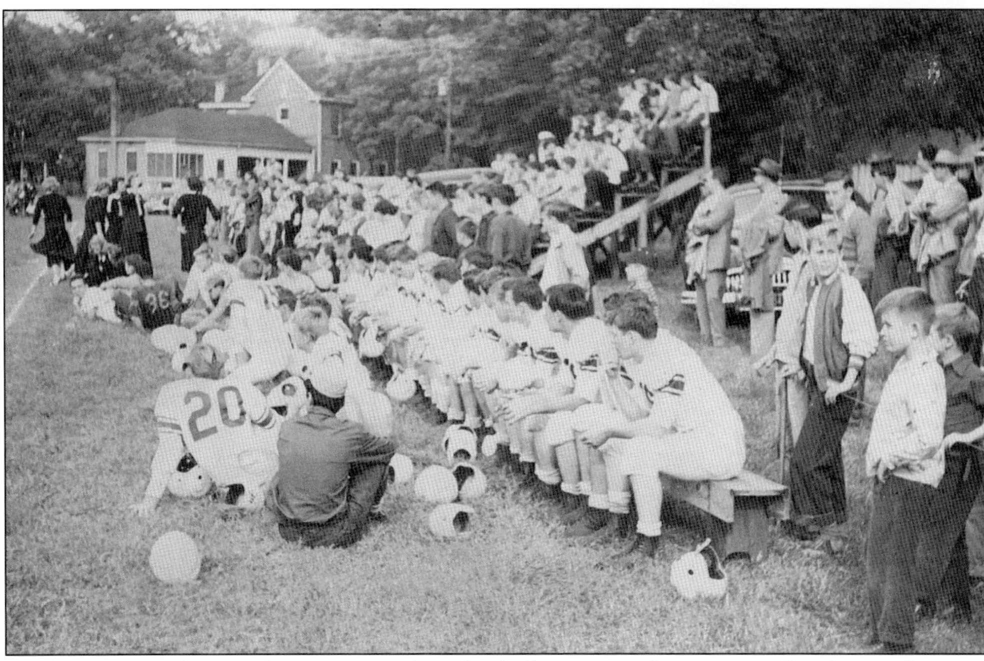

Mills Home was known for its outstanding football teams in the 1940s and 1950s. Mills Home was hosting Lexington when this sideline shot was made in 1947. Lexington is dressed in white in the foreground.

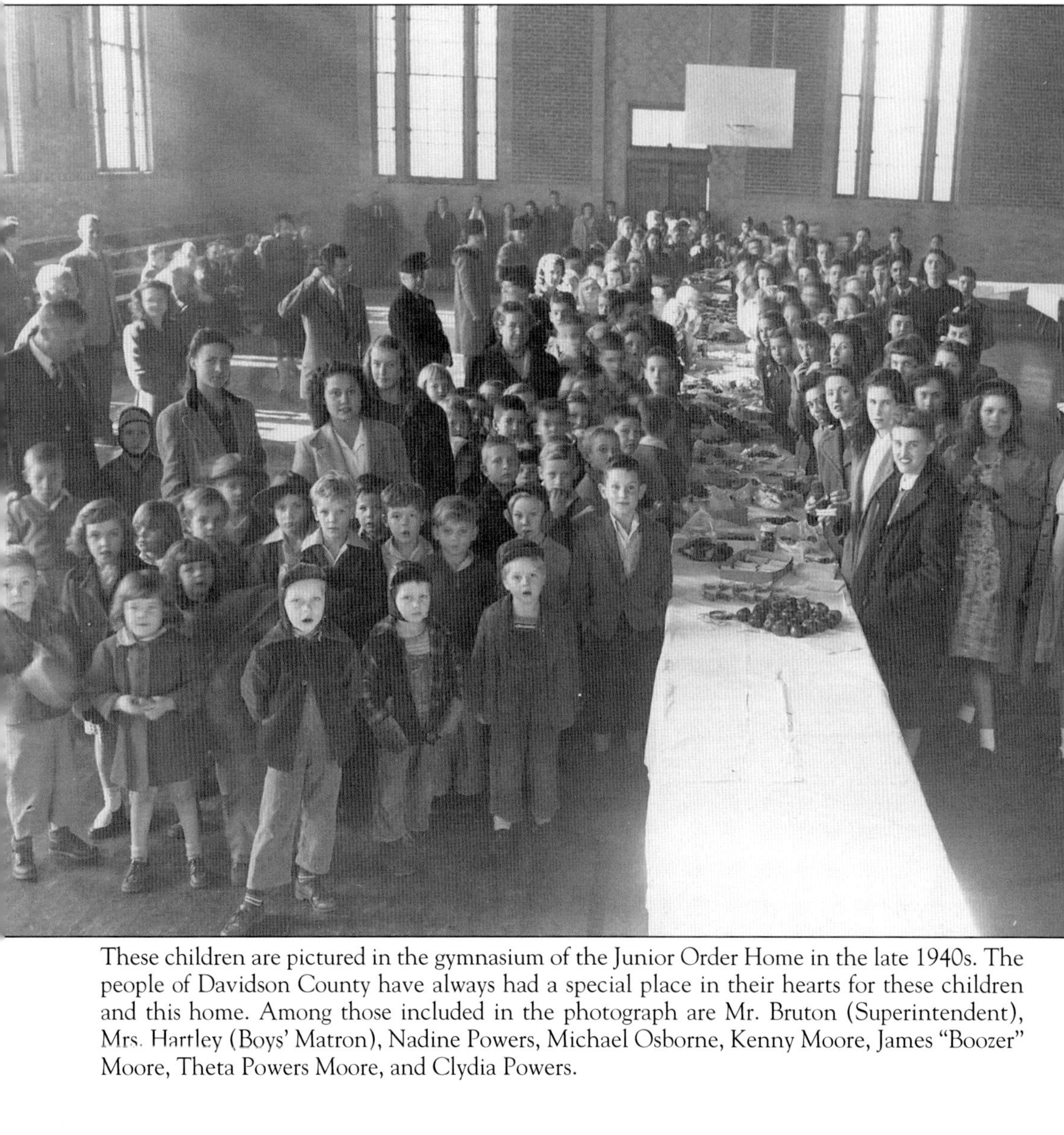

These children are pictured in the gymnasium of the Junior Order Home in the late 1940s. The people of Davidson County have always had a special place in their hearts for these children and this home. Among those included in the photograph are Mr. Bruton (Superintendent), Mrs. Hartley (Boys' Matron), Nadine Powers, Michael Osborne, Kenny Moore, James "Boozer" Moore, Theta Powers Moore, and Clydia Powers.

Six

Life in Davidson County

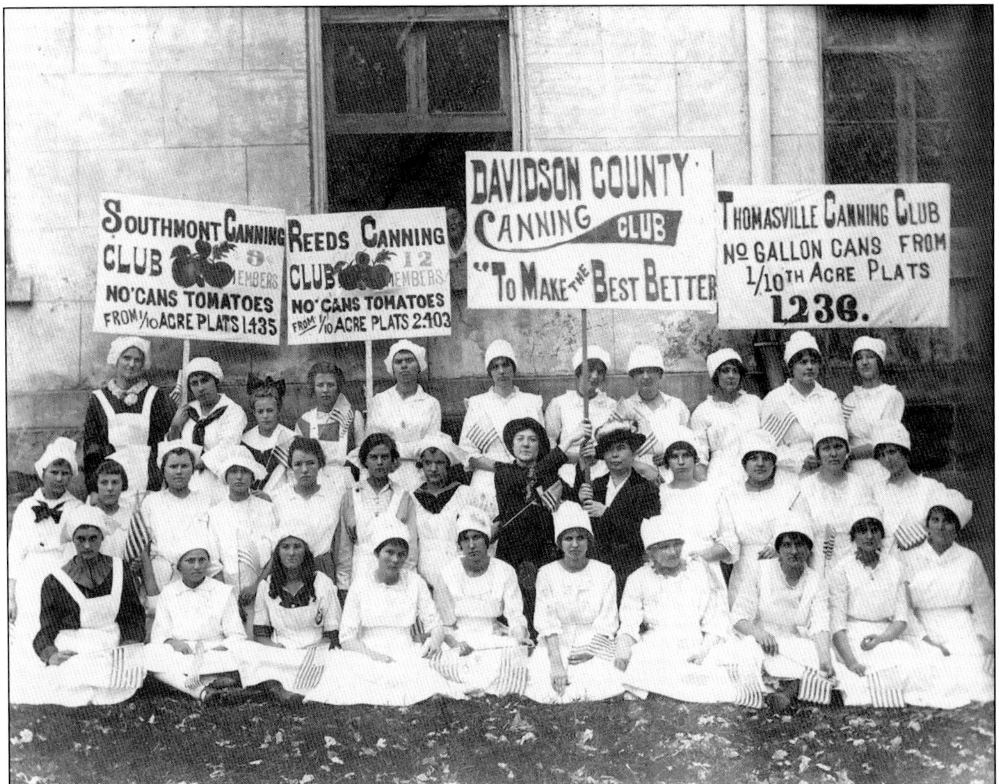

Canning clubs were the forerunners of 4-H Clubs. Miss Eunice Penny (in black suit, fifth from right, middle row) was the first Davidson County Home Agent and started the canning clubs in 1914. The girls in this 1915 photograph, made beside the old courthouse, were in tomato clubs, while the boys were in corn clubs.

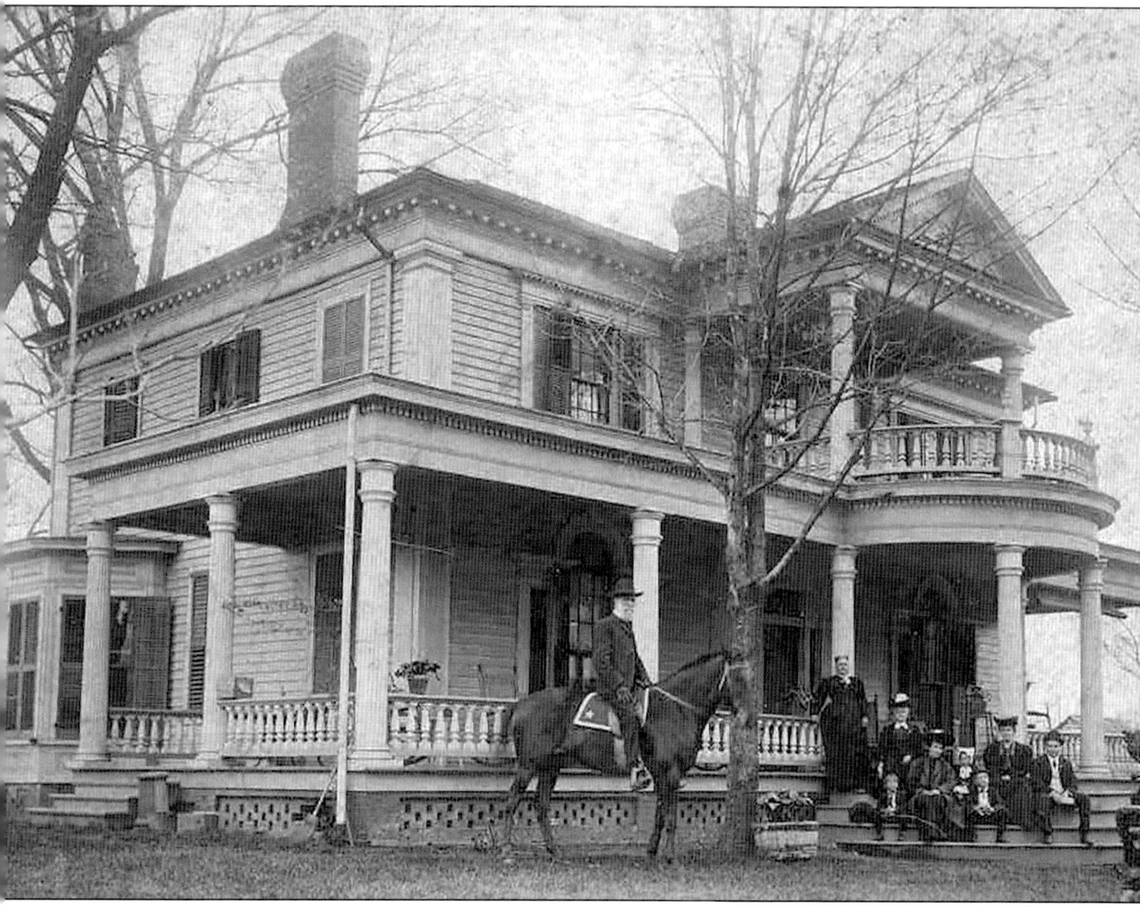

Col. Charles A. Hunt (on horseback) is pictured with his family at "The Homestead" in Lexington. The impressive Greek Revival home was built in 1834 by Dr. William Rainey Holt, whose daughter, Fannie Amelia, married Colonel Hunt in 1869. The immense Colonial Revival portico added shortly after 1900 was removed in the 1980s when this National Register house was restored to its original appearance. The house and its owners have long been associated with progress in 19th- and 20th-century Davidson County. Dr. Holt was one of North Carolina's most prominent and influential citizens before the Civil War, advancing such causes as medicine, business, education, religion, and transportation. He was a charter member of the North Carolina Agricultural Society, later serving as its president for eight years. His son-in-law, Colonel Hunt, was a founder in 1887 of the Wennonah Cotton Mill and of the Nokomis Cotton Mill in 1900.

Grimes Conrad was five years old when this picture was taken in front of his home in the Holly Grove in 1925. The house was built in 1903 by Nathaniel Green Conrad and is still standing on Nat Conrad Road. Wonder what Grimes was saying to his father's hunting dog?

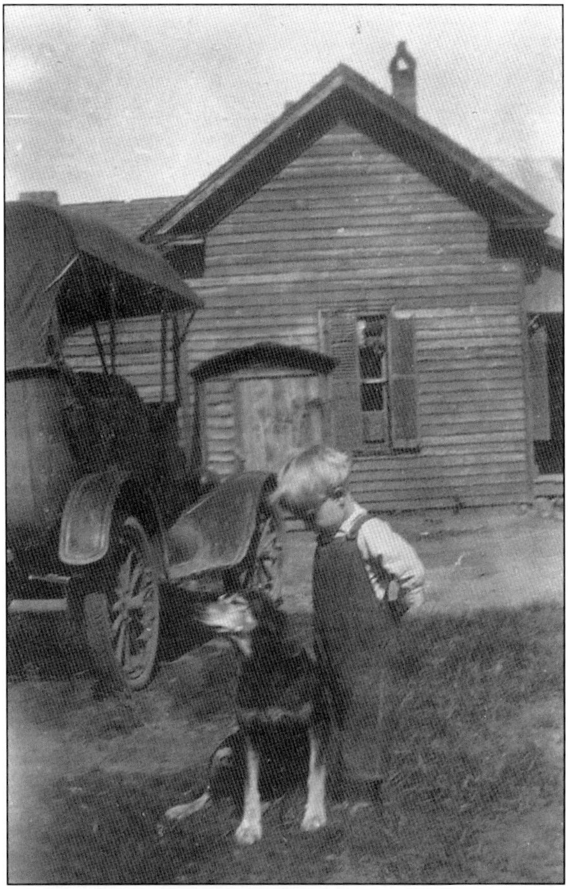

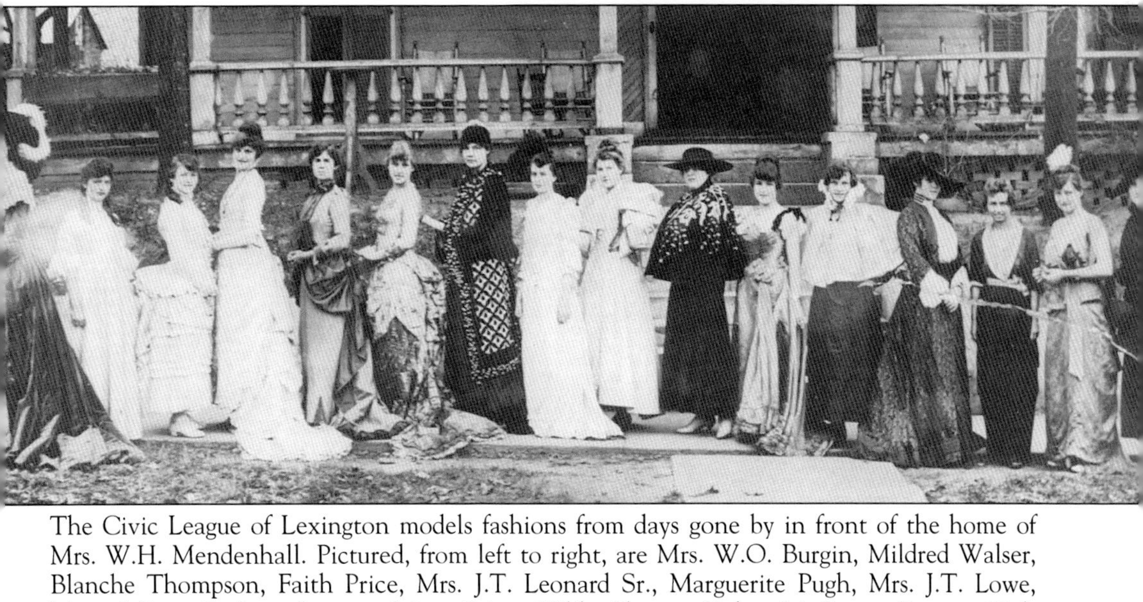

The Civic League of Lexington models fashions from days gone by in front of the home of Mrs. W.H. Mendenhall. Pictured, from left to right, are Mrs. W.O. Burgin, Mildred Walser, Blanche Thompson, Faith Price, Mrs. J.T. Leonard Sr., Marguerite Pugh, Mrs. J.T. Lowe, Mary Lillian Sink, unknown, Mary Price, Hilda Sheets, Helen McCrary, Frances Holt Mountcastle, Katherine Walker, Dorothy Mendenhall, and Ruth Fitzgerald.

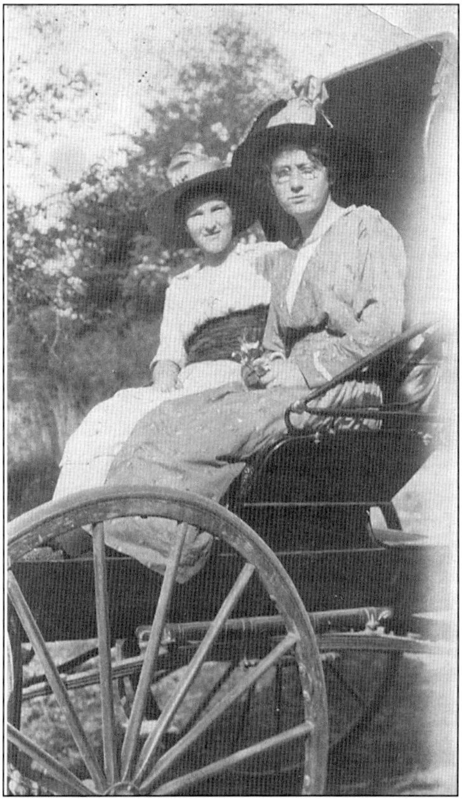

Berta Yarbrough Perryman (left) and Velna Tate are dressed up for a pleasant afternoon drive in this photograph made around 1915.

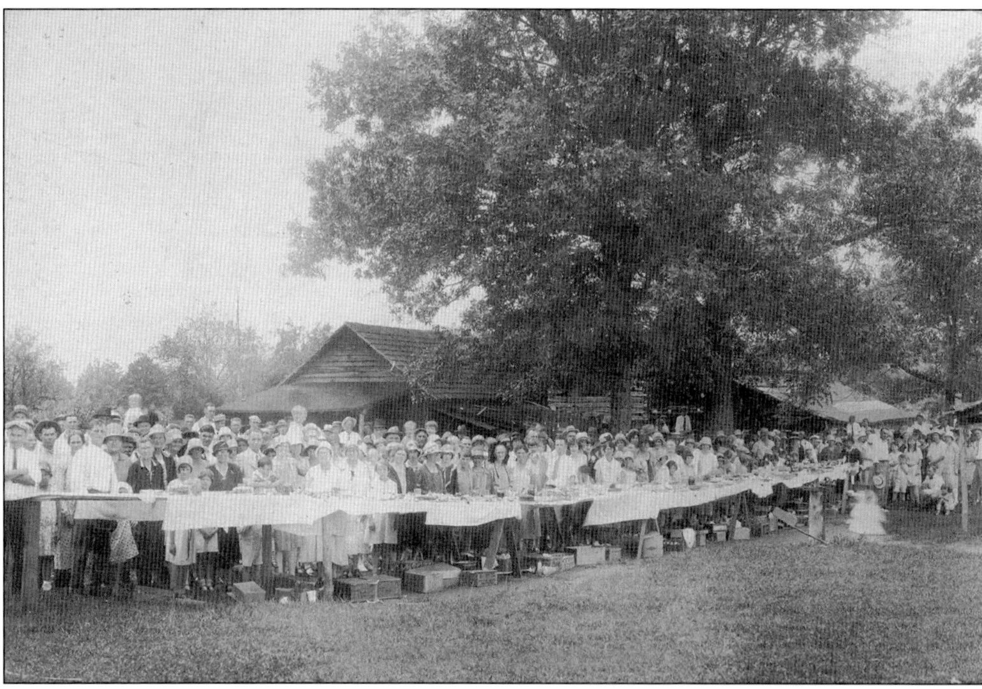

We all have fond memories of those wonderful family reunions. This is the Parker family reunion on August 26, 1928. Most everyone in the Parker family seems to be present.

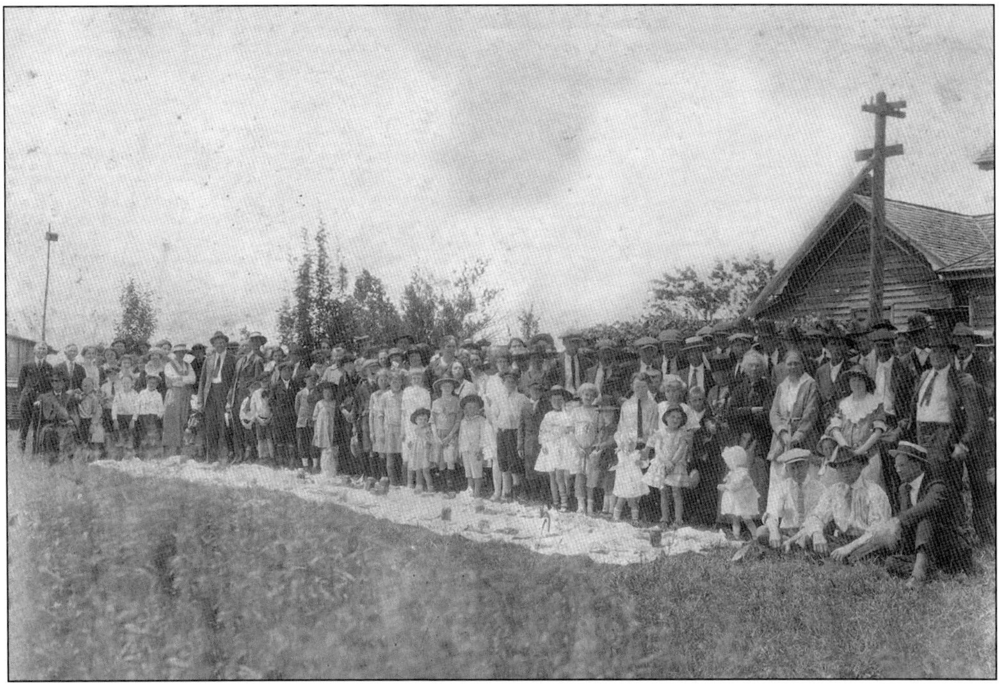

We don't know who these good people are or when the picture was made, but there is no doubt as to what they are doing. Yes, this is an authentic "Dinner on the Ground!"

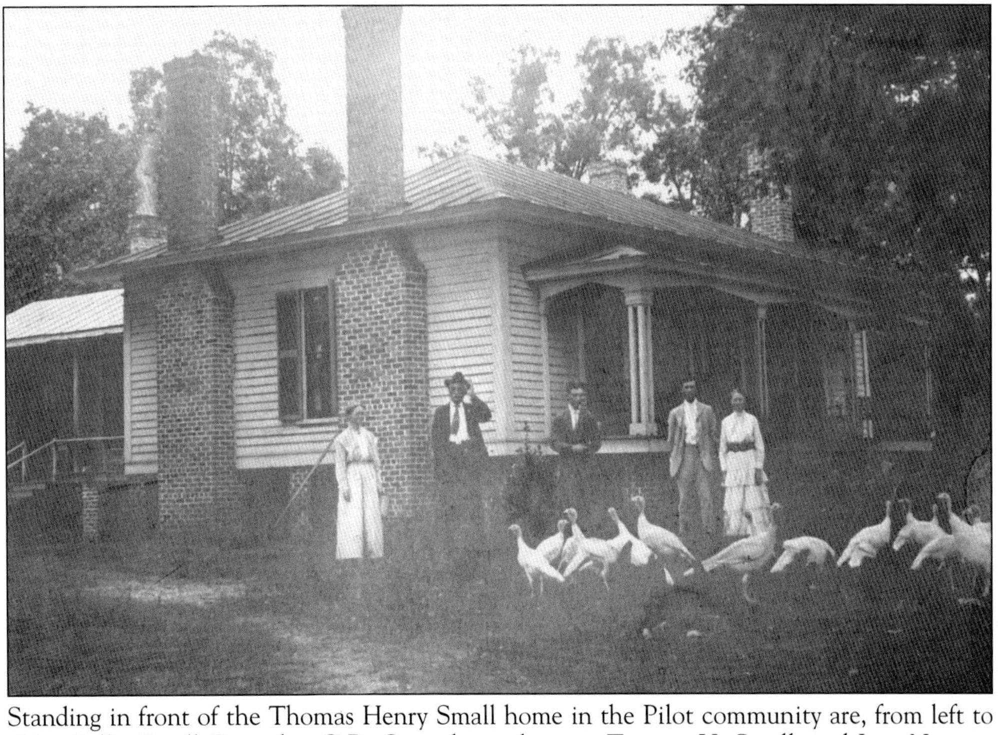

Standing in front of the Thomas Henry Small home in the Pilot community are, from left to right, Sallie Small Orrender, O.R. Orrender, unknown, Tommy H. Small, and Ivey Newton Small. The turkeys are unidentified.

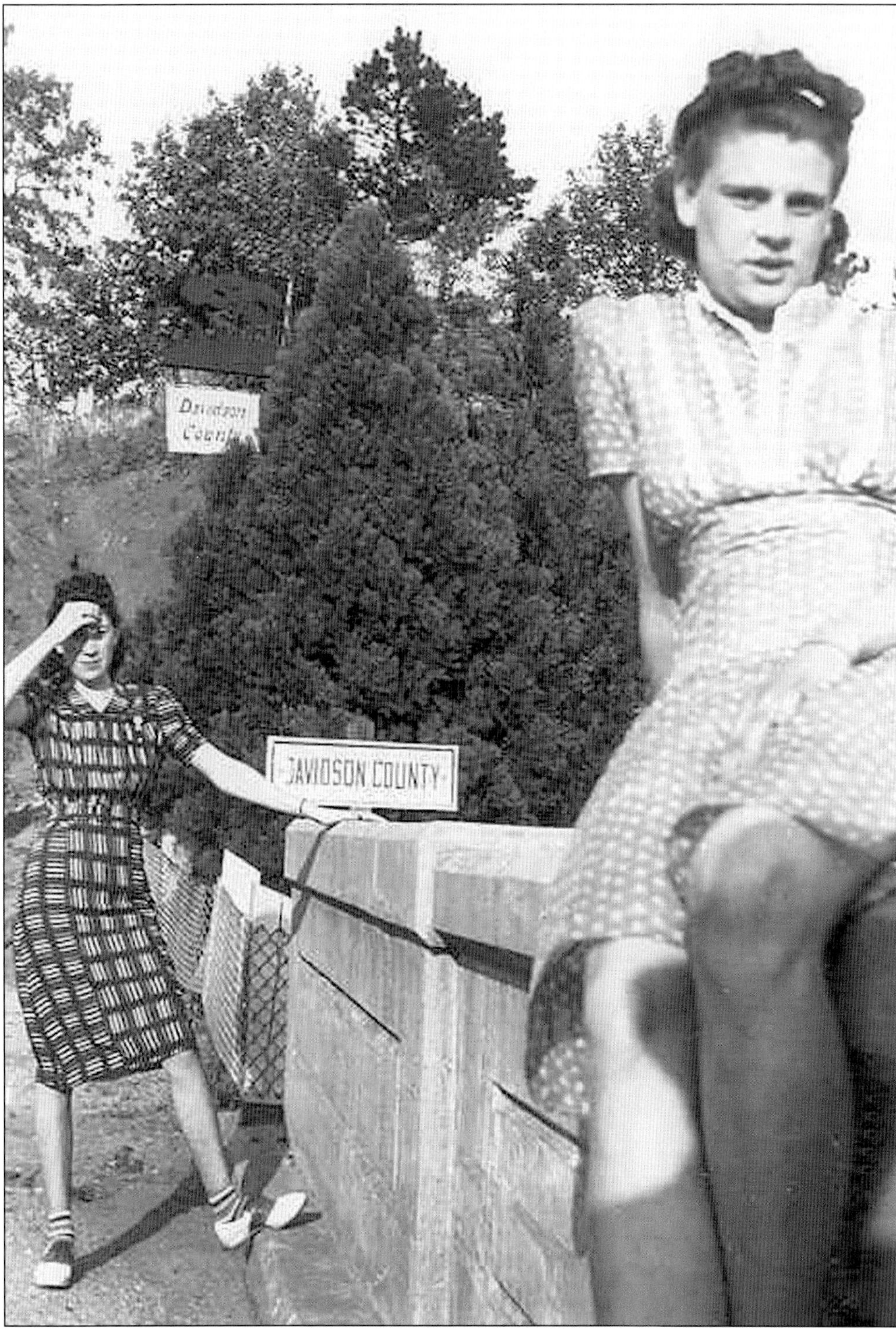

These two young women knew they were somewhere special when they reached the Davidson County line! Pauline Robbins (left) and Sarah Robbins pose on the Davidson-Rowan County line on old Highway 29 at the Yadkin River.

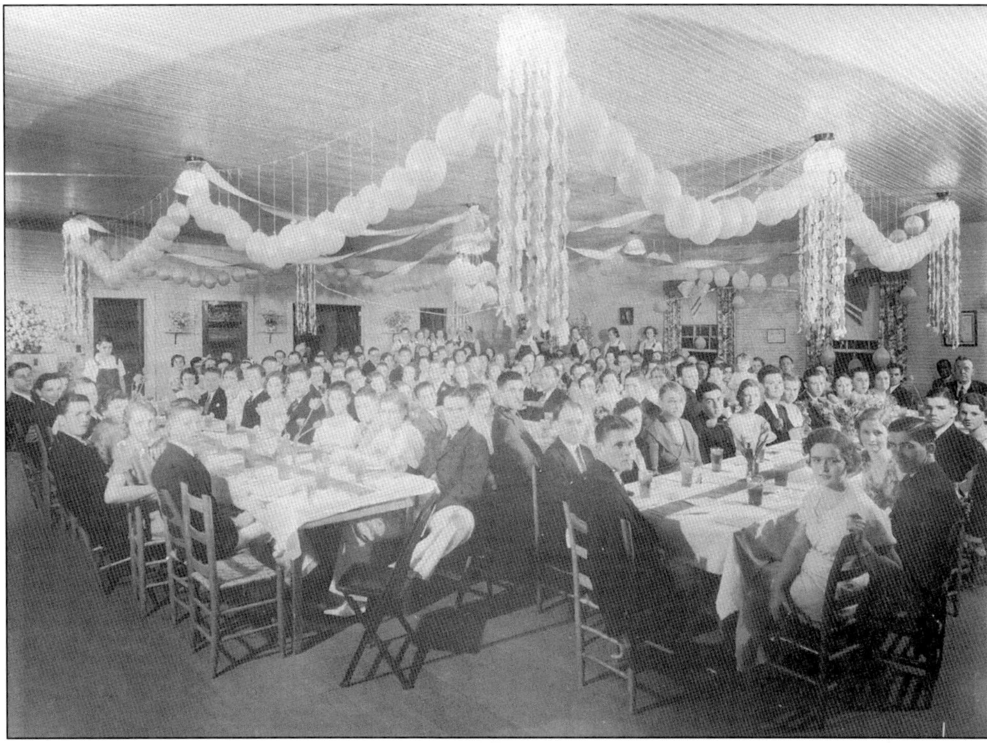

These young people were all dressed up for the Junior-Senior Banquet pose at Lexington High School in the late 1940s.

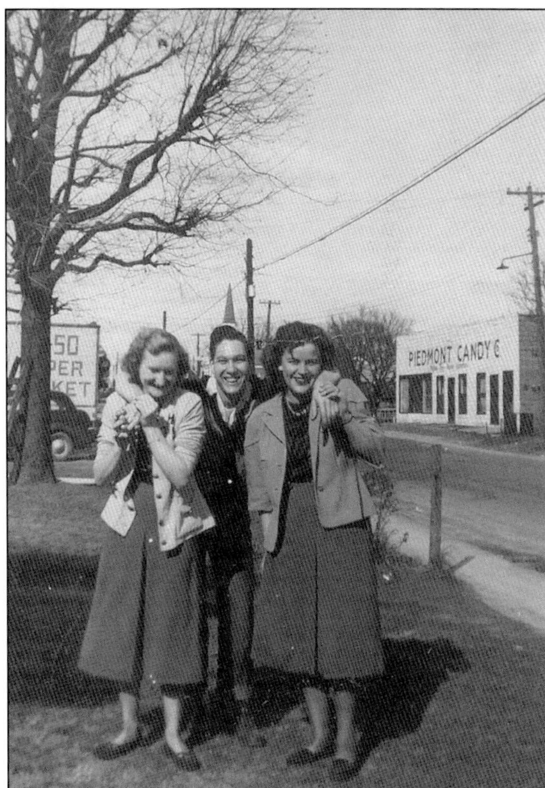

Margaret Cross Owens and her friends often gathered on Sunday afternoons at her home on Cotton Grove Road in Lexington. In this 1946 photograph, Margaret, Robert Palmer, and Ruth Goss smile for the camera. Behind them can be seen two area landmarks—the 50-50 Supermarket and Piedmont Candy Company.

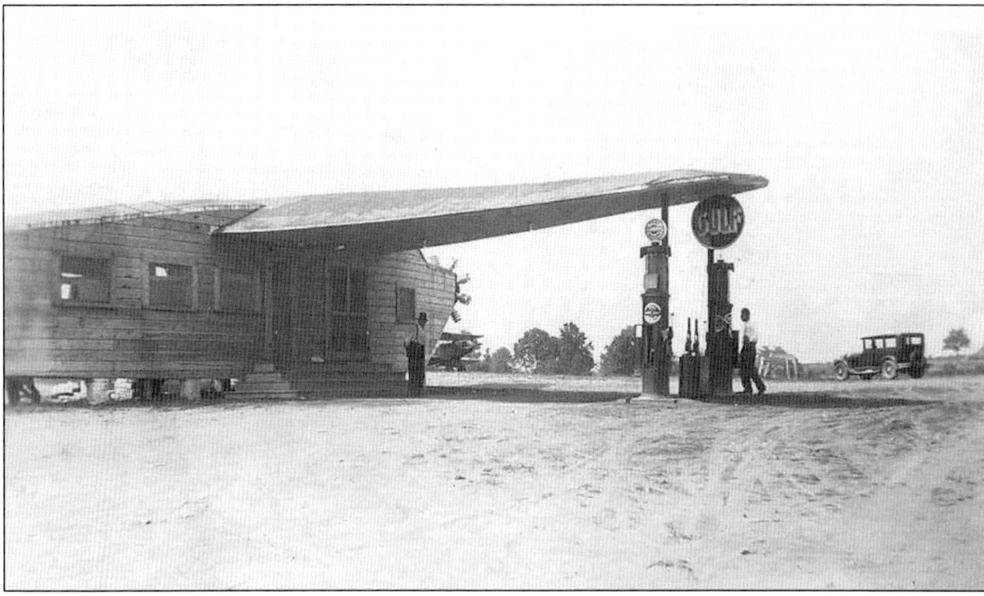

Zeb Grubb built this filling station south of Lexington during the 1920s. He liked airplanes and felt a business that resembled one would surely draw attantion and customers driving past on busy Highway 29. Note the bi-plane in the parking lot just beyond the "nose" of the station. Grubb also built a station shaped like an igloo on Highway 29. He was a pilot and was killed in 1949 when his private plane crashed into the Yadkin River.

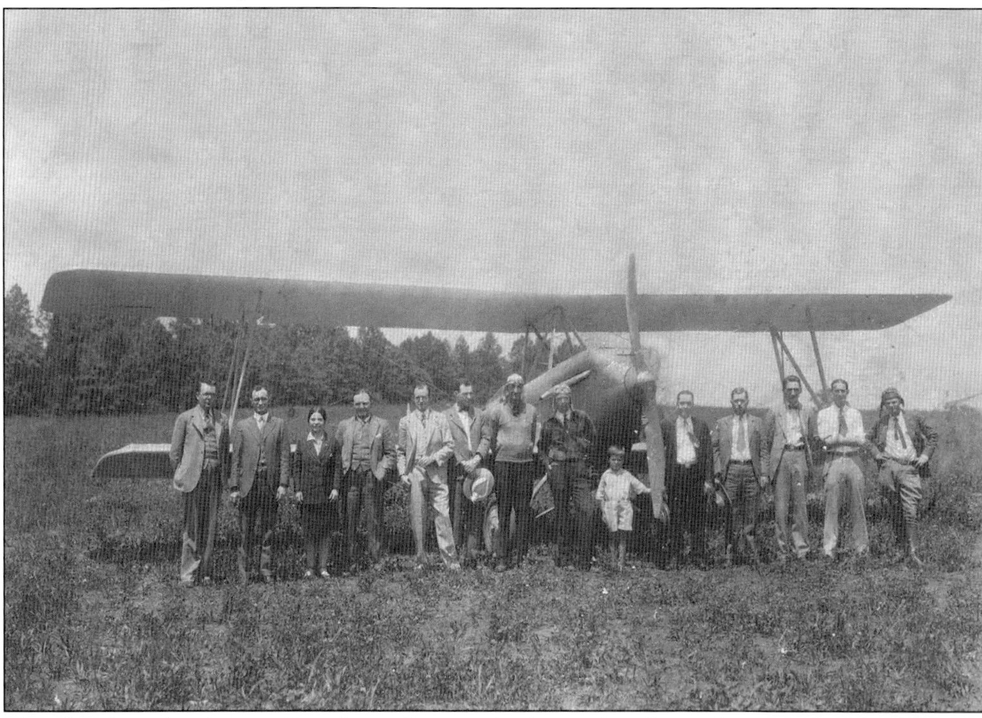

This bi-plane landed in Davidson County back in the days when airplanes were very much a novelty. The pilots, named Sam Yarborough and Gallimore, were greeted by this welcoming committee.

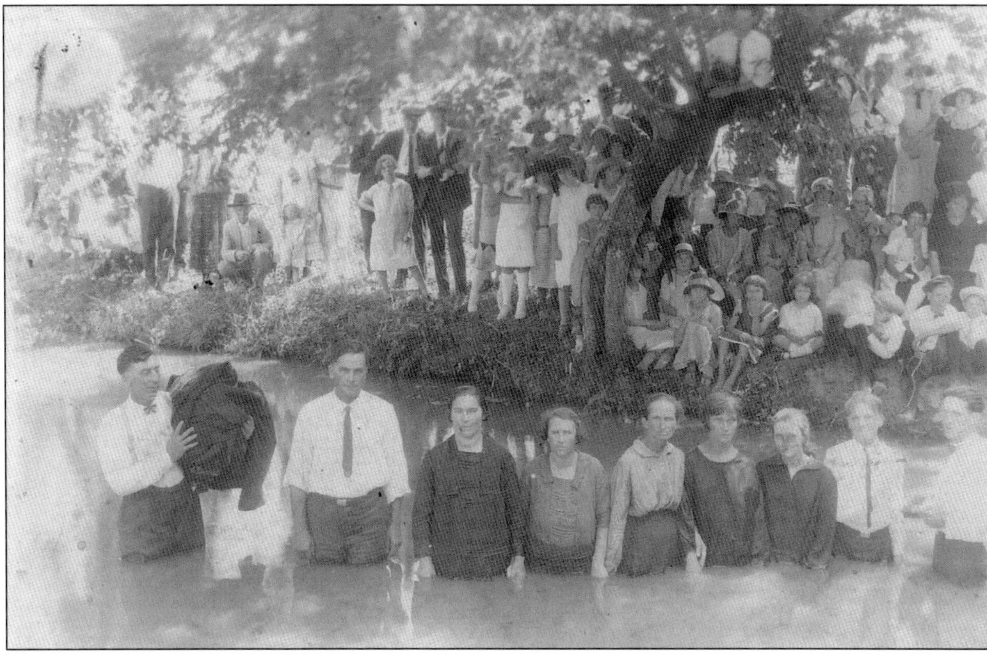

Members of Mt. Zion Pilgrim Holiness Church gather in the late 1920s for an old-fashioned baptism in a Davidson County creek. The fourth person from the left is Myrtle Gordon Bryant. The man on the far left appears to be responsible for keeping the coats dry!

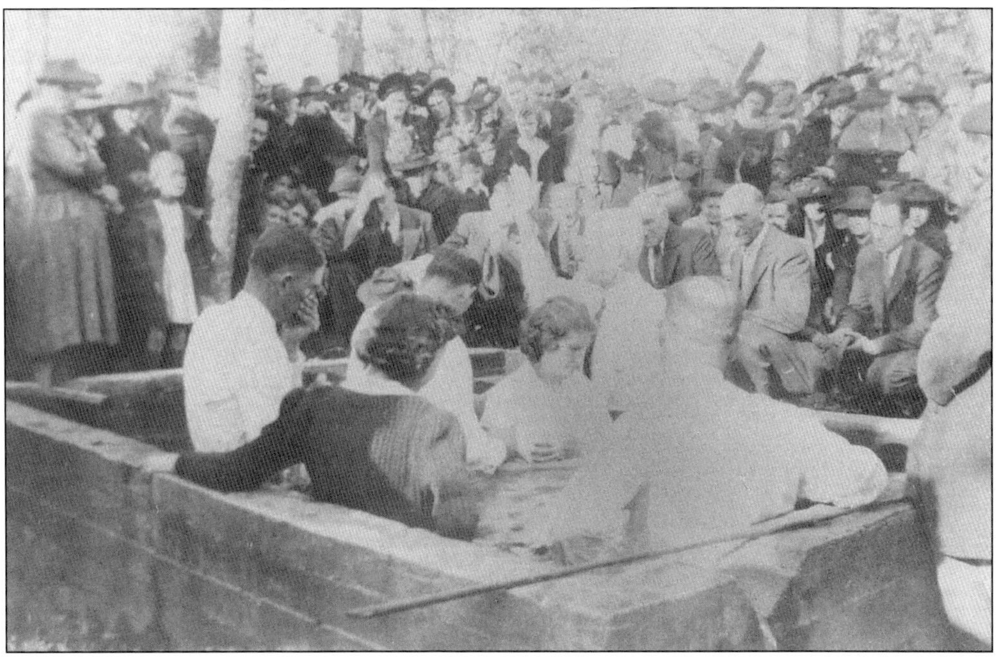

Not all baptisms took place in a river. Abbotts Creek Primitive Baptist Church used a pool built by Abbotts Creek Missionary Baptist Church on the Orrel farm. This 1944 picture shows the cement pool that replaced one built of wood in 1897. It was fed by a spring above the pool. Ola Clodfelter Williard and several members of her family are being baptized by Elder Fagg and Elder Moore (with his hands up).

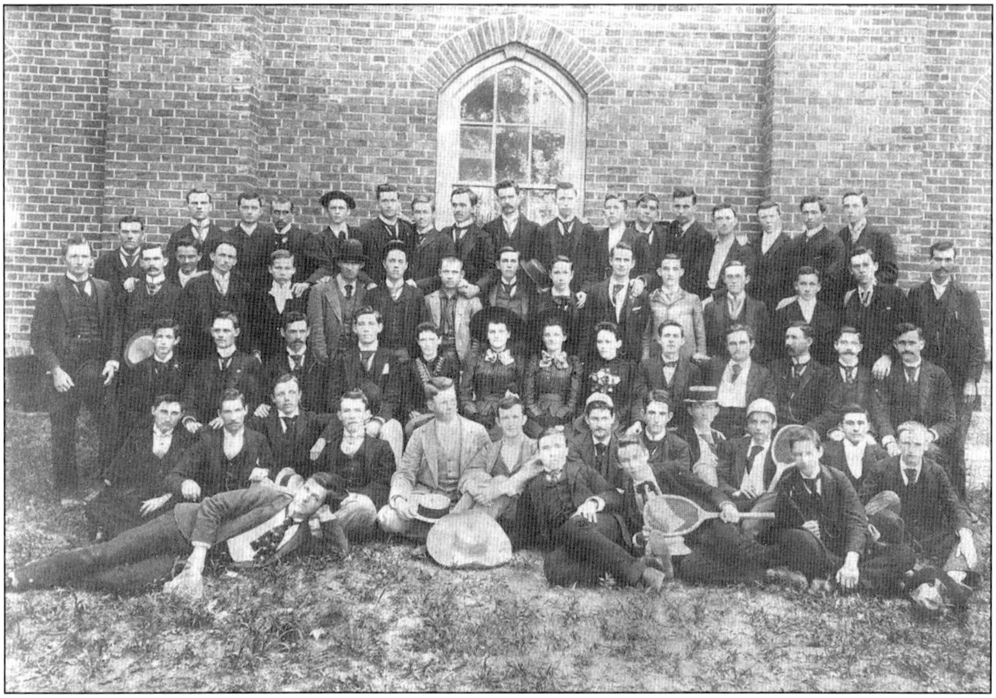

This picture is identified only as a Thomasville Sunday school class in the 1890s. The picture, however, raises two questions. There are four women in the middle of the group. Was this an early co-ed class? What about the two young men with racquets in their hands? Tennis anyone? It must have been an interesting class.

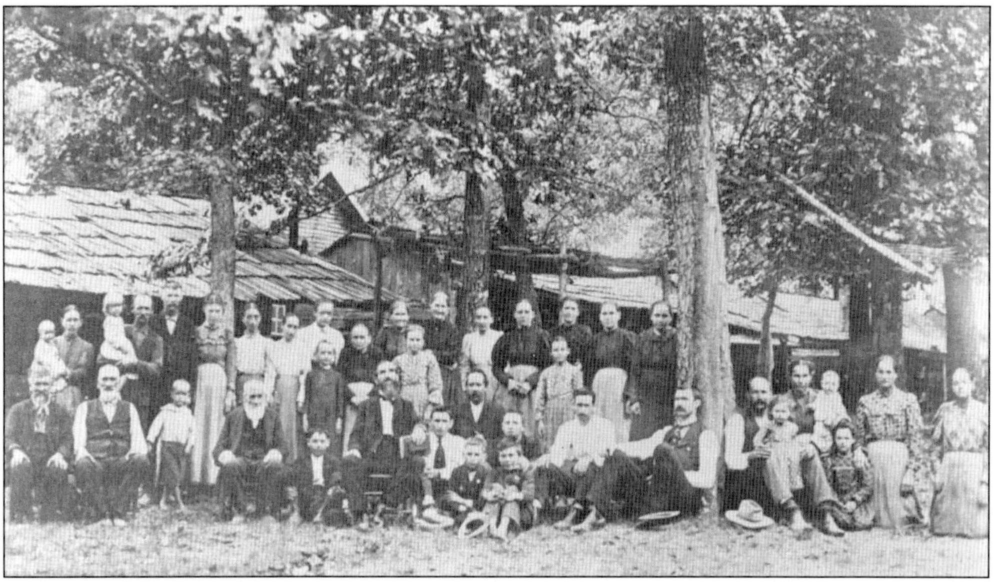

In the 1830s, several Methodist Protestant churches were organized in Davidson County in the Yadkin College settlement, Thomasville, Pleasant Garden, Lexington, and Reeds. The Chapel Hill Methodist Protestant Church, located a few miles east of Denton, was well known for its summer camp meetings, where families would stay several days to participate in services and fellowship.

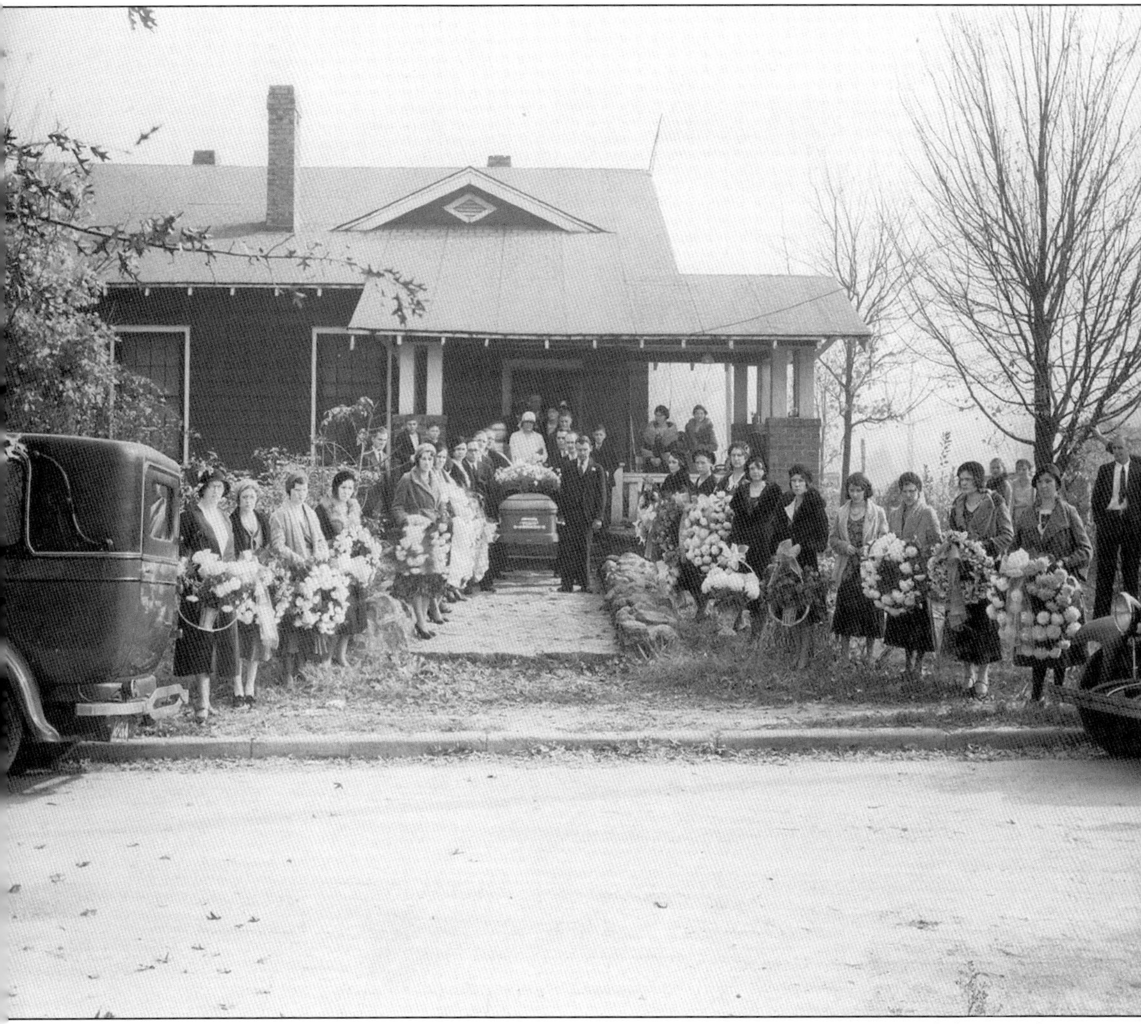

There is a time to be born and a time to die. Until recent times, many aspects of the ritual observance of a death took place in the home. This is a funeral in an Erlanger home in the 1930s.

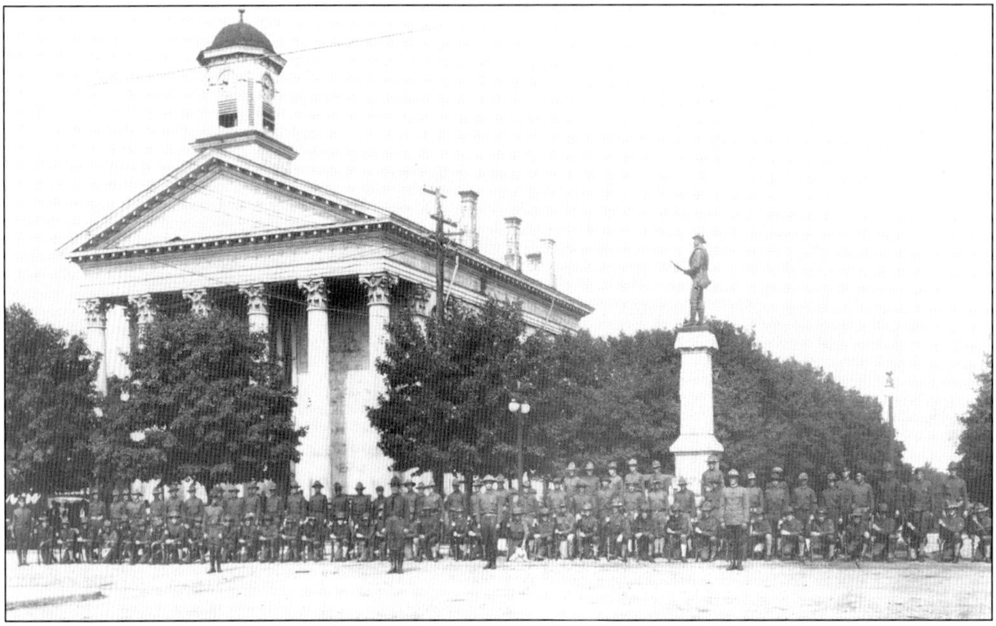

Nine hundred and thirty-two Davidson County residents faithfully served their country in the First World War—39 never came home.

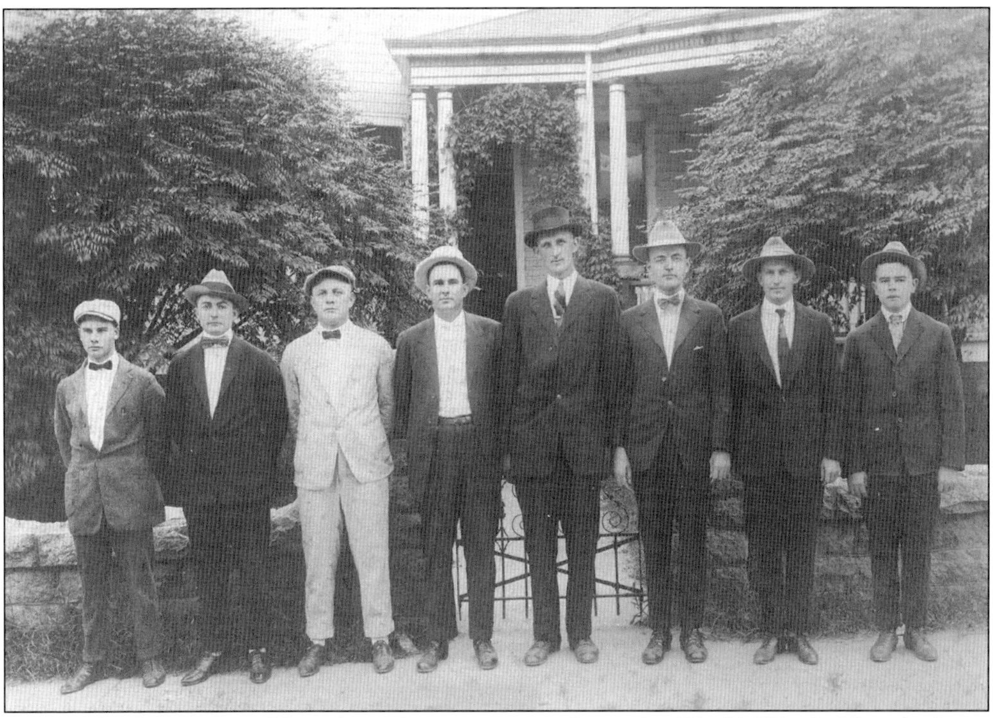

This is the first group of Davidson County men to leave for World War I. They had just completed their physical examination by Dr. E.J. Buchanan. From left to right are Arthur Thomason, Raymond Bowers, Mod Stout, Sam J. Welborn, Joe L. Everhart, Archie C. Dorsett, William E. Raper, and Raymond Ward. Dorsett was in the Hospital Corps and the rest were member of Battery E, 317 Field Artillery.

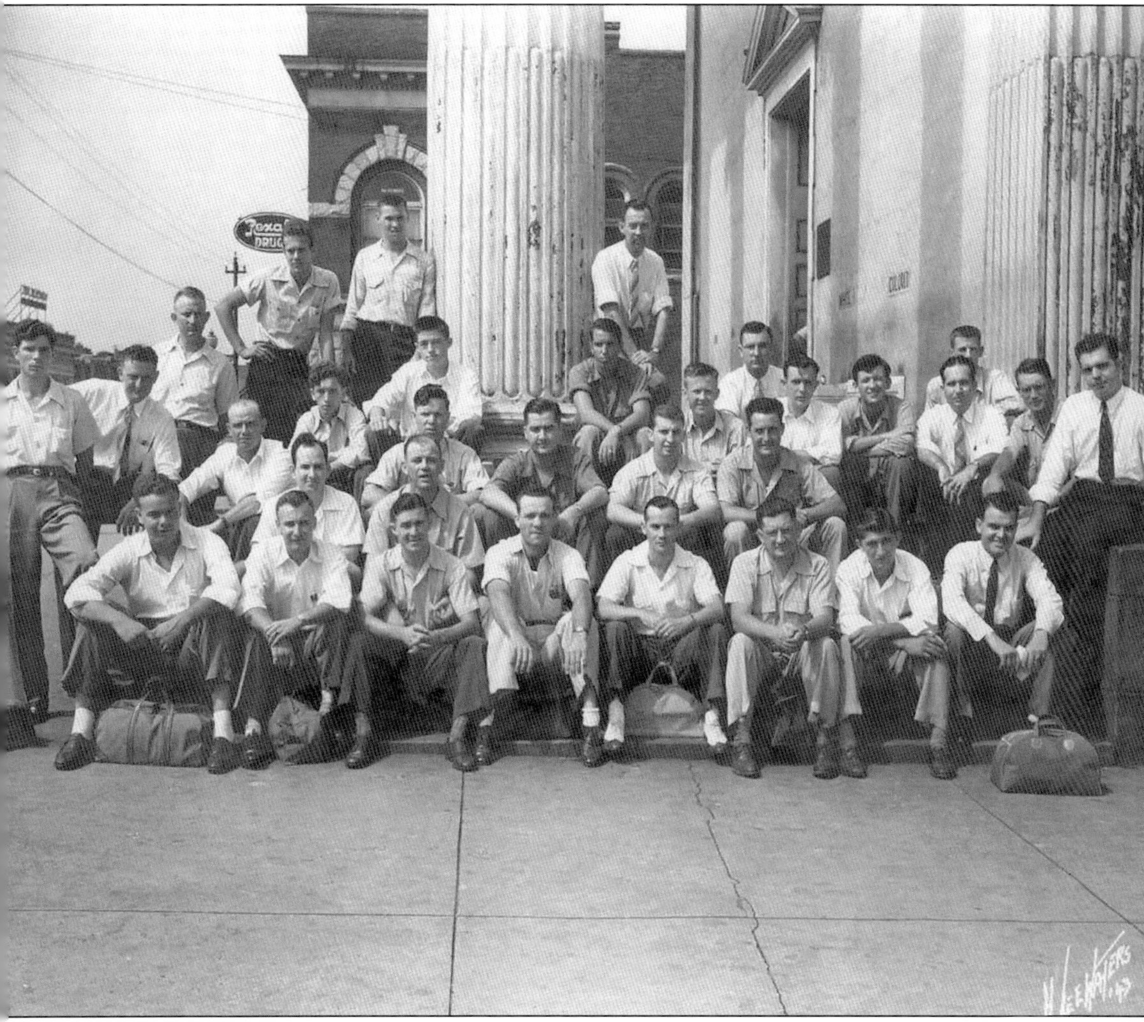

These Davidson County sons were reporting for service in World War II. Seventeen thousand, seven hundred and ninety-seven Davidson County residents were registered for military service during the war years. These men are, from left to right, as follows: (standing) Harold Miller, Dolen Swing, Lonnie Ward, Carroll Dorset, Melvin Everhart, and unknown; (seated, first row) Cleo Briggs, Garland Powell, Solomon Tesh, John Hines, William Frazier, Edgar Sink, John Leonard, and Cicero Lopp; (seated, second row) Fred Siceloff and George Mauney; (seated, third row) Robert Swing, Dermont Byerly, Oliver Young, Melvin Dry, and John Story; (seated, fourth row) Archie Lanning, Sam Hooks Jr., George Ijames, Henry Link, Edgar Hinkle, Bruce Hartley, William Raker, Don McLaurin Jr., William Lopp Sr., Robert Hubbs, and Harold Sledge. The man in the center top is unidentified.

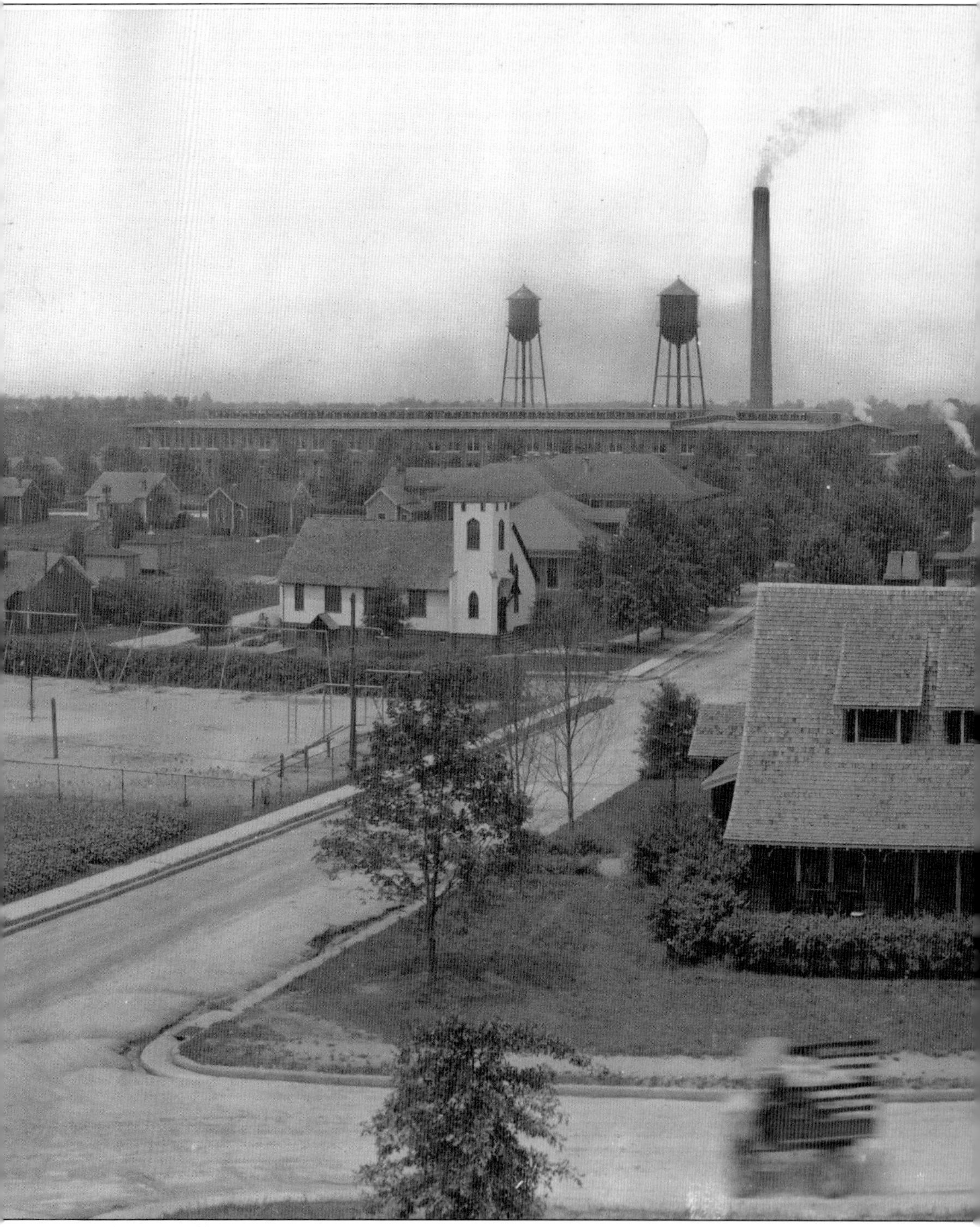

Erlanger Village was planned around the mill with construction beginning in 1913. The Lexington *Dispatch* reported on May 21, 1913: "The houses are to be built along different lines and monotony will be avoided as much as possible. The map of the village shows that no two houses exactly alike will stand side by side. In fact, there will hardly be two houses alike in the

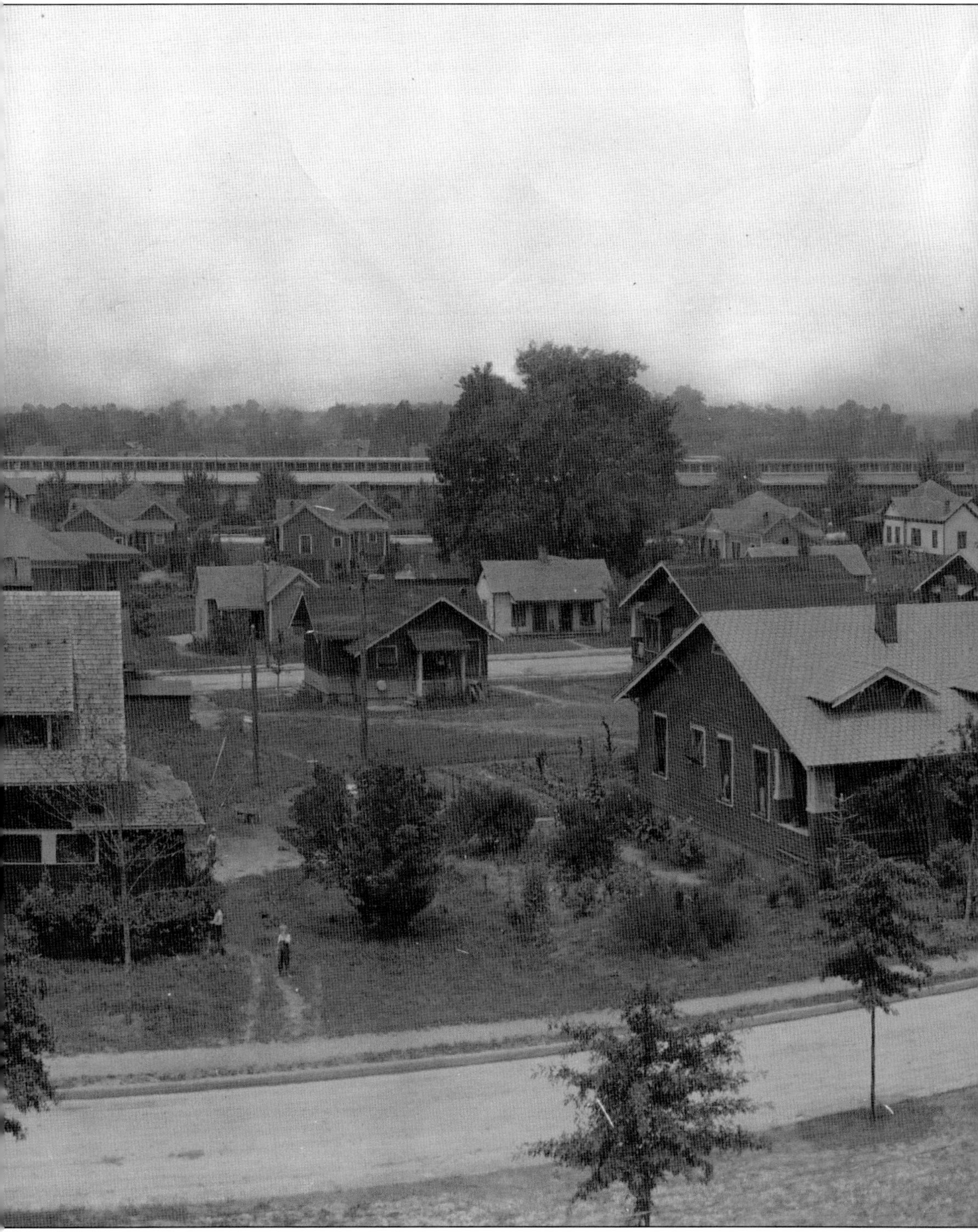

same block. Sameness in painting will also be avoided and a cheerful, pleasing color scheme will be worked out. Erlanger village is to be in a class by itself. Provision is made for a big park over in the woods toward the railroad and there will be a fine ball park east of the mill."

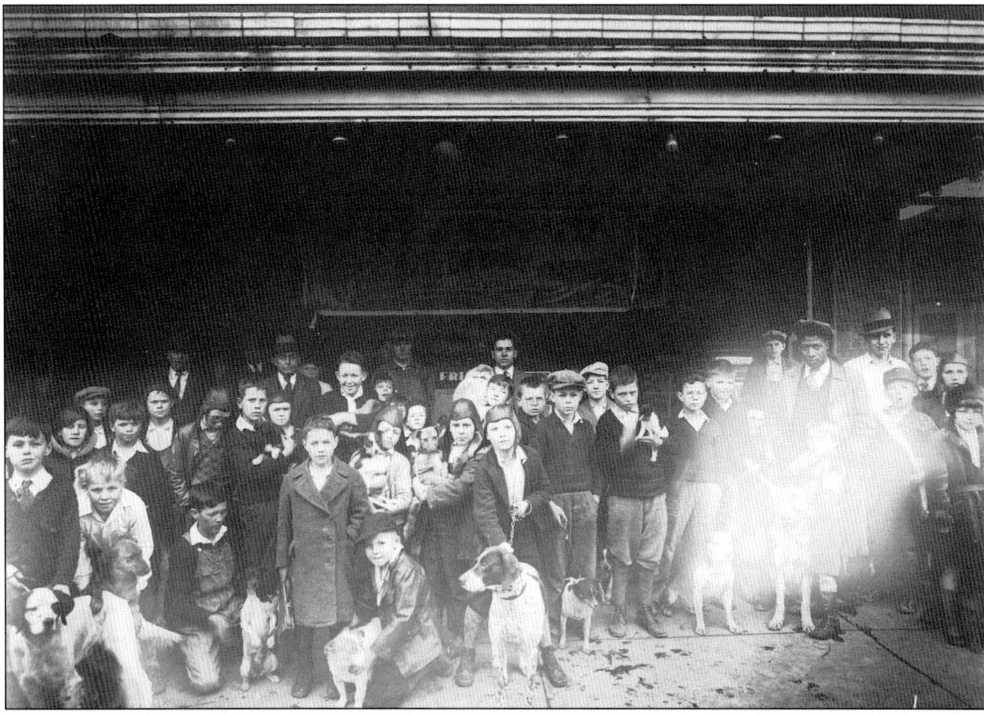

The Carolina Theater sponsored a Rin Tin Tin contest for the kids. The children were invited to bring their dogs, with the prize being awarded to the one that looked the most like the famous acting canine, Rin Tin Tin.

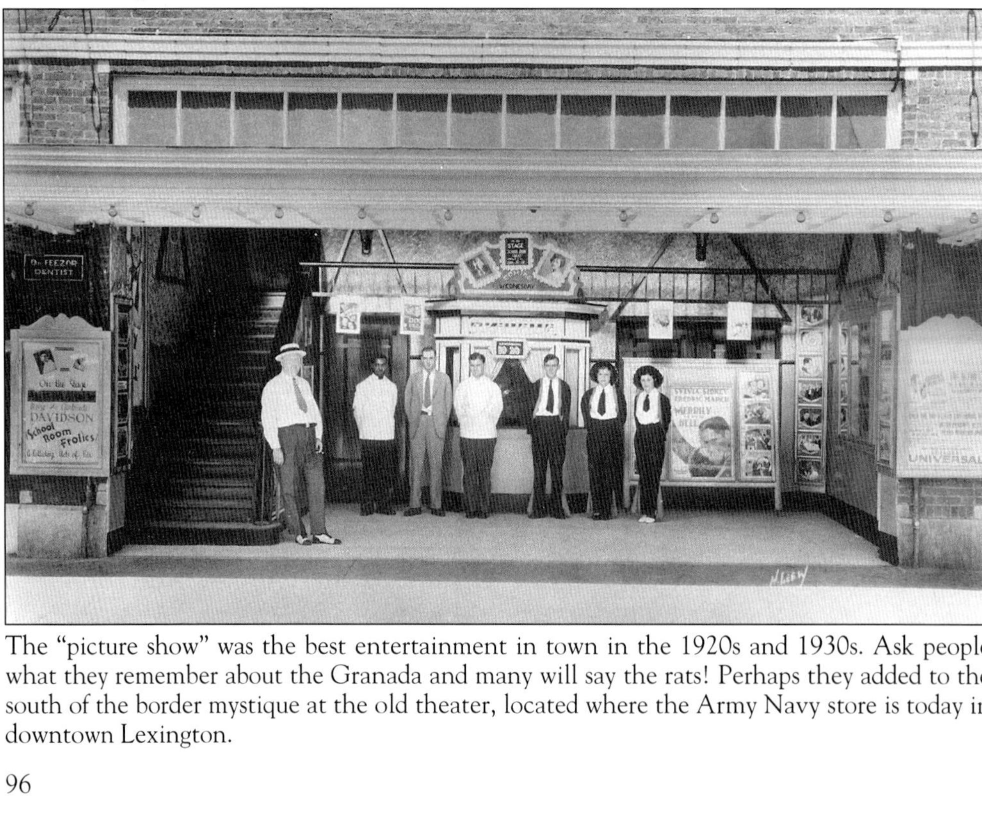

The "picture show" was the best entertainment in town in the 1920s and 1930s. Ask people what they remember about the Granada and many will say the rats! Perhaps they added to the south of the border mystique at the old theater, located where the Army Navy store is today in downtown Lexington.

The 1950 Skull & Bone Queen and her court were "Queen" Edwina Lanier Saunders (seated) and, from left to right, Louise Gordon Miller, Gwendolyn Thomason Pearson, and Vera Cureton.

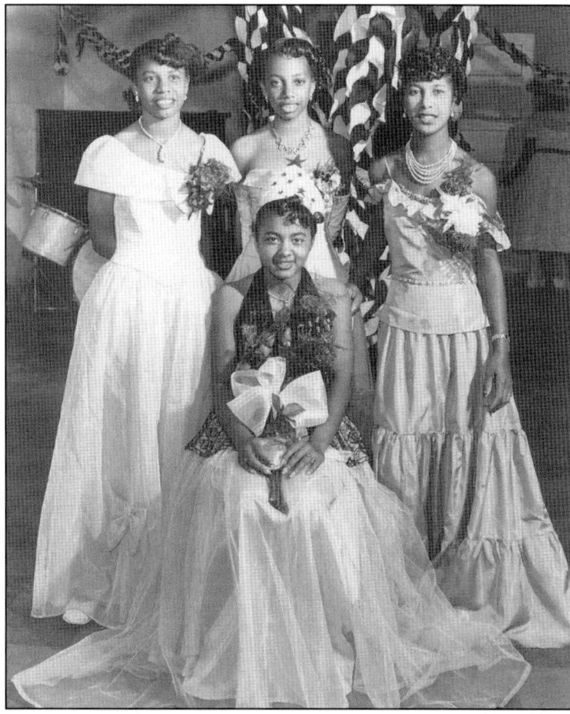

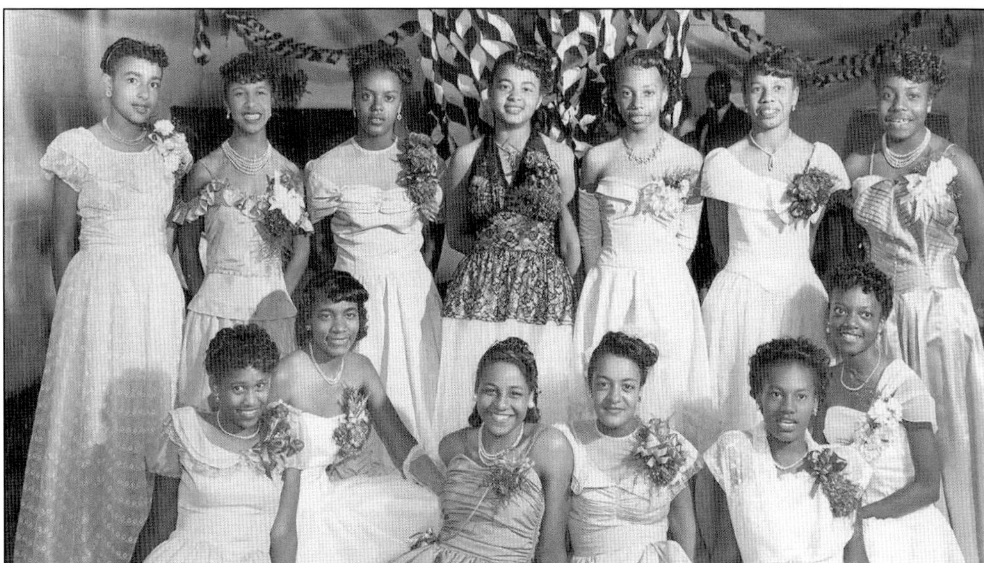

When Miss Helen Roberts came to Dunbar School on Fourth Street in Lexington, she established the Skull and Bone Club to recognize student excellence in character as well as academic performance. The club was comprised of 12 members, 4 students each from the 10th, 11th, and 12th grades. Club members in 1950 pictured here, from left to right, are as follows: (seated) Pauline Gooden Hargrave, Helen Robert Long (faculty advisor), Margaret Hairston Weeks, Frances Jones Mack, Alberta Barker Harvey, and Betty Brummell Cunningham; (standing) Henrietta Peoples, Vera Cureton, Emma Jones Graham, Edwina Lanier Saunders, Gwendolyn Thomason Pearson, Louise Gordon Miller, and Lizzie Brown.

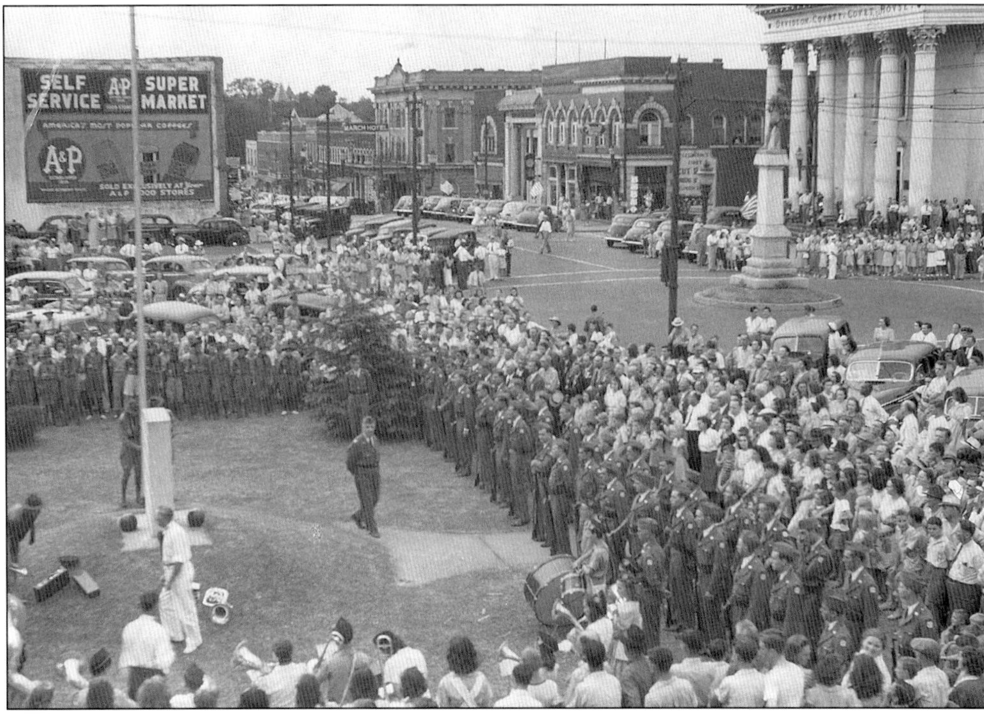

The Veterans Memorials on the square in Lexington have seen many assemblies of servicemen and citizens who wish to remember Davidson County soldiers who served their country. This large crowd includes a band, color guard, and many observers crowding the square and old courthouse steps. This picture was probably taken between 1945 and 1950 because the Man on the Monument is still located in the middle of Main and Center Streets.

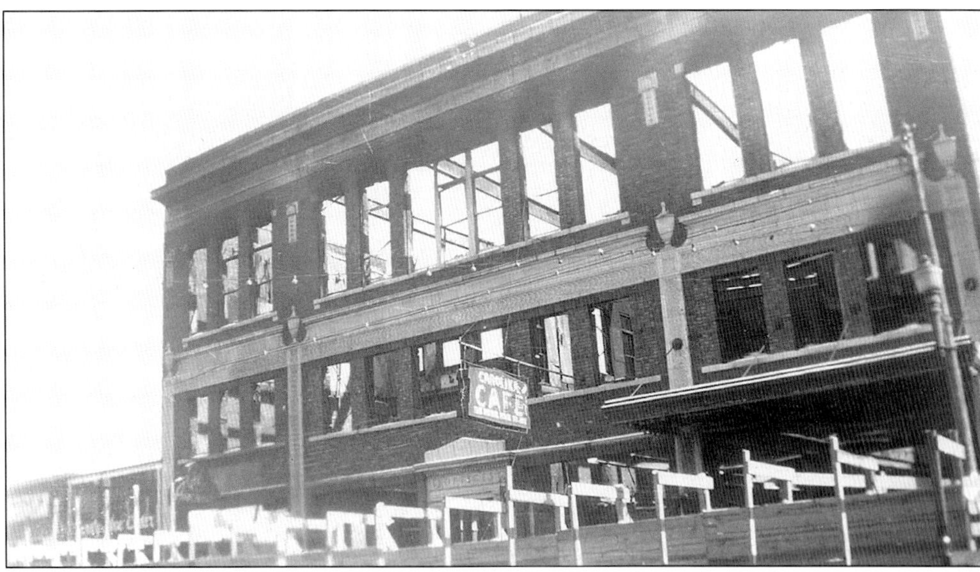

On December 5, 1945, the Carolina Theater in Lexington burned. The loss was estimated at $350,000, making it the worst fire since United Furniture suffered a $400,000 loss in May 1936. The fire call was received at 4:20 a.m. on a night plagued by sleet and snow. The fire department used so much water on the fire that the water pressure in town dropped drastically.

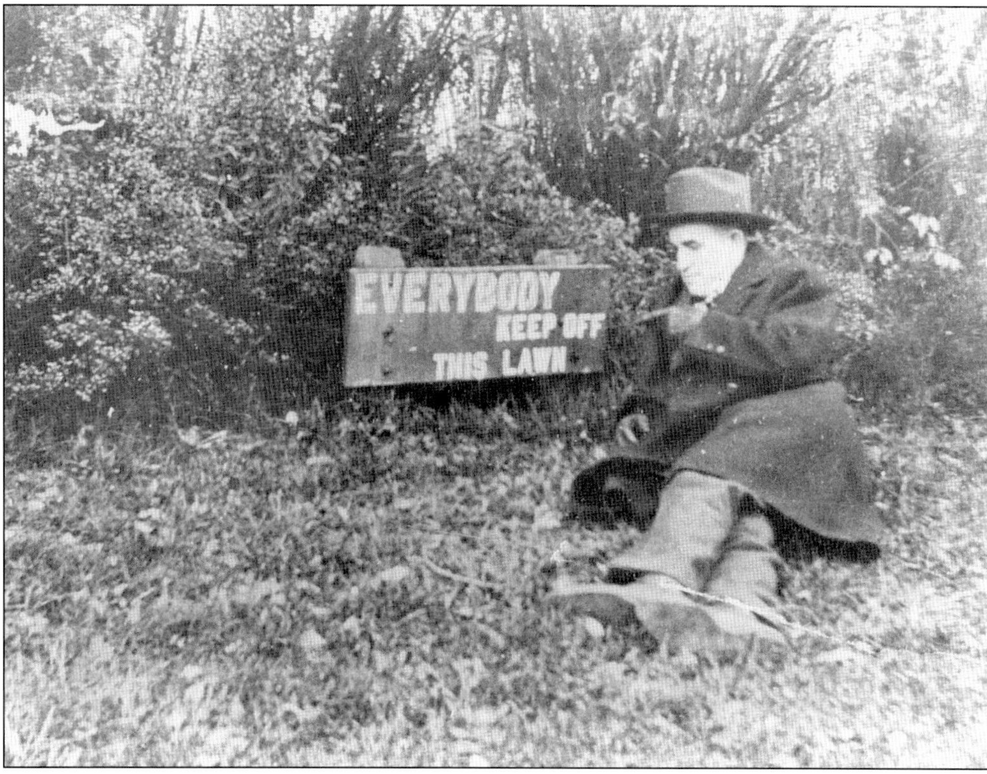

In 1908, a Lexington City ordinance was passed charging a $1 fine for walking on the grass. Slingshots were banned and you could not play marbles on the sidewalks. A person who went to church "in a state of intoxication" was fined $25 and anyone who disturbed a musical or theatrical performance by loud talking, hissing or snoring was fined $5.

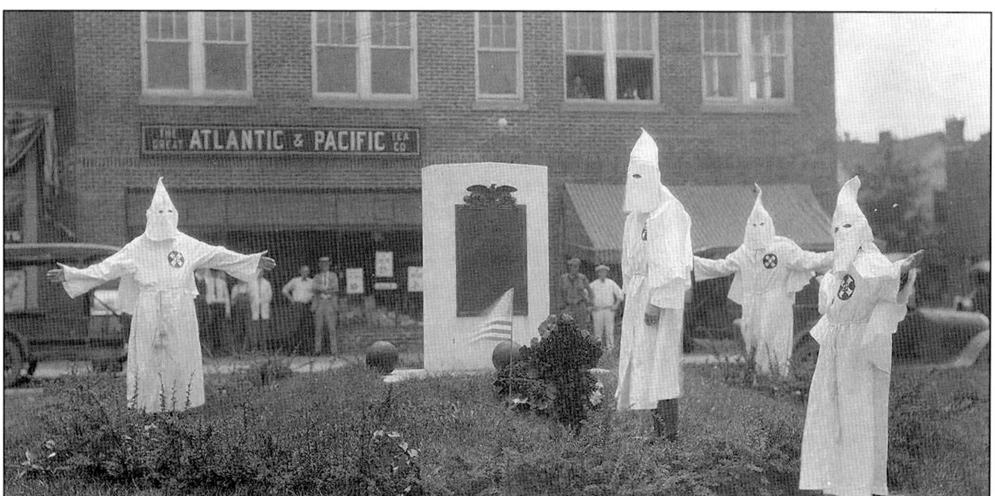

Hatred and racism have surfaced at times in Davidson County. This Ku Klux Klan rally took place in the 1930s on Court Square. Unfortunately, the KKK is not restricted to history books. They rallied at the courthouse as recently as the summer of 1998.

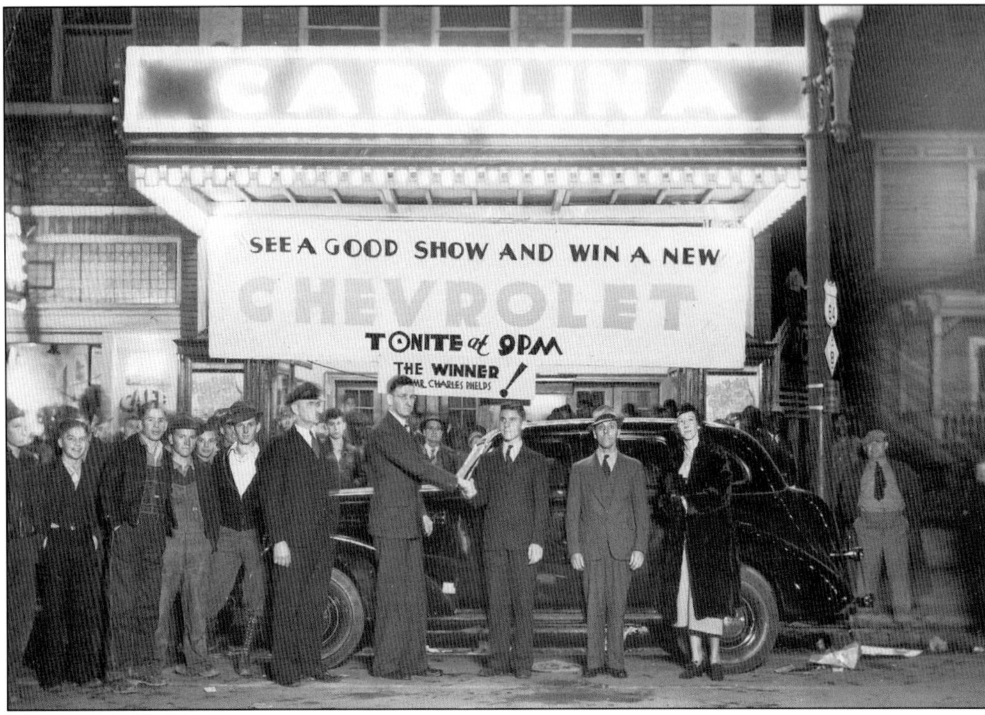

If you want to draw a large crowd, give away a new car. It seems that everyone in town turned out to have a chance to win this new 1933 Chevrolet. Charles Phelps was the winner and stoically poses here to receive his prize.

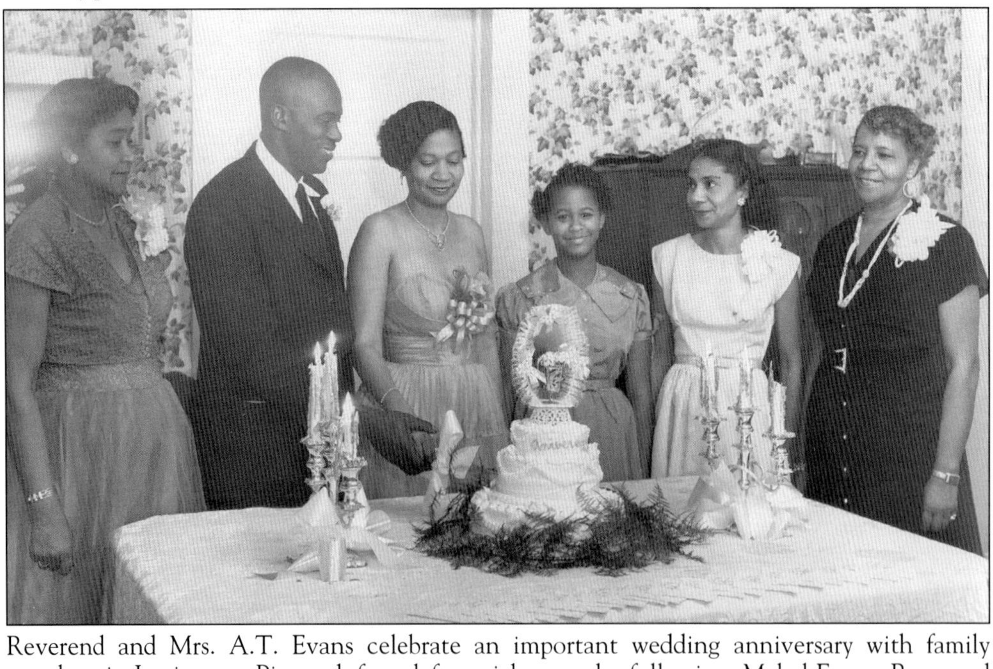

Reverend and Mrs. A.T. Evans celebrate an important wedding anniversary with family members in Lexington. Pictured, from left to right, are the following: Mabel Evans; Reverend Evans; his wife, Lillie Mae Evans; their daughter Annette Evens; Jessie Miller; and Hildred Moore. Reverend Evans was pastor of First Baptist Church for many years.

Adelaide Hargrave Gordon poses with her uncle, R.S. Hargrave, and a dog named Jack. This picture, taken about 1902, appears to have been taken in Lexington. The sign in the left background reads, "B. Shemwell Co." Baxter Shemwell was a well-known figure in Davidson County who started a wagon works in Lexington about 1870.

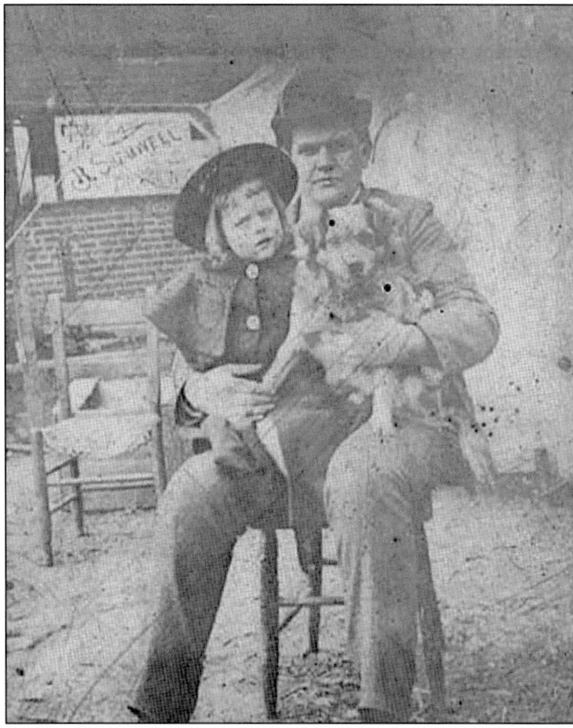

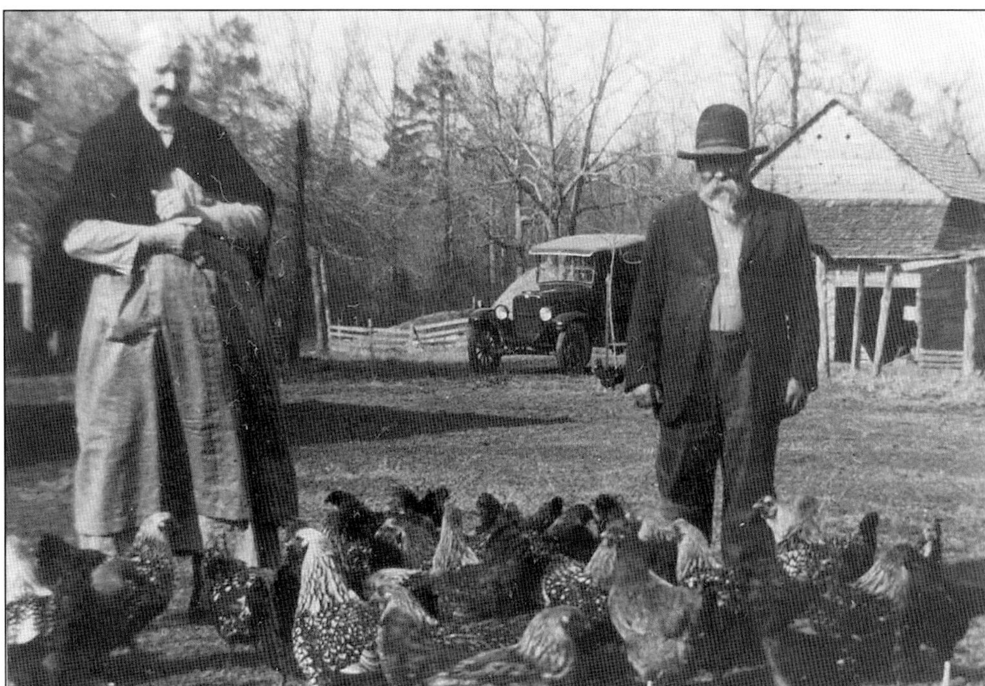

This 1923 photograph was made in Handy, south of Denton on the farm of Alice and William Thomas Morris. The elderly couple feeds their chickens; Mrs. Morris holds the feed in her apron.

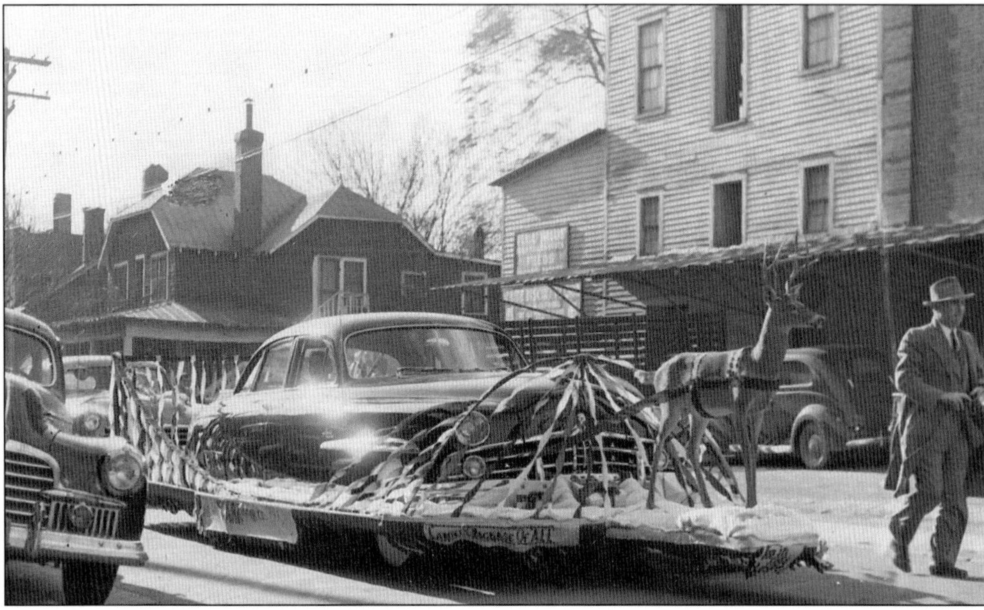

This parade photo shows the love affair we have always had with our cars. It also records information of now vanished buildings in Lexington. In the background, to the right, is Grimes Mill, the first roller mill in North Carolina. The wood addition added to the original brick structure, now used by Central Carolina Bank, was later removed. The float is one block away from the square.

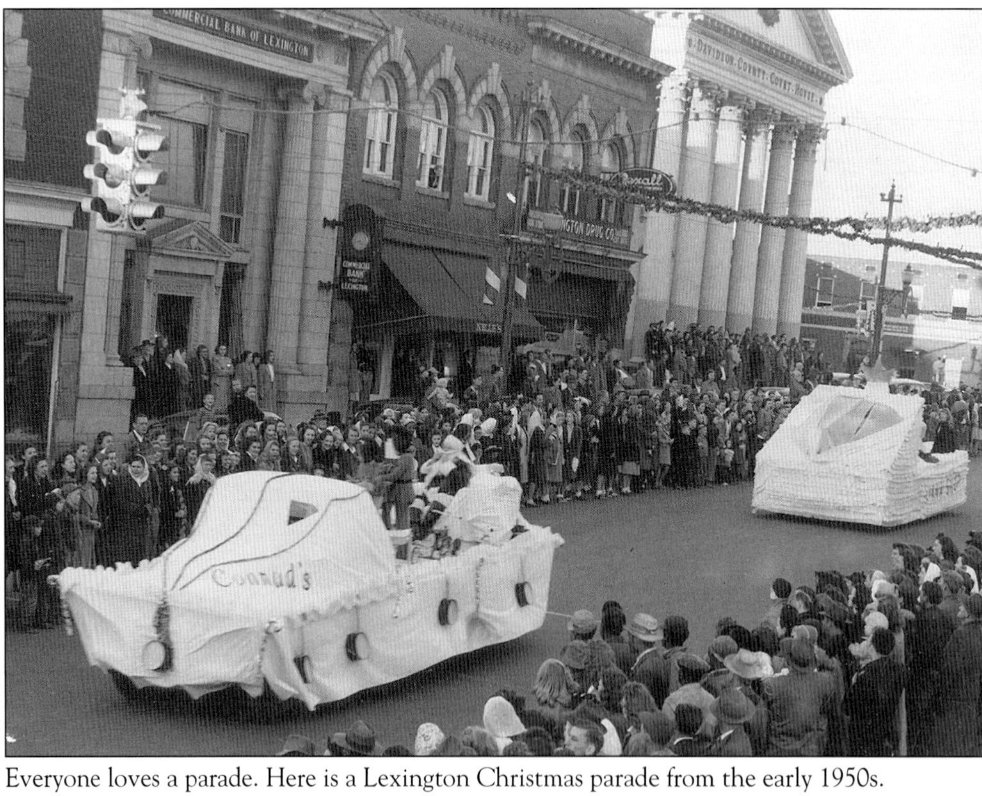

Everyone loves a parade. Here is a Lexington Christmas parade from the early 1950s.

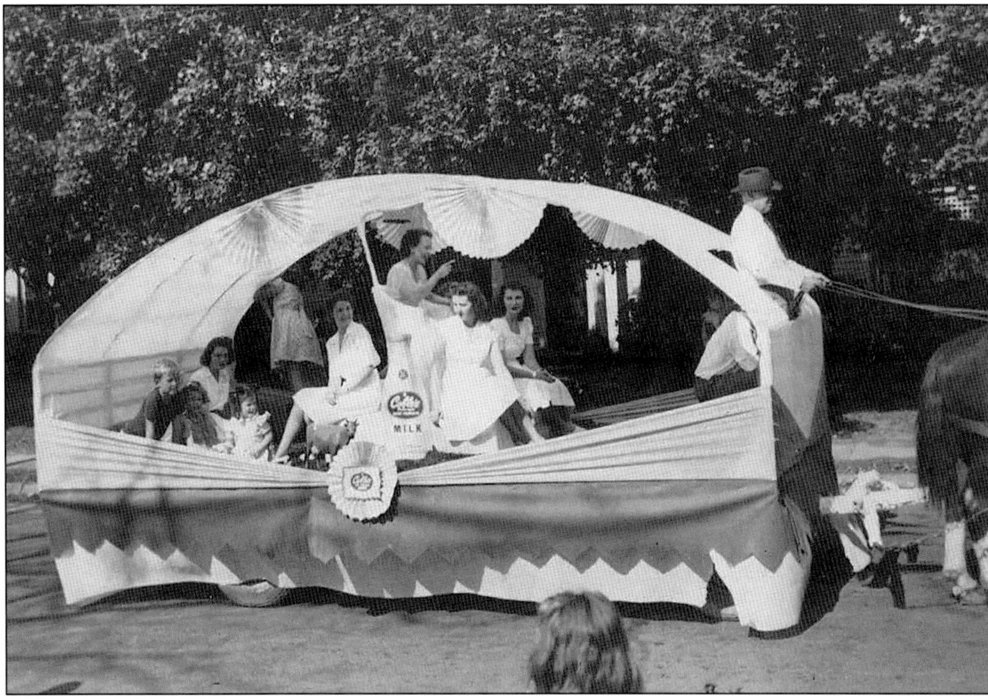

Coble Dairy helped make this 1945 parade special with this elegant float. Mrs. George Coble is on the top seat. Frances Miller Ebelein is in front of her, facing the camera, and Maxine Moore Blaylock is to her right, looking backwards. Mary Jo Davis Shoaf is behind Mrs. Coble. The children in the back are Eddie Coble, Libby Coltrane Sink, and Georgeanna Coble Jordan Bingham.

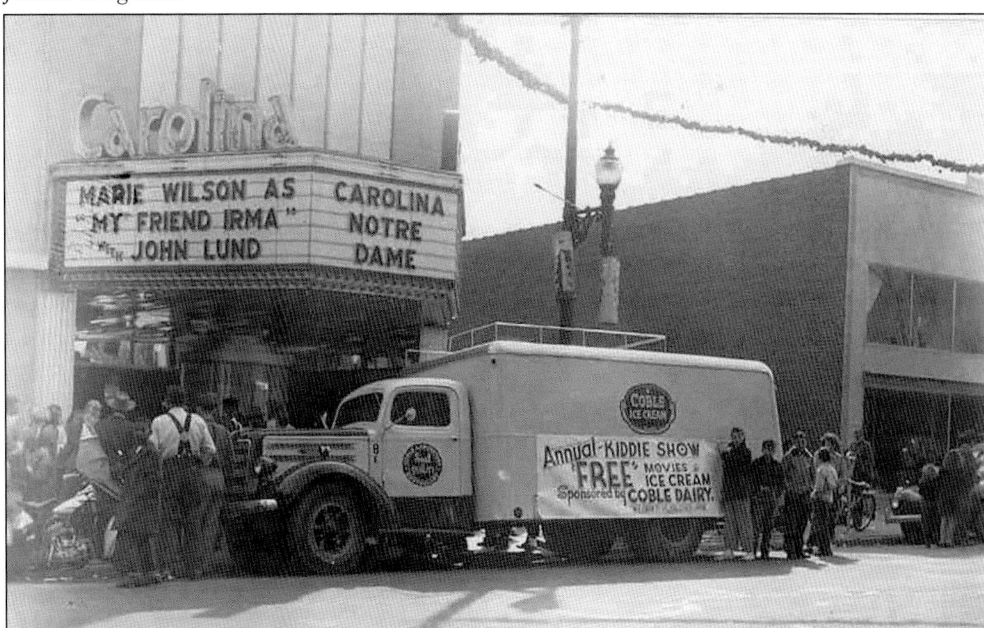

Coble Dairy would sponsor Saturday matinees for children at the Carolina Theater in Lexington. You not only saw a free movie, but enjoyed free ice cream, too!

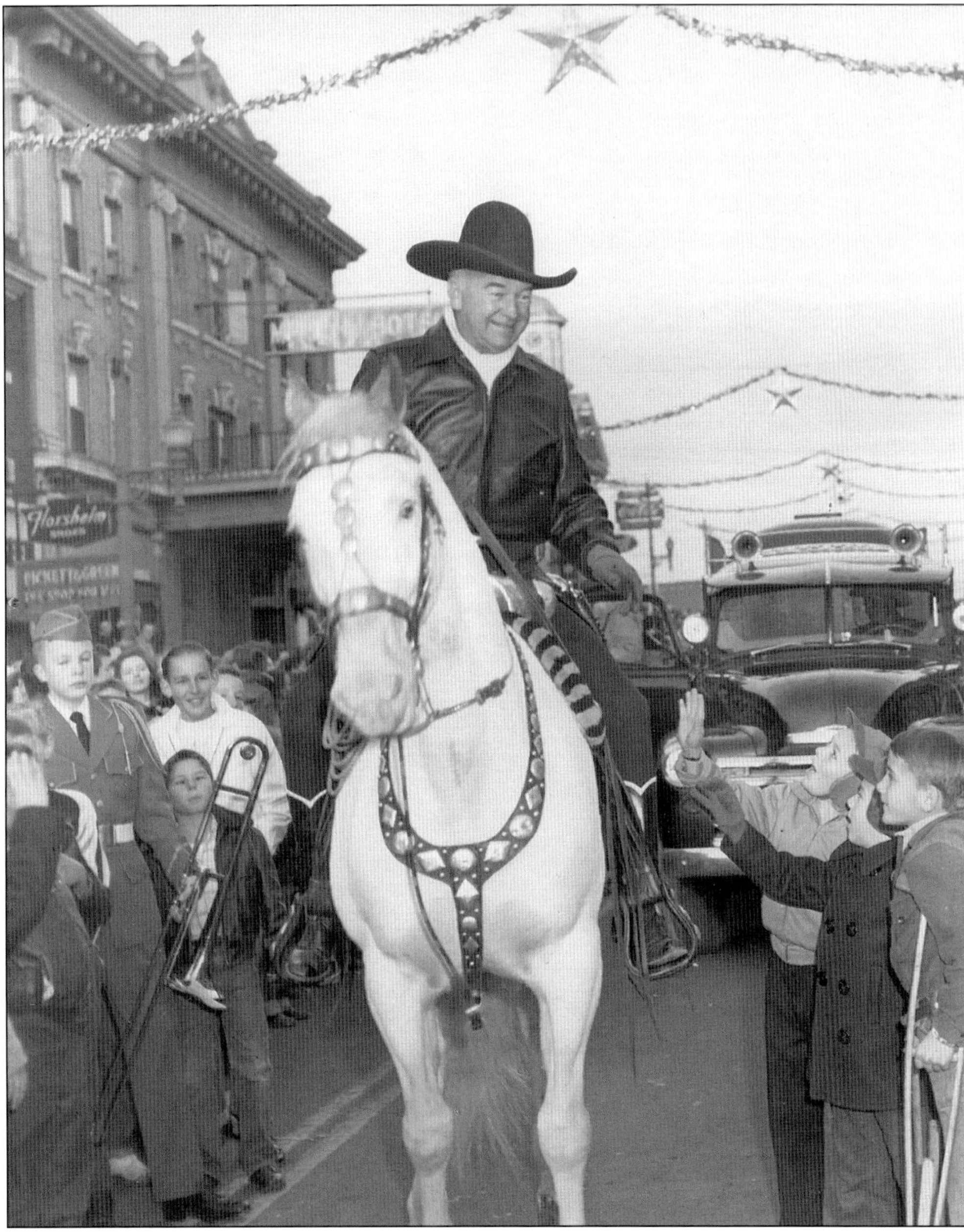

Famous television and movie star Hop-Along-Cassidy is greeted by some of his young admirers in this Lexington Christmas parade from the 1950s.

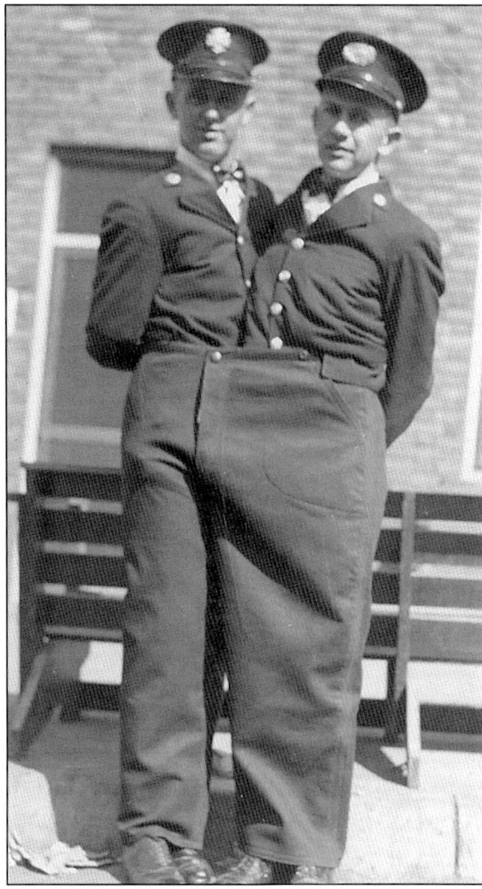

Speaking of some big shoes to fill? There was always time for some fun at the Lexington Fire Department. One of these firemen later became Lexington's chief, Norman Owen.

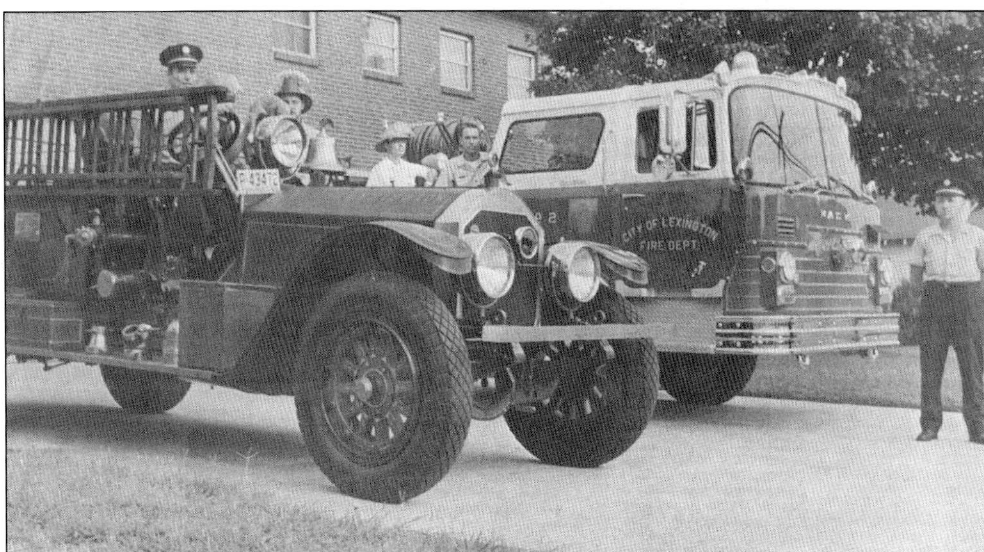

Out with the old and in with the new. The 1922 American La France truck was sent back to the factory and rebuilt following the 1926 fatal wreck (see Chapter 9). It was placed back in service and served Lexington until the 1960s, when it was replaced by the modern truck.

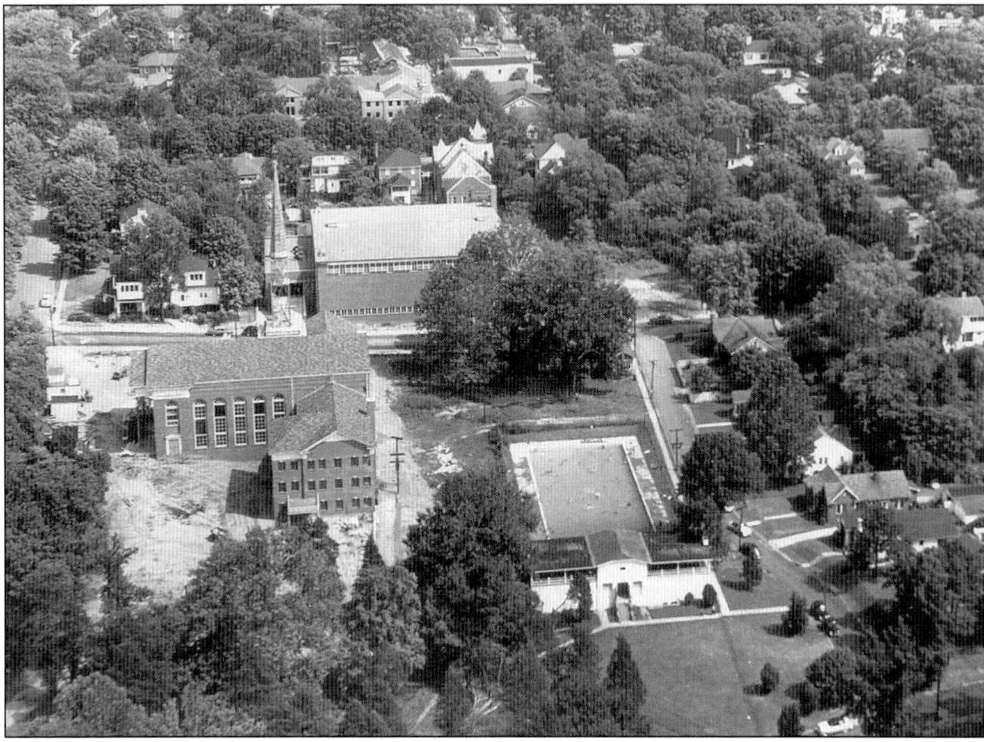

Three major Lexington landmarks are seen in this 1954 picture. The new First Baptist Church can be seen under construction in the foreground. Directly behind the church is the recently completed YMCA. Near the top of the picture is the back of the new First Methodist Church. These three new buildings represented an investment of almost $2 million that year. Note the old municipal swimming pool, which was full of happy children when this picture was taken.

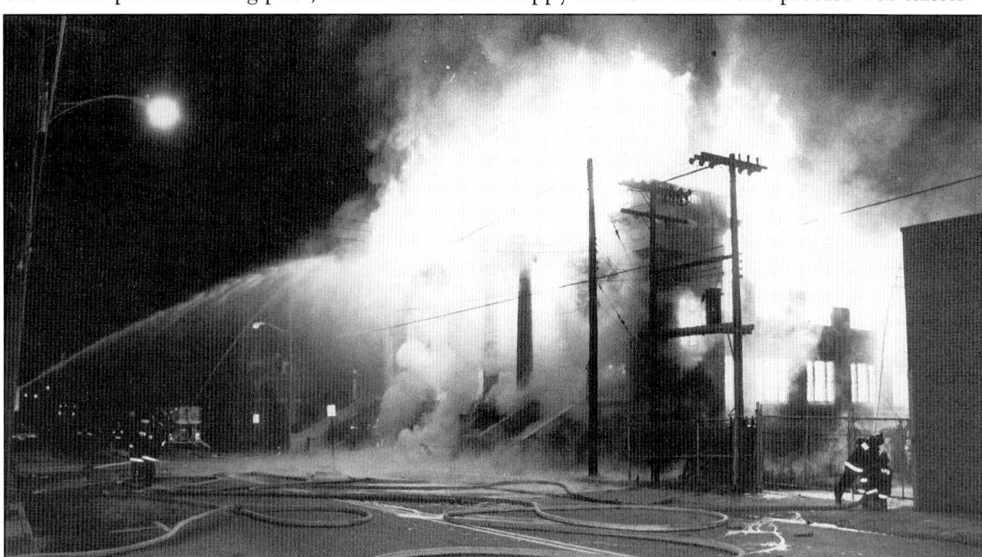

This night shot of the burning Thomasville Civic Center on Randolph Street in 1976 shows the city's fire department fighting to contain the blaze. The building, which was a complete loss, was formerly a church and stood on the site of the present public library.

In 1963, racial disturbances around the country also affected Lexington. A man was shot and killed behind First Reformed Church, and racial tensions were at a fever pitch. The next Sunday, police were required to protect the worshippers at historic St. Stephen's Church.

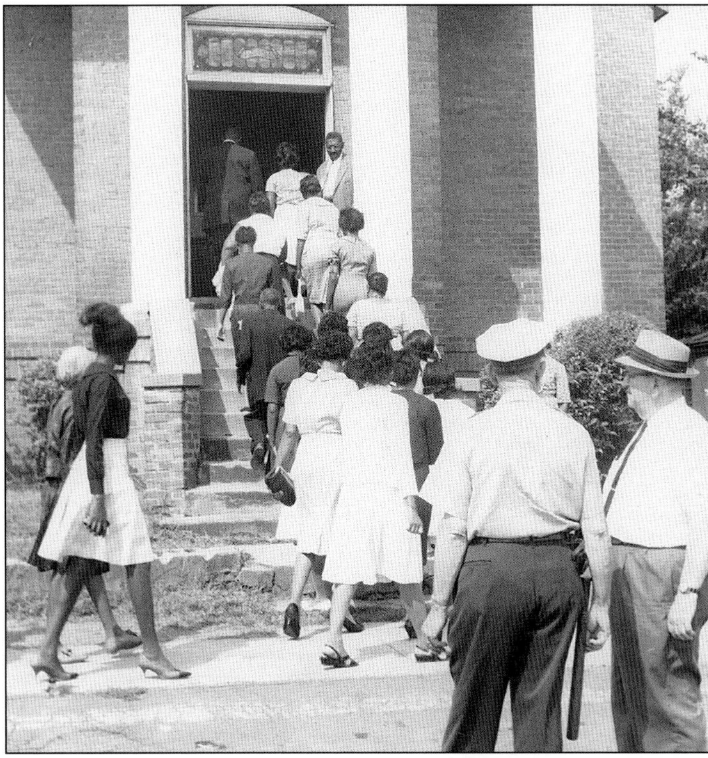

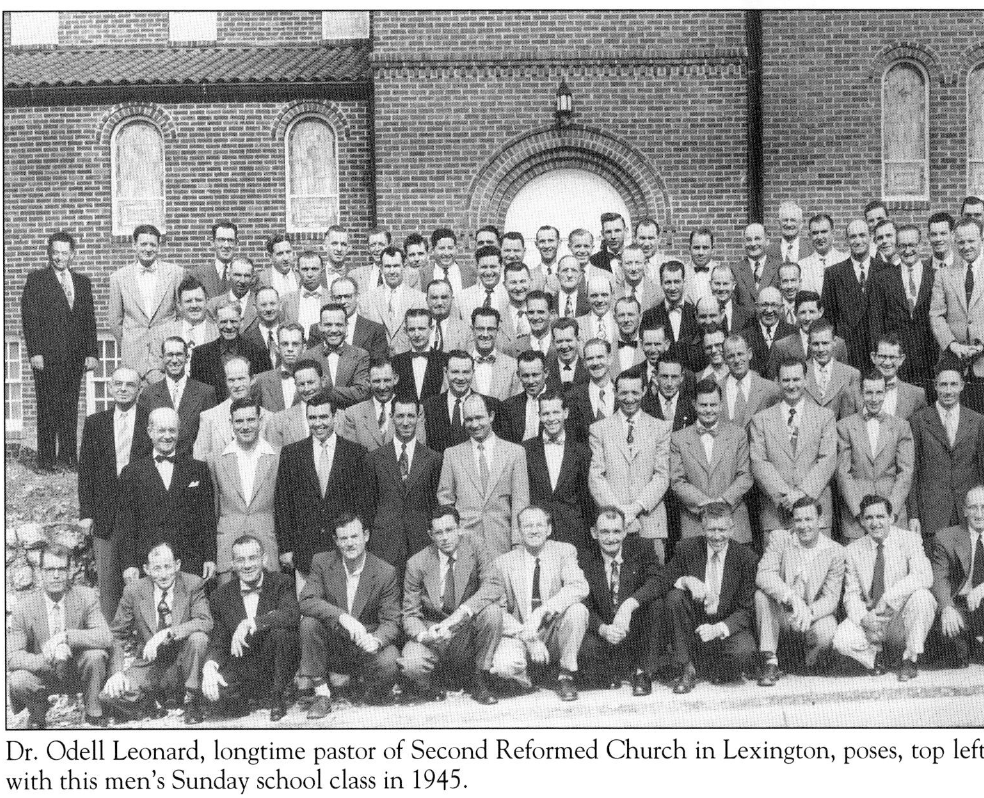

Dr. Odell Leonard, longtime pastor of Second Reformed Church in Lexington, poses, top left, with this men's Sunday school class in 1945.

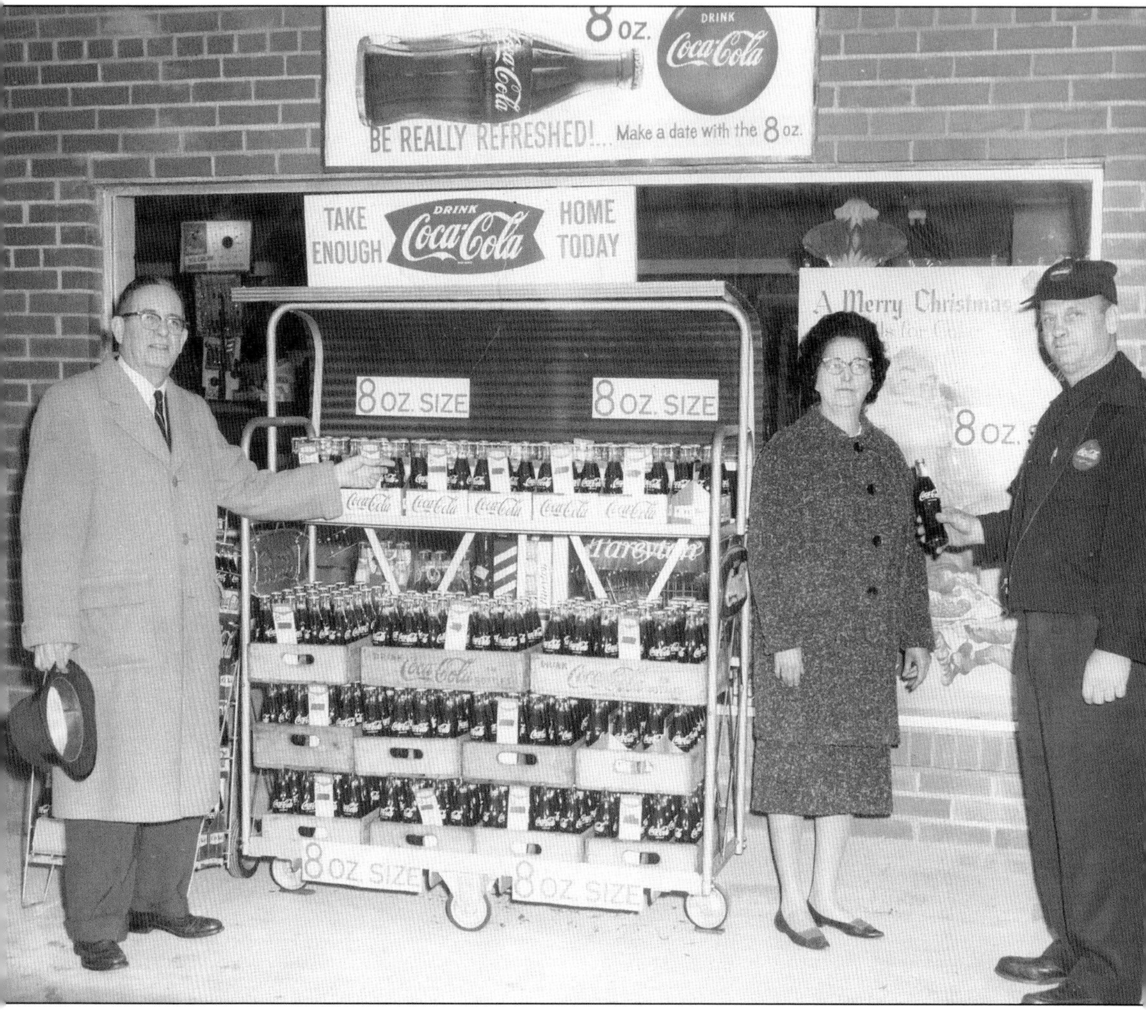

Remember when Coca-Cola came in small bottles? The 6-ounce bottle, still favored by many, was giving way to the new 8-ounce bottle when this late 1961 photograph was taken. The Lexington bottling plant was the first in North Carolina to bottle the new-size Coke, and McBride's Curb Market was selected as the first store to retail it. Pictured, from left to right, are Tom Snider, local Coca-Cola executive; Laura McBride, store owner; and Jake Briggs, local Coca-Cola route supervisor.

Tobacco was a primary crop for many Davidson County farmers when this picture was made in 1955 on the James Ray Clodfelter farm on the Old Greensboro Road near Thomasville. Nanny Hunt Clodfelter and James Ray Clodfelter are holding their grandsons, Dwight Lee (the baby) and Ray Von Clodfelter.

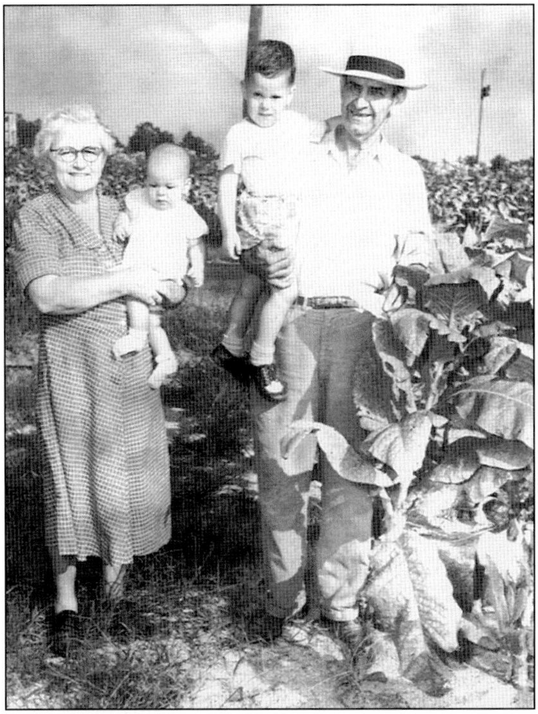

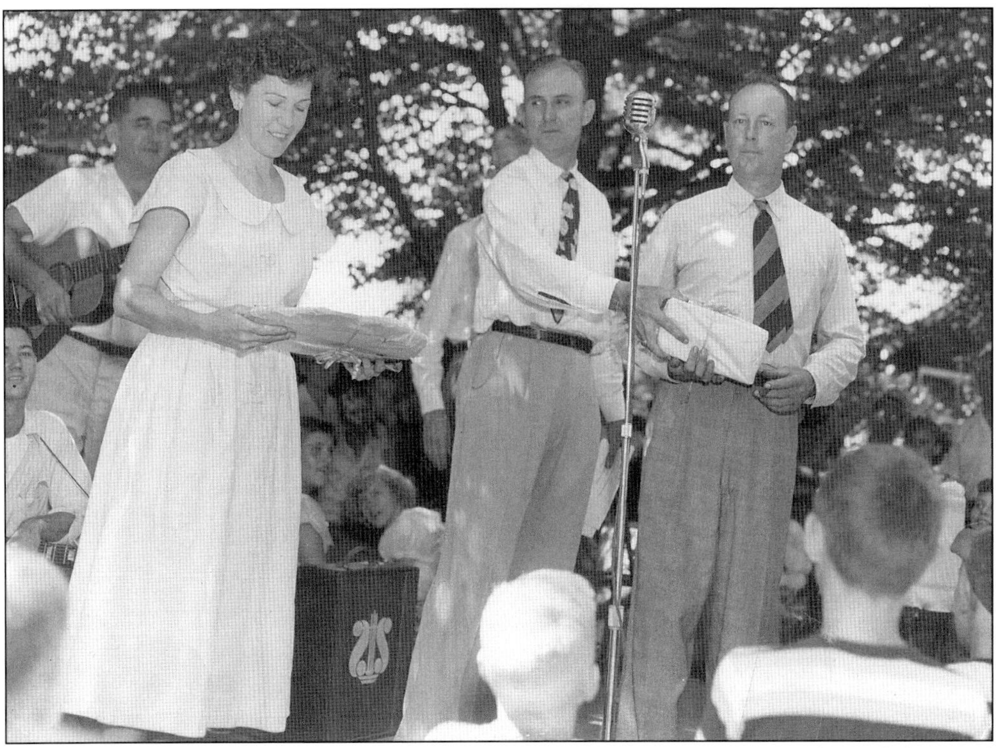

It was Erlanger Day in 1947 when Conrad Hinson, personnel director at the mill, honored Helen Hames Rogers and Clifford Gurley for being the first girl and boy born in Erlanger. Both were born in 1915.

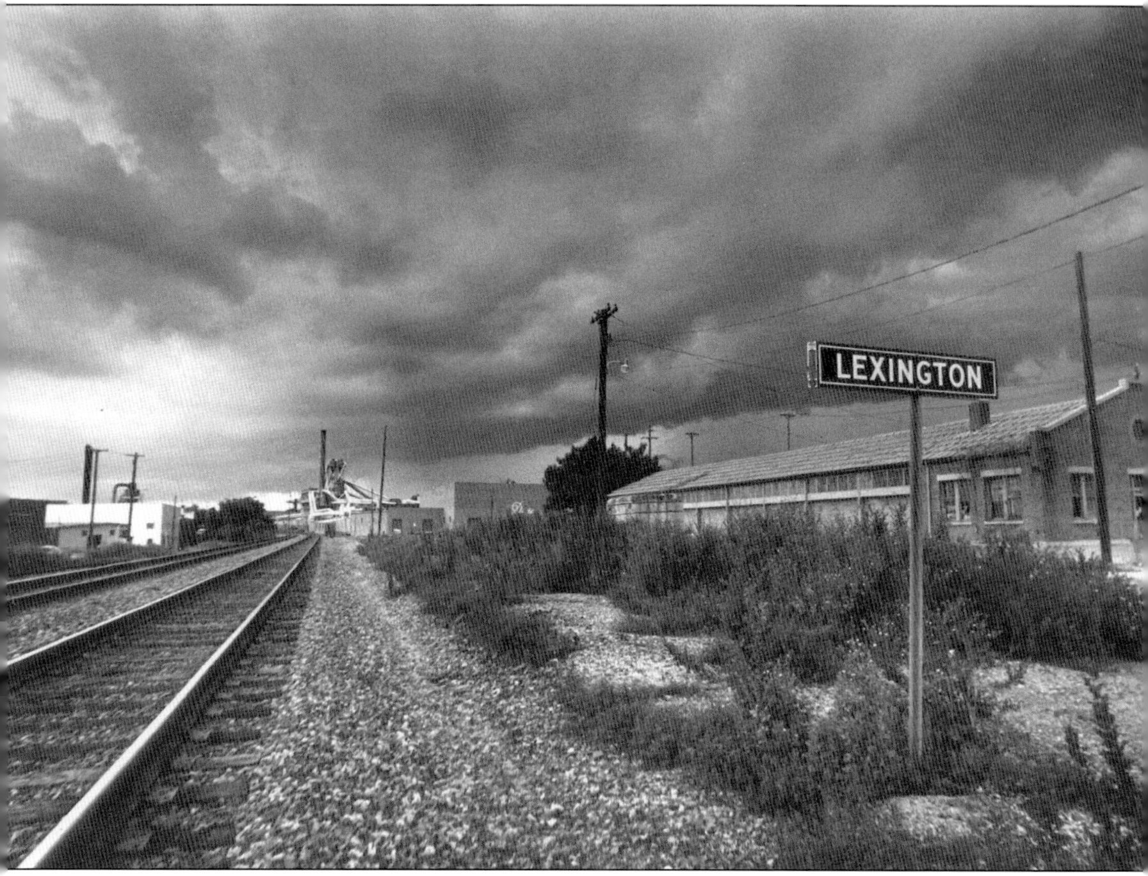

For almost 150 years, the railroad has been a focal point for both Lexington and Thomasville. On March 26, 1941, the first modern silver streamlined passenger train passed through Davidson County. In Lexington, teachers and students from Cecil and Holt Schools joined hundreds of other cities that turned out to catch a glimpse of the "Southerner" on its inaugural run. Four years later, in April 1945, thousands of Davidson County residents stood by the railroad tracks to see President Franklin D. Roosevelt's funeral train pass through.

Seven

Davidson County Distinctions

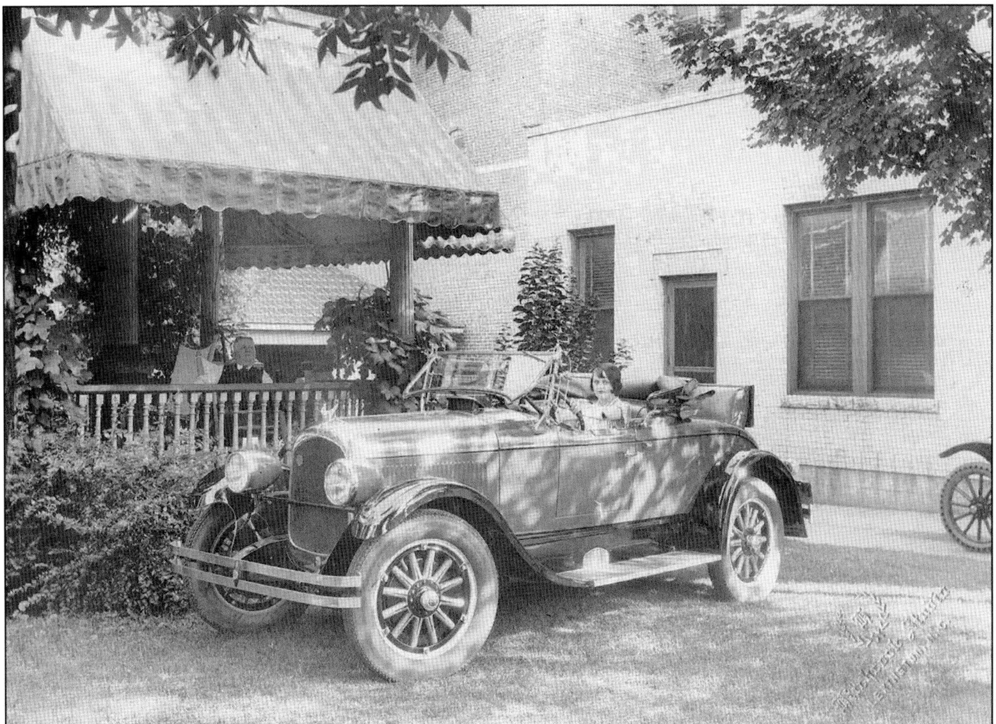

This 1925 Chrysler Roadster set a land speed record for a non-stop automobile run between Lexington and Jacksonville, FL. Automobile dealer C.C. Gray and John "Salty" Trice left Lexington one midnight wearing goggles for the 559-mile journey. They arrived in Jacksonville at 12:35 p.m., averaging 48.7 miles per hours. Gray's sister-in-law, Helen Buchanan, is pictured behind the wheel with her father, Dr. E.J. Buchanan, on the porch. Along the route the men distributed handbills describing the commercial and industrial advantages of Lexington.

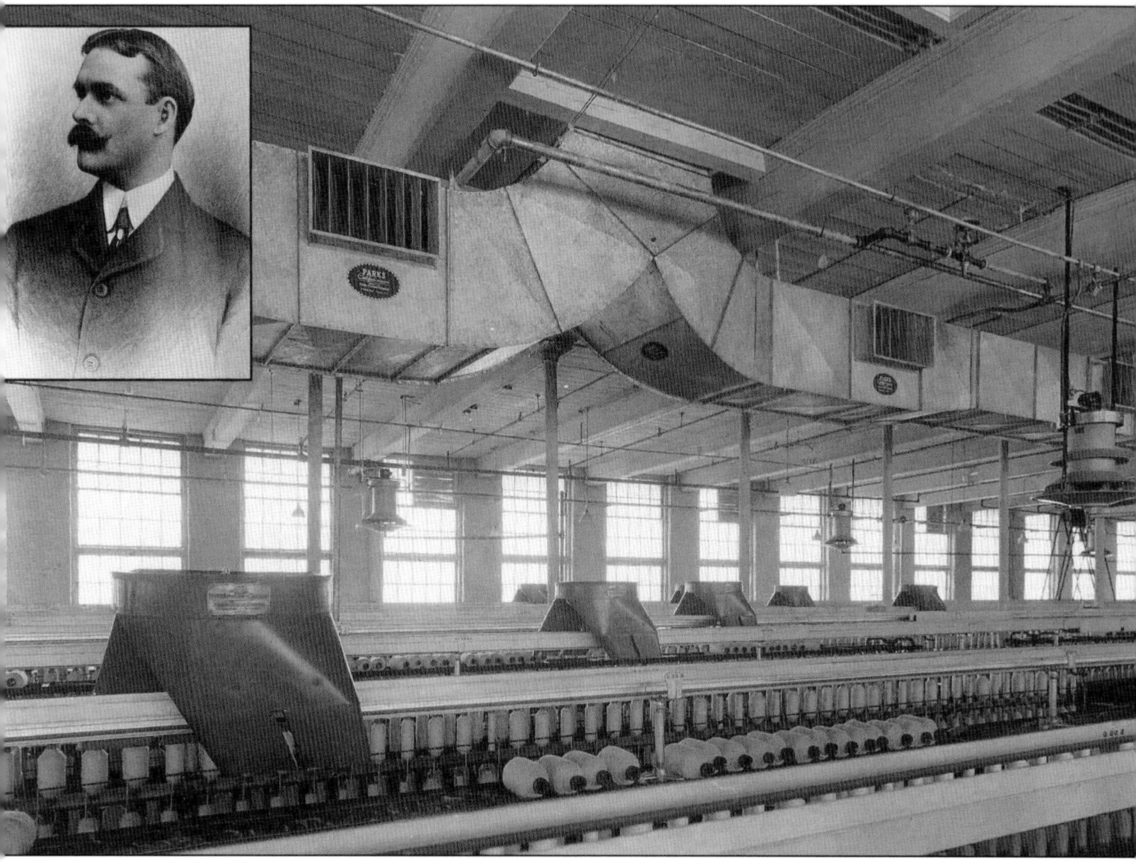

Stuart Cramer was born in Thomasville in 1868. The grandson of the town's founder, John W. Thomas, Cramer was an engineer and inventor who pioneered the development and improvement of textile mills. Between 1895 and 1905 he designed and/or equipped nearly one-third of all the new cotton mills built in the South. He patented "air-conditioning" for textile factories, defining his invention as humidification, air cleaning, and heating and ventilation. Cramer's work had a profound influence on the urbanization of the South, keeping jobs, factories, and people from leaving the region for other parts of the country. He founded the town of Cramerton, near Charlotte, creating the first model mill village where residents enjoyed some of the best conditions then known in mill housing.

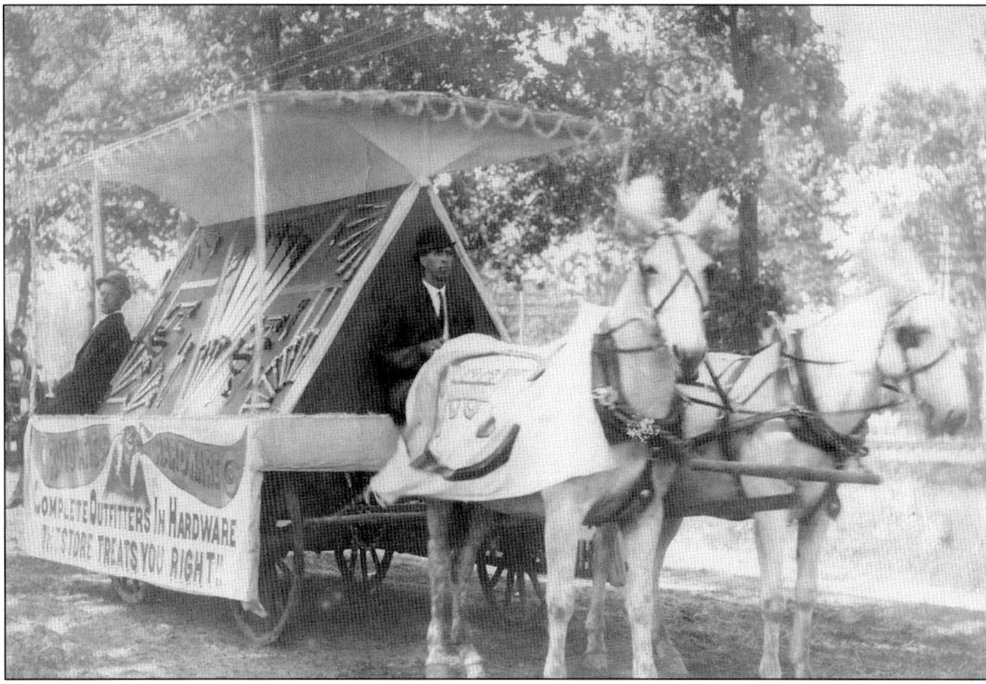

Thomasville held the first Everybody's Day in October 1908. It was the earliest street festival in the state of North Carolina. O.E. Swicegood, a representative of the Acme Company, steered this float in the 1908 parade for the Thomasville Hardware Company.

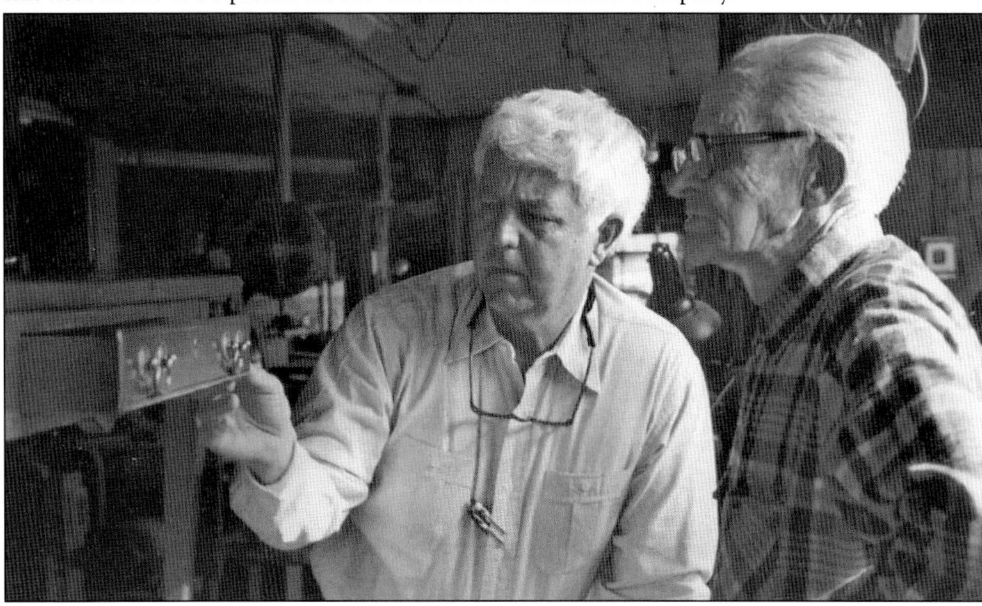

Artist Bob Timberlake did not begin painting full-time until the age of 33. His watercolors have been exibited widely and in 1980 he became the first artist from the South to design a Christmas stamp for the Postal Service. In 1990 he launched a comprehensive furniture line based on his designs through Lexington Furniture Industries. Here Timberlake is shown with Fred Craver, a local master craftsman who produced handmade furniture reminiscent of earlier 19th-century cabinetmakers in Davidson County.

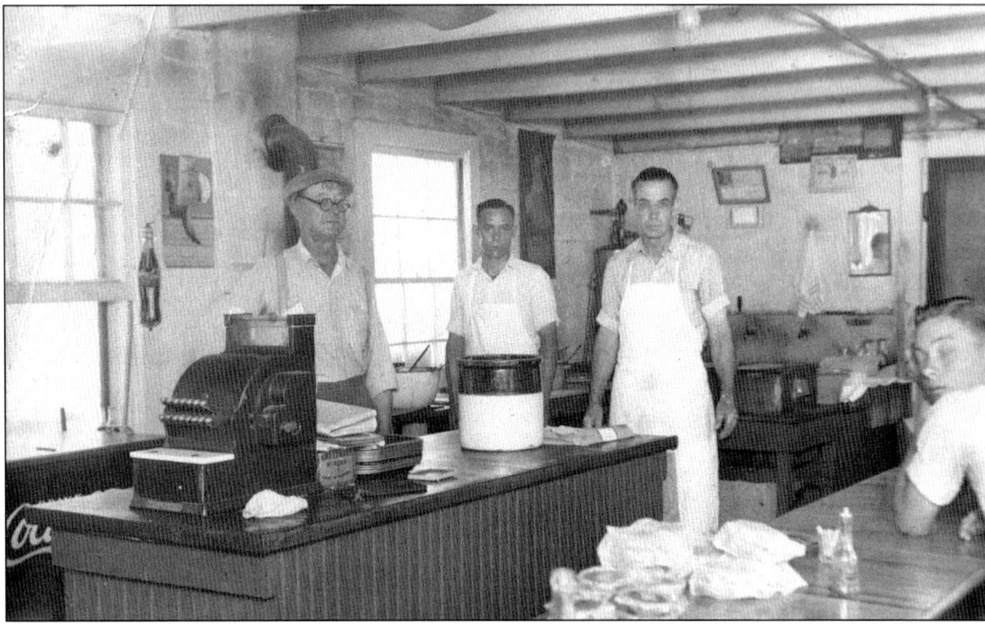

Sid Weaver is known as the "Father of Lexington Style Barbecue." He started selling barbecue from a tent on the corner of West Center and Greensboro Street in 1916. At first, he was open only when court was in session and for special occasions, but he later built a permanent building at the same location. Sid Weaver is the man with glasses to the left. Clay Johnson (middle) and Zeke Roberts are also behind the counter. The young customer is Lewis Farmer.

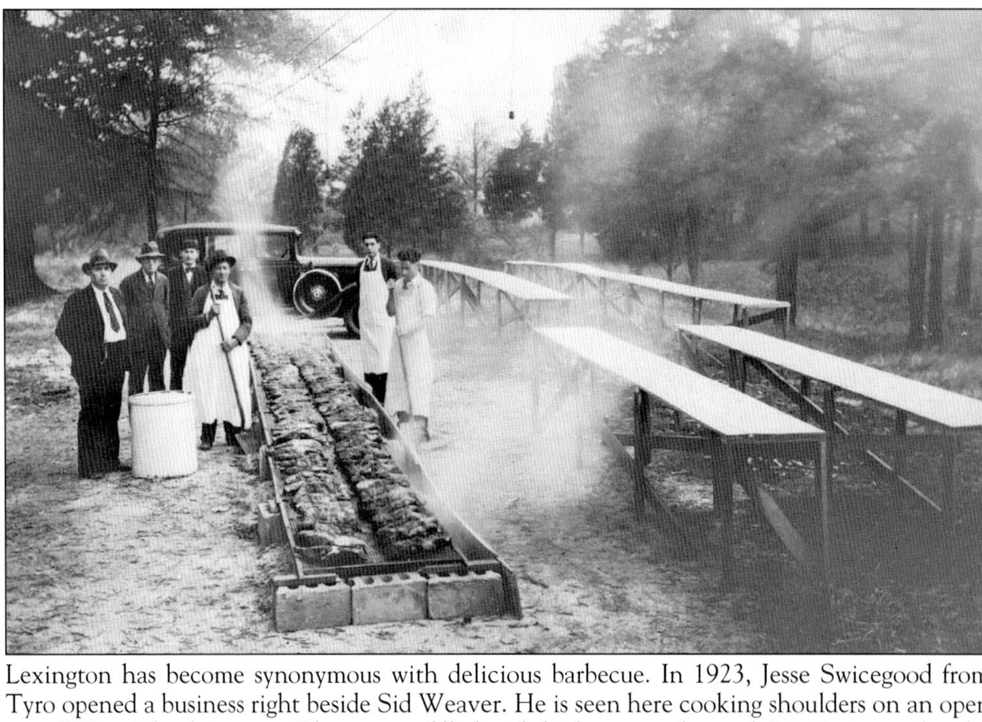

Lexington has become synonymous with delicious barbecue. In 1923, Jesse Swicegood from Tyro opened a business right beside Sid Weaver. He is seen here cooking shoulders on an open pit off West Third Avenue. The pit was filled with hickory or oak wood. Mr. Swicegood is the man in the apron on the left.

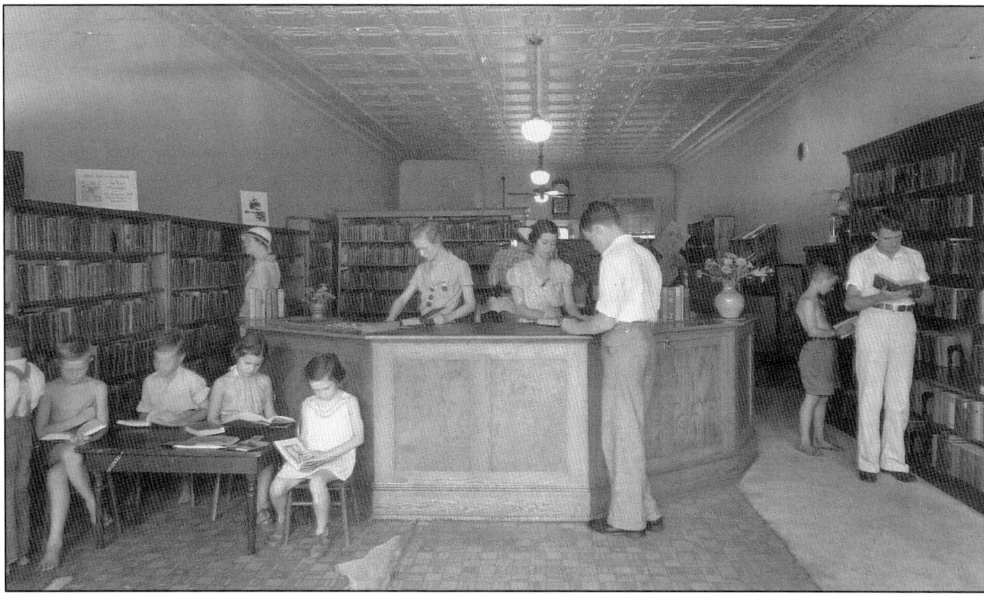

On October 23, 1928, the Davidson County Library opened in Lexington in Burgin's store with 700 books, 2 tables, and 8 chairs. The next day the Thomasville branch opened in the Thomasville High School Library with 200 books. The library was the result of a campaign from both the Lexington and Thomasville Woman's Clubs. Davidson County Commissioners appropriated $5,000, while the city of Lexington gave $1,200 and the city of Thomasville, $800. The Lexington Woman's Club donated many books from a previous effort in 1923 to open a library at the March Hotel. The Davidson County Library was the first library in the South to extend services to all people, regardless of race.

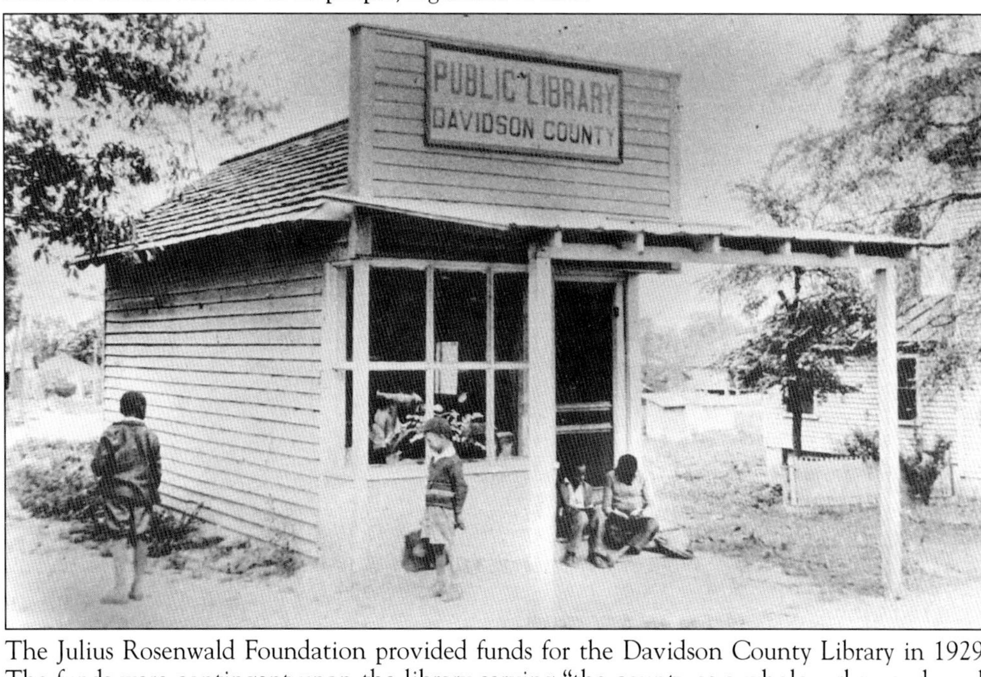

The Julius Rosenwald Foundation provided funds for the Davidson County Library in 1929. The funds were contingent upon the library serving "the county as a whole, urban and rural, colored and white." Here is the "colored" library in Thomasville in 1928.

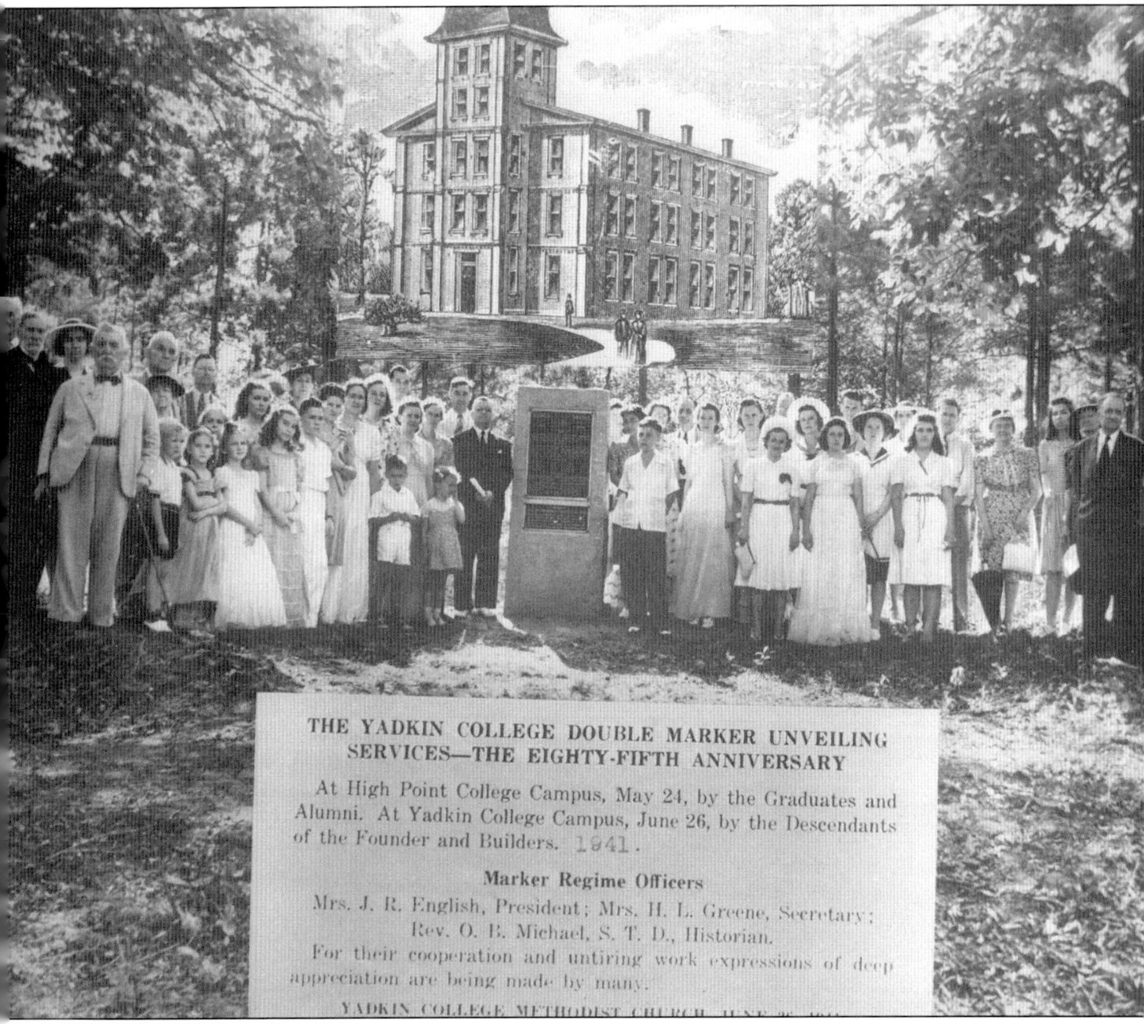

Henry Walser had a dream—to build a school of higher learning in Davidson County. Receiving little support from the Methodist Conference in 1852, he declared that he would build the school himself. He served as chairman of the trustees for the first 25 years of the school's existence and was succeeded by his son, Gaither Walser.

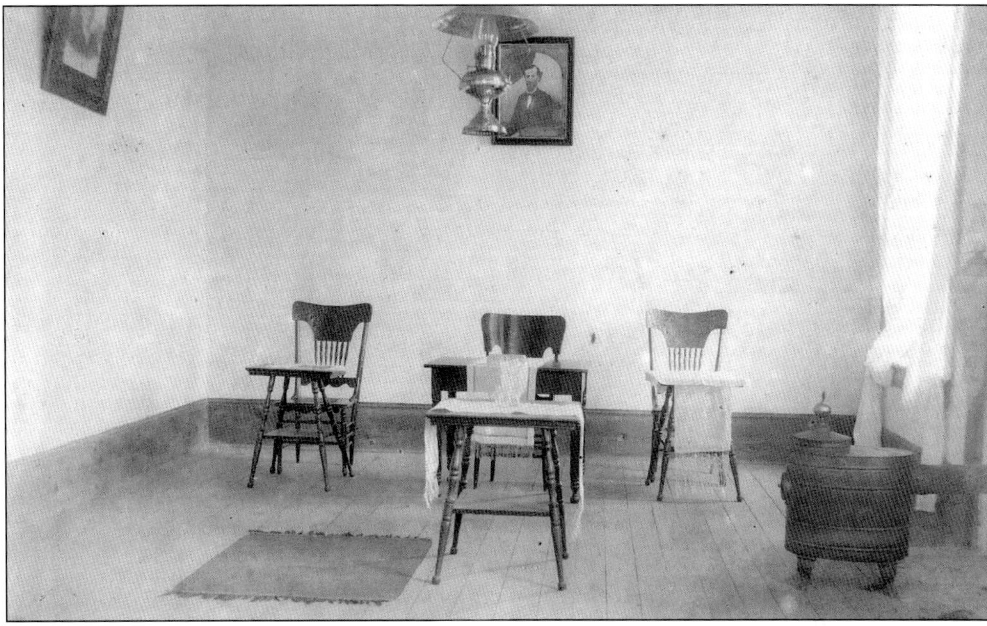

Yadkin College was once the social and intellectual center of Piedmont North Carolina. Located on the banks of the Yadkin River, the school opened in 1855. Honorable Zeb Vance Walser, North Carolina state attorney general and an 1879 graduate, said of his alma mater, "It was one of the great schools in the state; in fact, it came near being the greatest school in the state." This photograph shows the debating hall at Yadkin College.

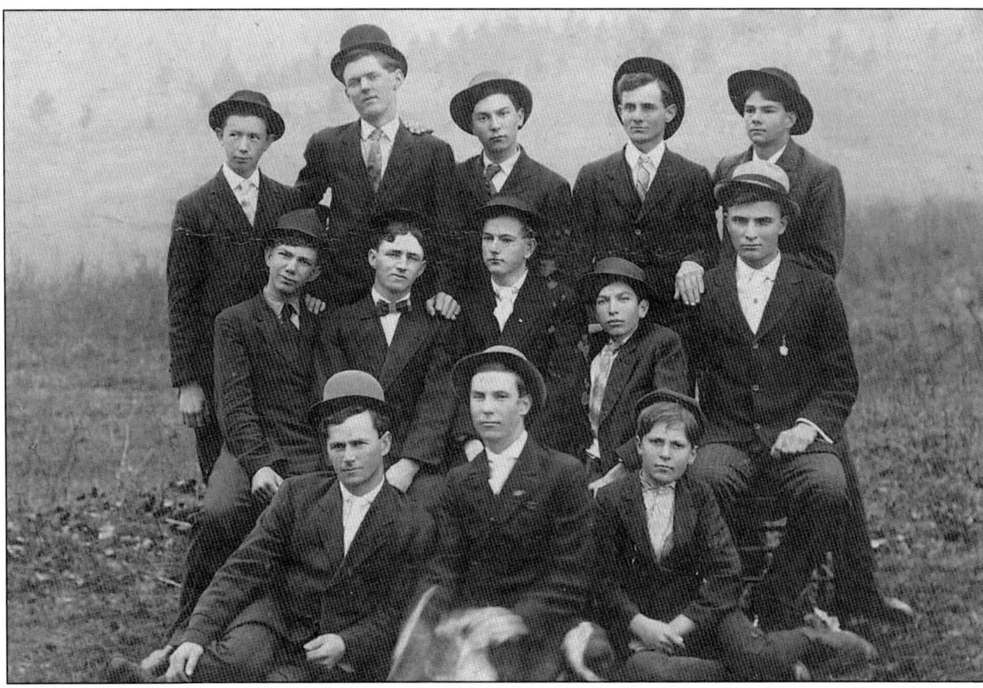

Yadkin College was most progressive for its time. Although not pictured in this group of students, in 1878, female students were admitted, making Yadkin College one of the first co-educational college in the South!

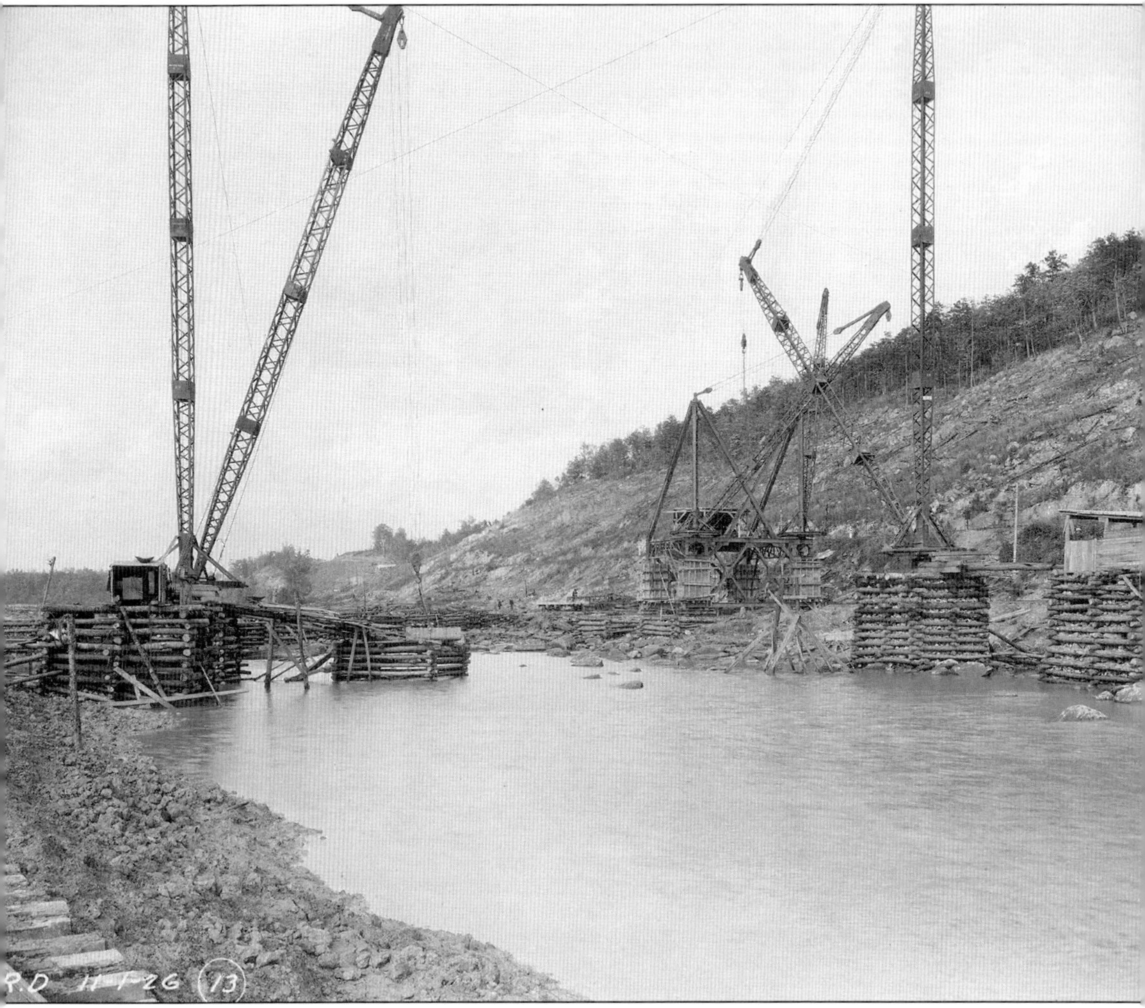

The High Rock Dam on the Yadkin was built by the Tallassee Power Company in 1925–27. Approximately 2,000 men worked on the 16-month project and over 1,000 acres of land were cleared to create a new lake that has become one of North Carolina's favorite recreational areas. The lake waters covered historic Trading Ford, where Gen. Nathaniel Greene's army escaped from the pursuit of Lord Cornwallis.

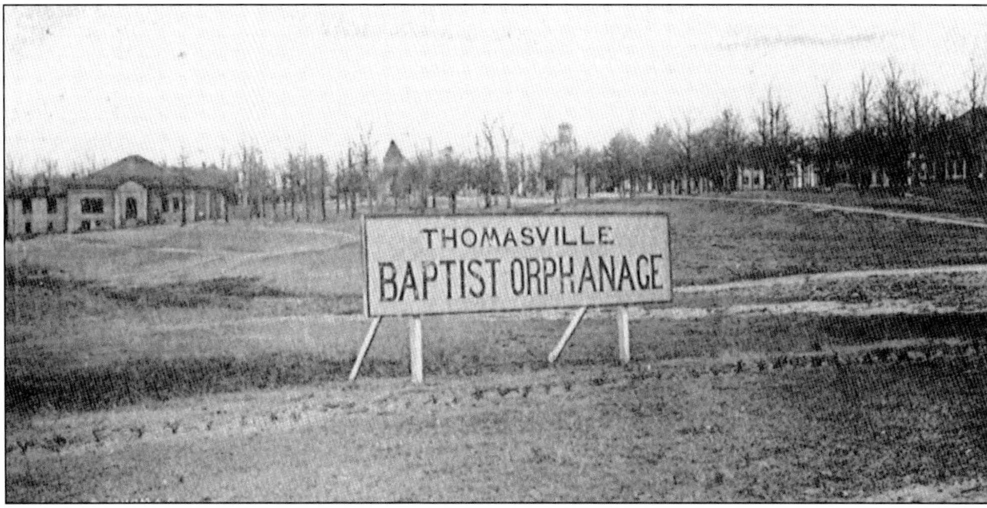

Davidson County is home to two excellent children's homes. There were many orphans in the late 19th century. John H. Mills, founder of the Oxford Masonic Orphanage in 1874, led the Baptists of North Carolina to establish the Thomasville Orphanage in 1885. The Junior Order Orphanage opened in Lexington in 1928. Through the years thousands of children have found love and support in the two children's homes of Davidson County.

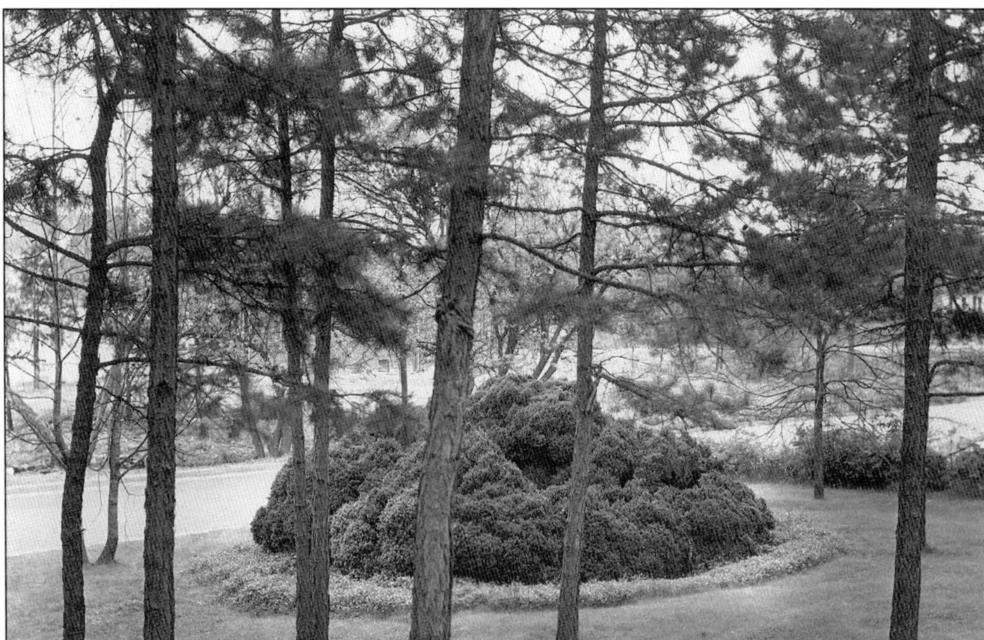

Did you know that the largest single-stem English boxwood in the United States was located at the Don Walser home on Williams Circle in Lexington? The boxwood was originally located on the Walser farm near Silver Valley. In 1922, government officials expressed interest in purchasing the boxwood for the newly constructed Lincoln Memorial in Washington, but the expense of transporting the huge plant was prohibitive. In April 1936 Don Walser obtained a special highway permit and transported the 12-ton plant to this home in Lexington. The boxwood measured over 100 feet in circumference and people came from all over the country to document its claim.

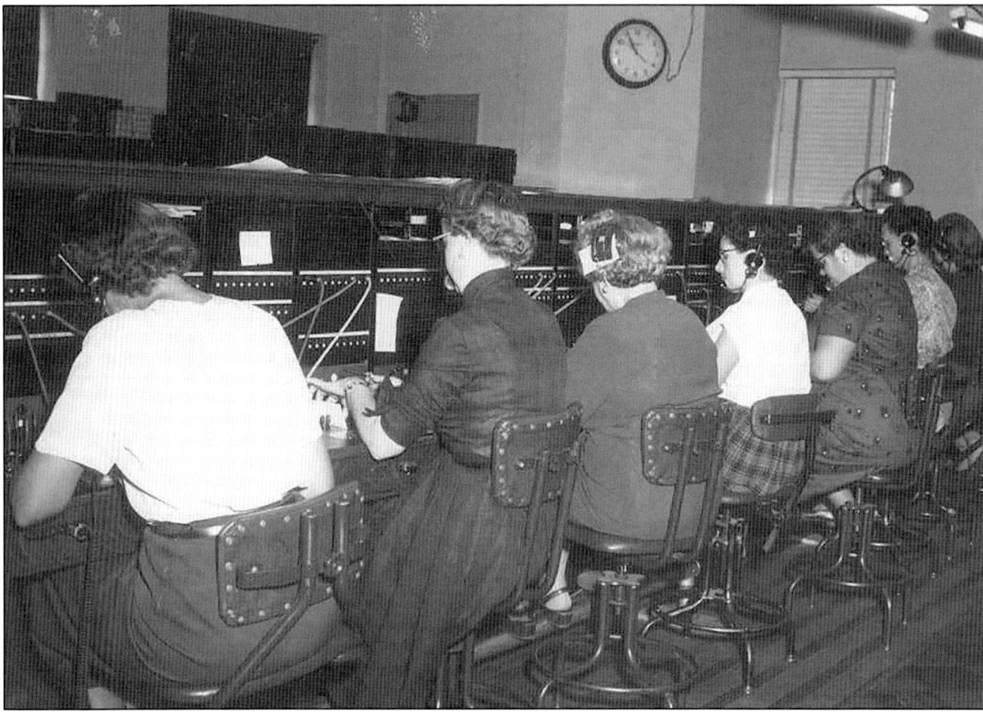

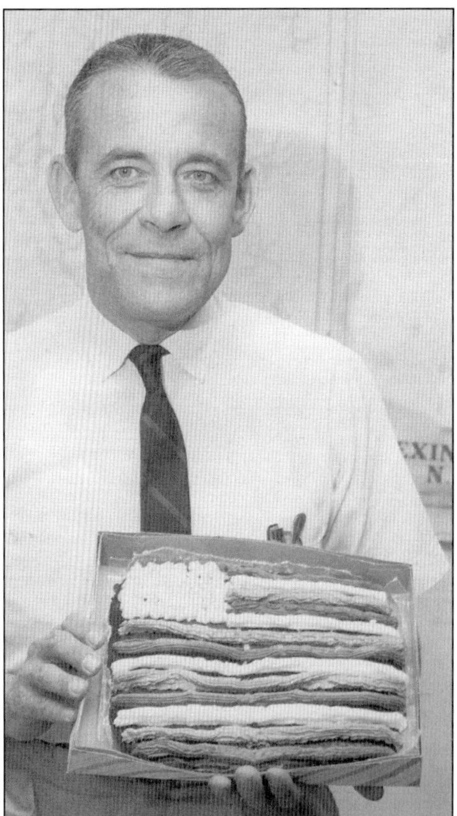

The Lexington Telephone Company, incorporated in 1896, became the second telephone system in the state and one of the first in the country to offer direct dialing in June 1921. Working side by side to connect calls in 1960 are, from left to right, switchboard operators Mildred Morgan, Dot Lingle, Ollie Mendenhall, Eve Hinson, Peggy Williams, Caldonia Carter, and Mary Swing.

H. Cloyd Philpott was a candidate for lieutenant governor when this picture was made in 1960. Mrs. Thomas Kimbrell made the candy flag complete with 50 stars. Most political observers agree that Mr. Philpott would have later been elected governor if not for his untimely death.

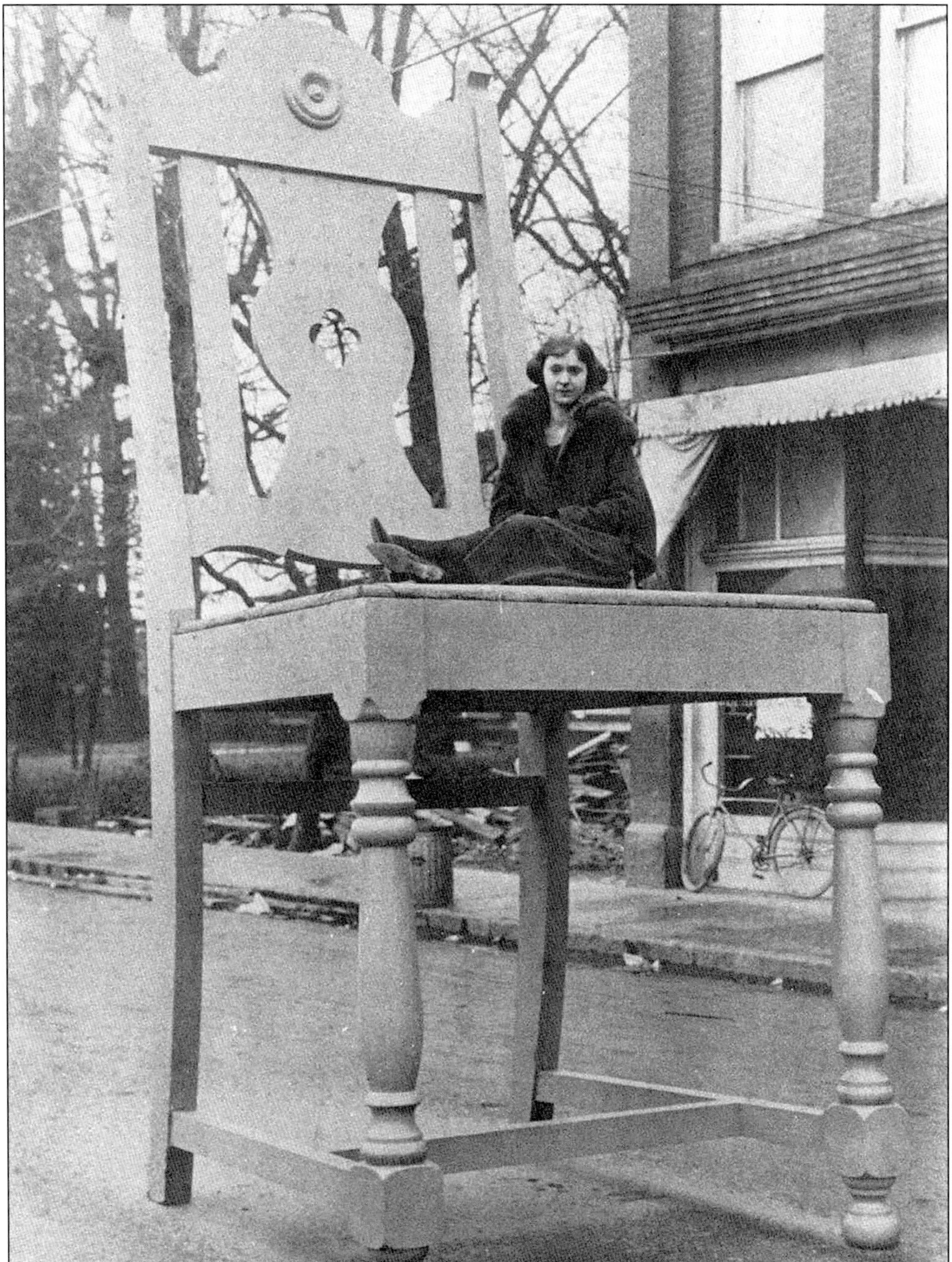

The original "Big Chair" measuring 13 feet was built in 1922. That year Thomasville, with a population of only 6,000, was producing more chairs than any city in the country. Charles M. Sturkey of the *Chairtown News* falsely boasted on a trip to Spartanburg, SC, that Thomasville had planned to build the world's largest chair. The Spartanburg paper reported his comments and national papers picked up the story. Sturkey was forced to ask the Rotary Club to start the project, which they did. This is the original chair before it was mounted beside the railroad. Sadie Blair Fouts, a secretary at Standard Chair, is pictured in the lofty seat.

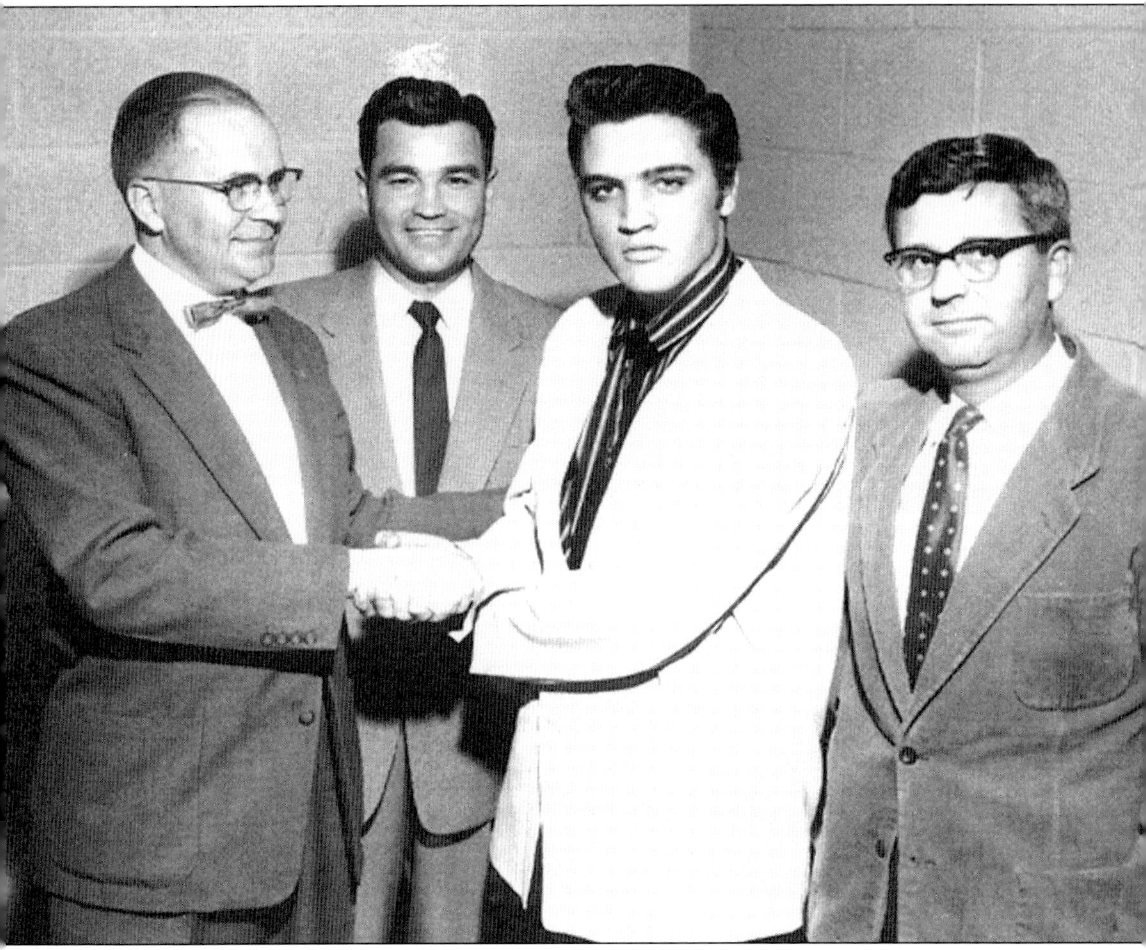

The Lexington Civitan Club thought singer Eddie Arnold was coming for a fund-raising concert. But when Arnold had to cancel, Col. Tom Parker called to say that a new young singer by the name of Elvis Presley would be taking his place. Dr. L.C. Harpe and the members of the Civitan Club had never heard of Elvis. But the young people had, and on the night of March 21, 1956, nearly 5,000 screaming fans packed the Lexington YMCA to hear the rising star. Unfortunately, the Civitan Club had made a deal with the Colonel to accept $200 in lieu of a percentage of the gate. But nevertheless, Dr. Harpe, Don Leonard, and Haynes Sherron (left to right) did have their picture made with Elvis. Almost half a century later, people still remember where they were "the day Elvis came to Lexington."

Eight

FALSE ALARM AT MIDNIGHT

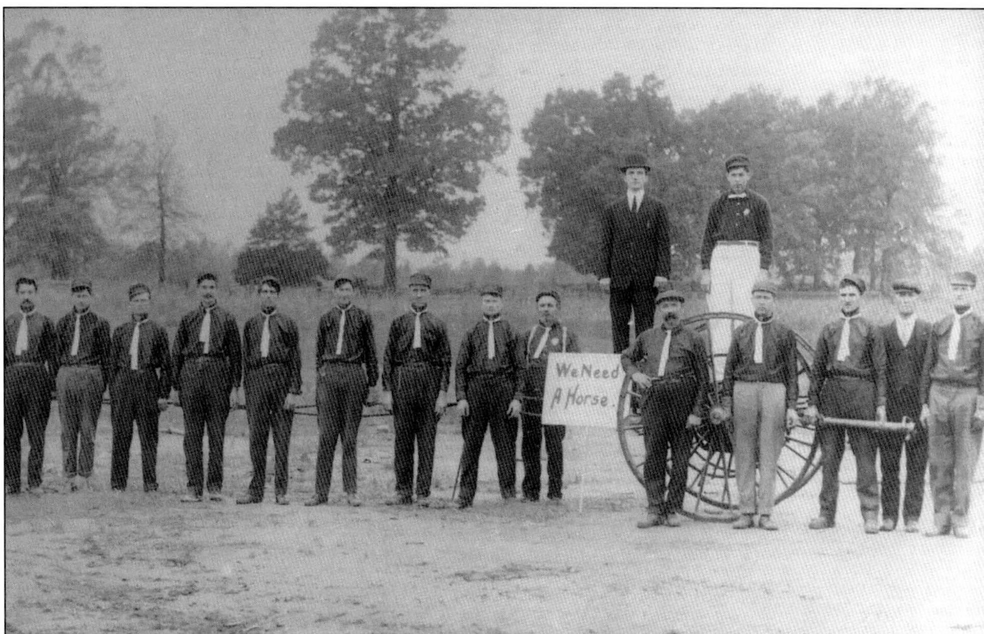

The city of Lexington had two fire companies for many years. The No. 1 Company was downtown and the No. 2 Company was at Wennonah Cotton Mills. This is the Reel Company, which was organized in 1905. The firemen had to pull the heavy reel by hand, so they started a campaign for a horse. The fire chief, J.F. Spruill, is standing on the cart beside the assistant chief, J.W. Broadway. The firemen from left to right are Charlie Swing, Sol Godfrey, Jake Palmer, C.B. Yates, Charles Phiefer, Charles Coggins, George Milsap, Ernest Taylor, Ed Hoskin, Will Link, Lindsay Link, Robert Swing, O.C. Kinney, and Lindo Hardister.

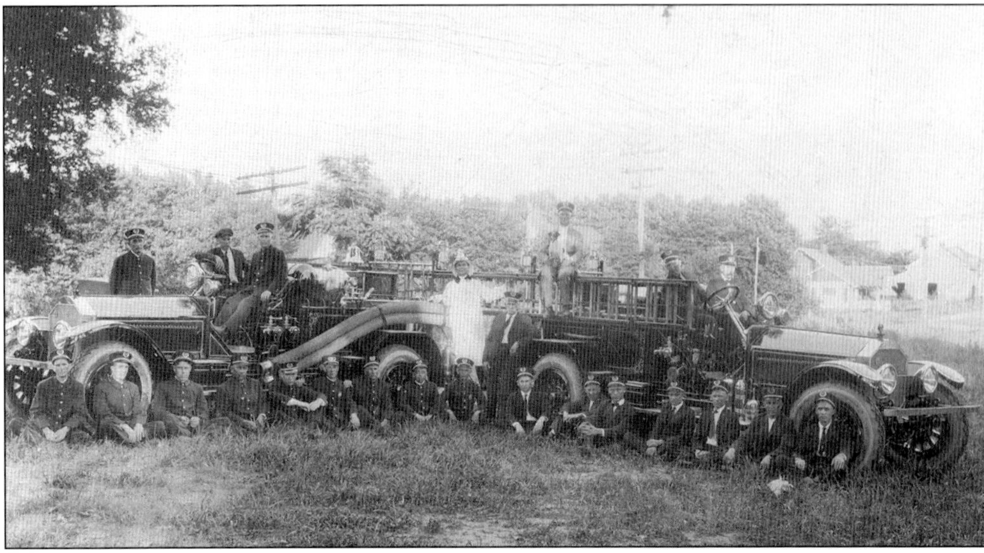

In April 1922, the city of Lexington purchased two new American La France 750-gallon pumper trucks. The Wennonah Company was first told the city could not afford two trucks, but after an appeal, the city commissioners agreed to purchase a second truck if Wennonah could raise $5,000. Mr. W.E. Holt and Mr. J.V. Moffitt Sr. agreed to contribute the $5,000 on behalf of Wennonah Mills. The America La France Company also reduced the cost of the second truck by $1,000. These two trucks, the latest in firefighting equipment, cost the city only $18,000.

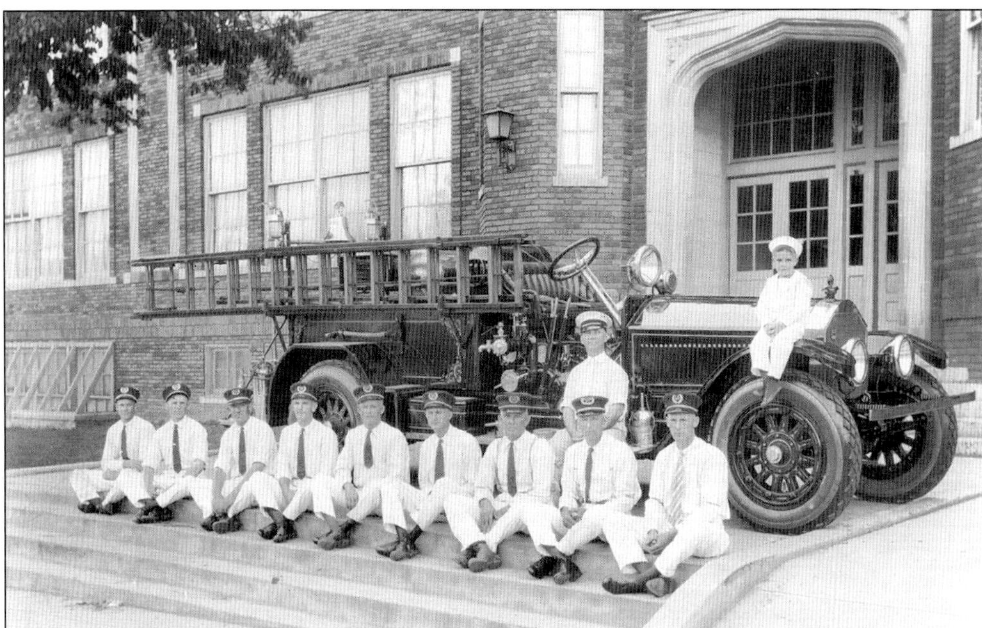

The Wennonah department was known as the No. 2 Company. Here is their new truck in 1922 in front of the new Lexington High School. Firemen from left to right are J.L. McCarn, O.B. Yarbrough, Ray Hill, Howard Michael, Henry "Freight Train" Gibson, Riley Cope, D.C. Cope, Henry Yarbrough, and J.C. Yarbrough. Fire Chief Dr. A.E. Brannock is pictured on the running board and his son Frankie is on the front fender.

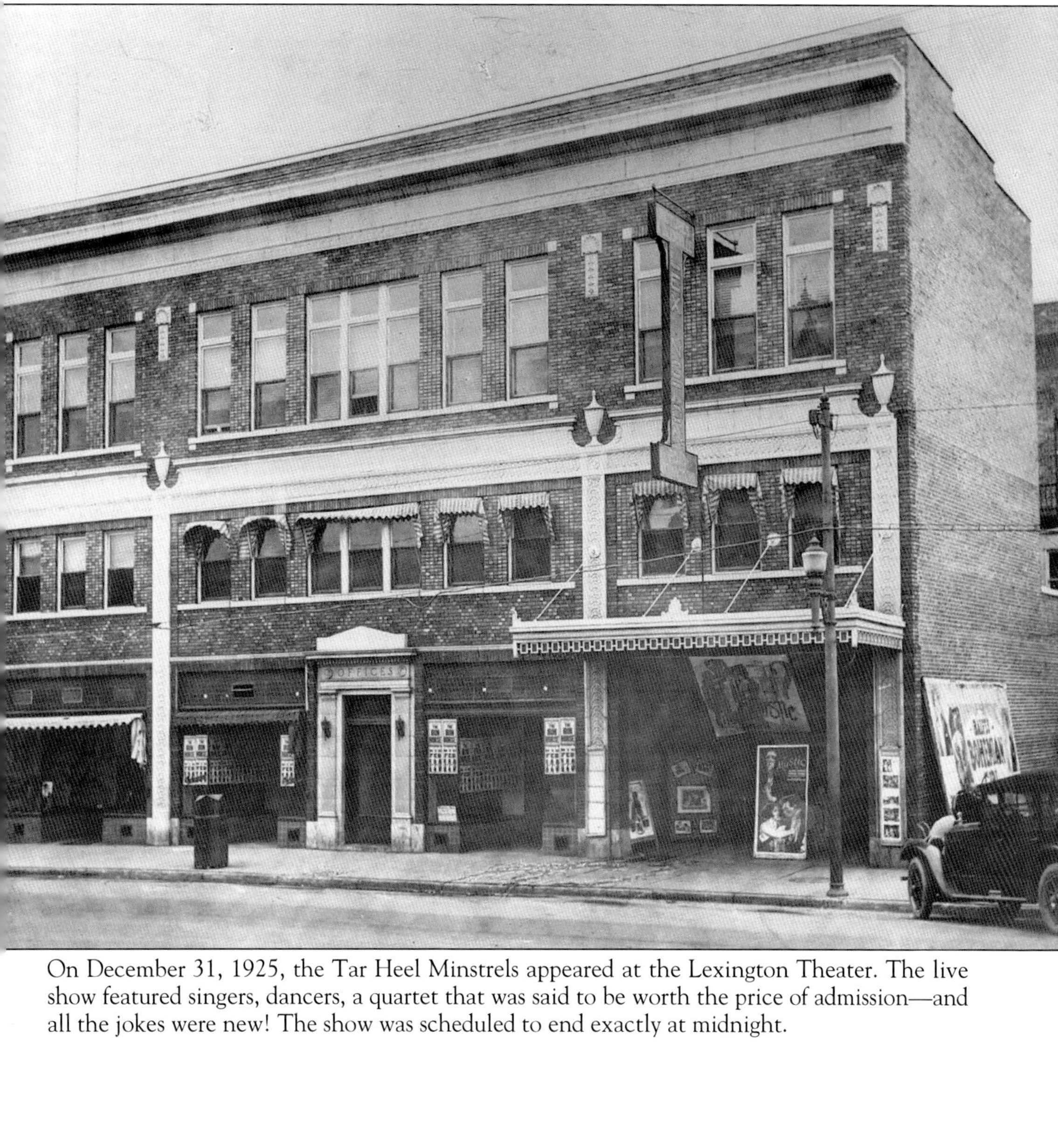

On December 31, 1925, the Tar Heel Minstrels appeared at the Lexington Theater. The live show featured singers, dancers, a quartet that was said to be worth the price of admission—and all the jokes were new! The show was scheduled to end exactly at midnight.

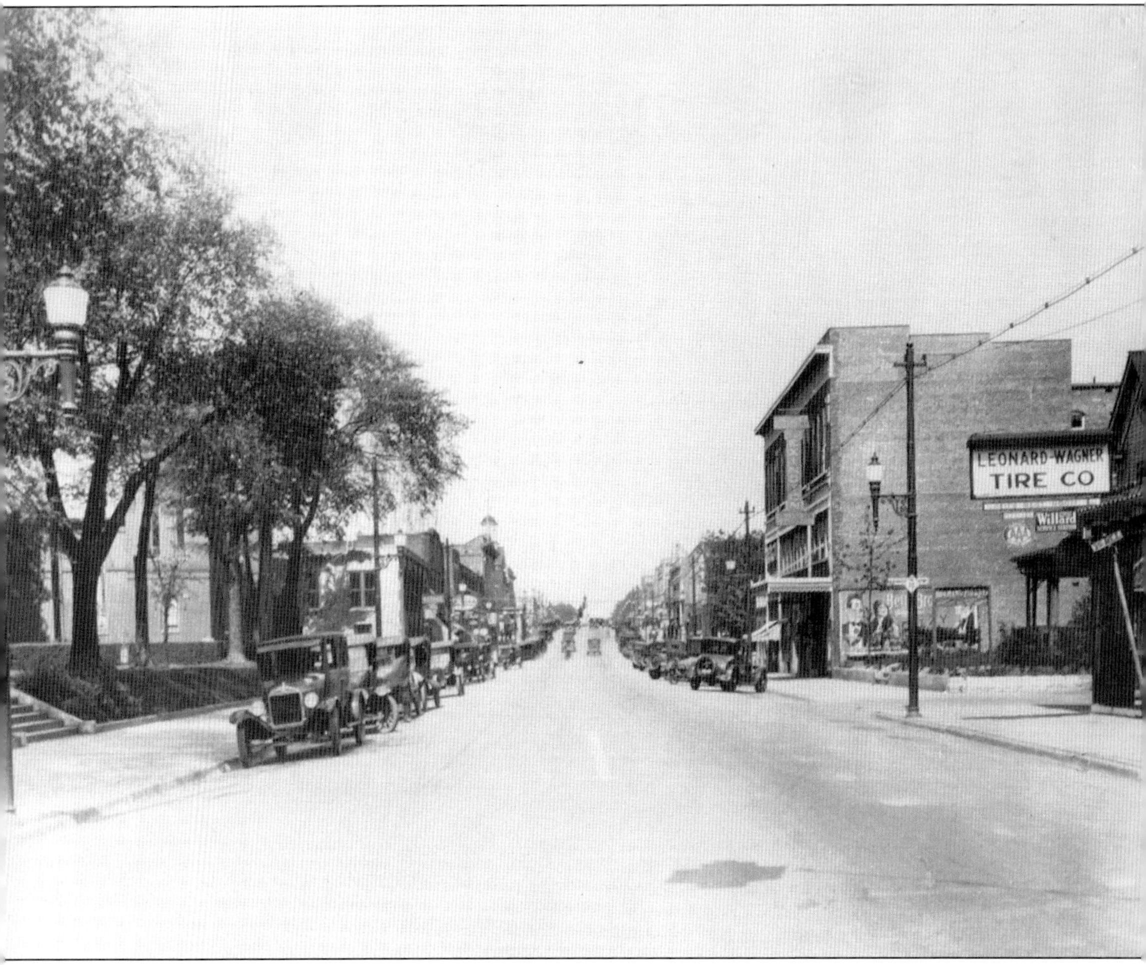

Cars parked on both sides of the street left little room in 1925. Precisely at midnight, an alarm was received at the Wennonah station from Raleigh Road at box 21. The No. 2 truck was responding to the alarm, coming north on Main Street. The driver, Henry Yarbrough, was forced to hold the fast-moving truck in the middle of Main Street due to the cars. As the firetruck approached Third Avenue, a car was in the intersection attempting a left-hand turn. Hearing the truck behind him, the driver aborted his left-hand turn and turned to the right to get out of the way. It was a cold night and the car stalled.

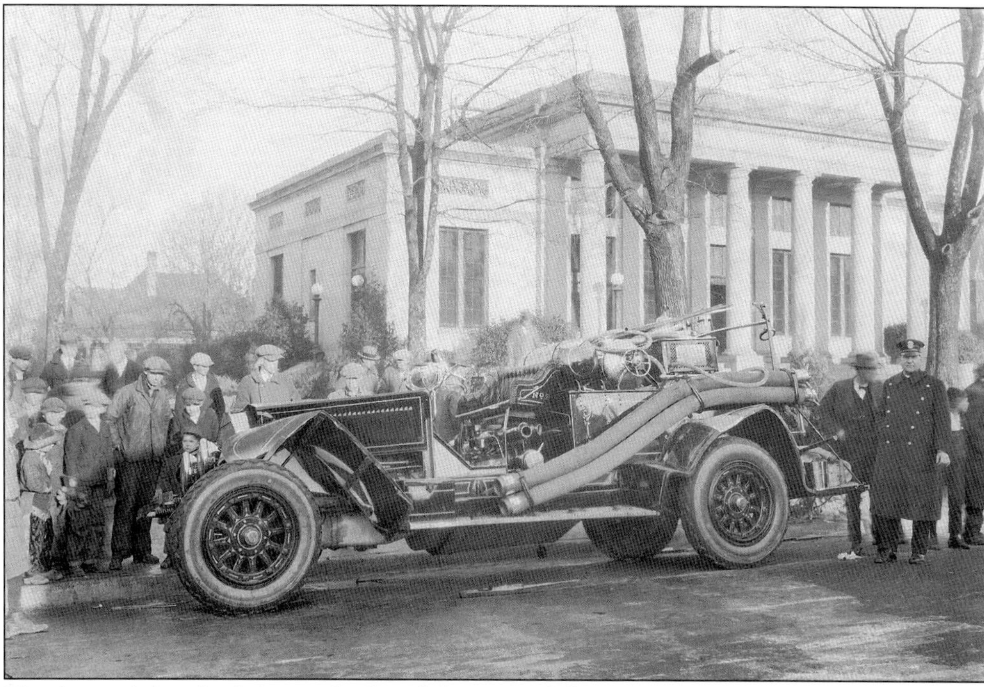

The firetruck hit the left rear fender of the car and flipped over two or three times. It was a terrible scene as the people exited the theater. D.C. Cope was killed instantly. Henry Gibson was lying in the middle of West Third Avenue. Ed Cope was lying in the middle of Main Street. Howard Michael was thrown onto the grass in front of the post office. Howard Michael and Ed Cope died within minutes of being transported to the hospital.

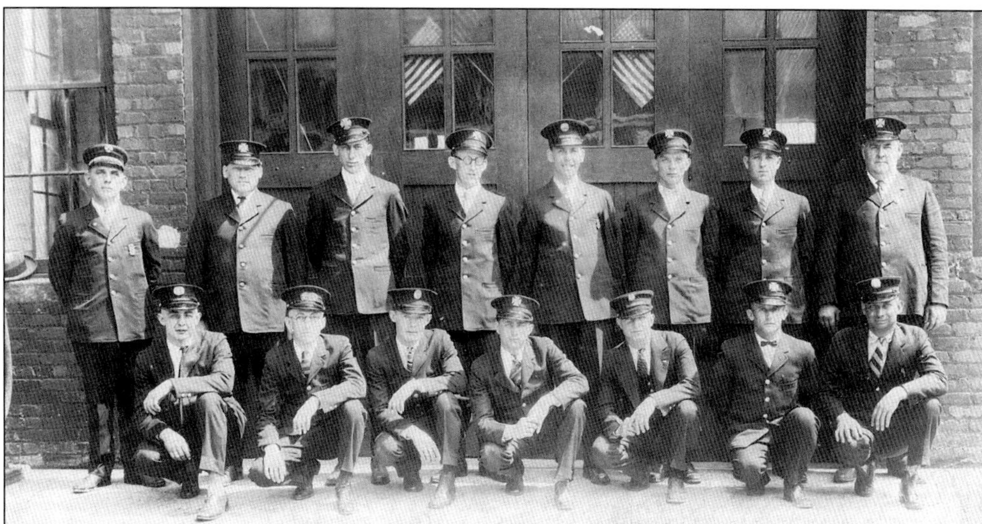

The Thomasville Fire Department helped with the funerals following the tragedy. This photograph of that department was taken in 1924 in front of the old fire station at the corner of Commerce and East Guilford Streets. From left to right are the following: (front row) Fred Sullivan, Tom Clinard, Howard Sullivan, Crater Lookabill, Grady Underwood, A.L. McCrary, and Carl Jackson; (back row) Chief Tomlinson, Wade Welch, Lewis Godbey, Paul Clinard, C.L. White, Lindsay Loftin, Herman Leonard, and H.W. Armsworthy.

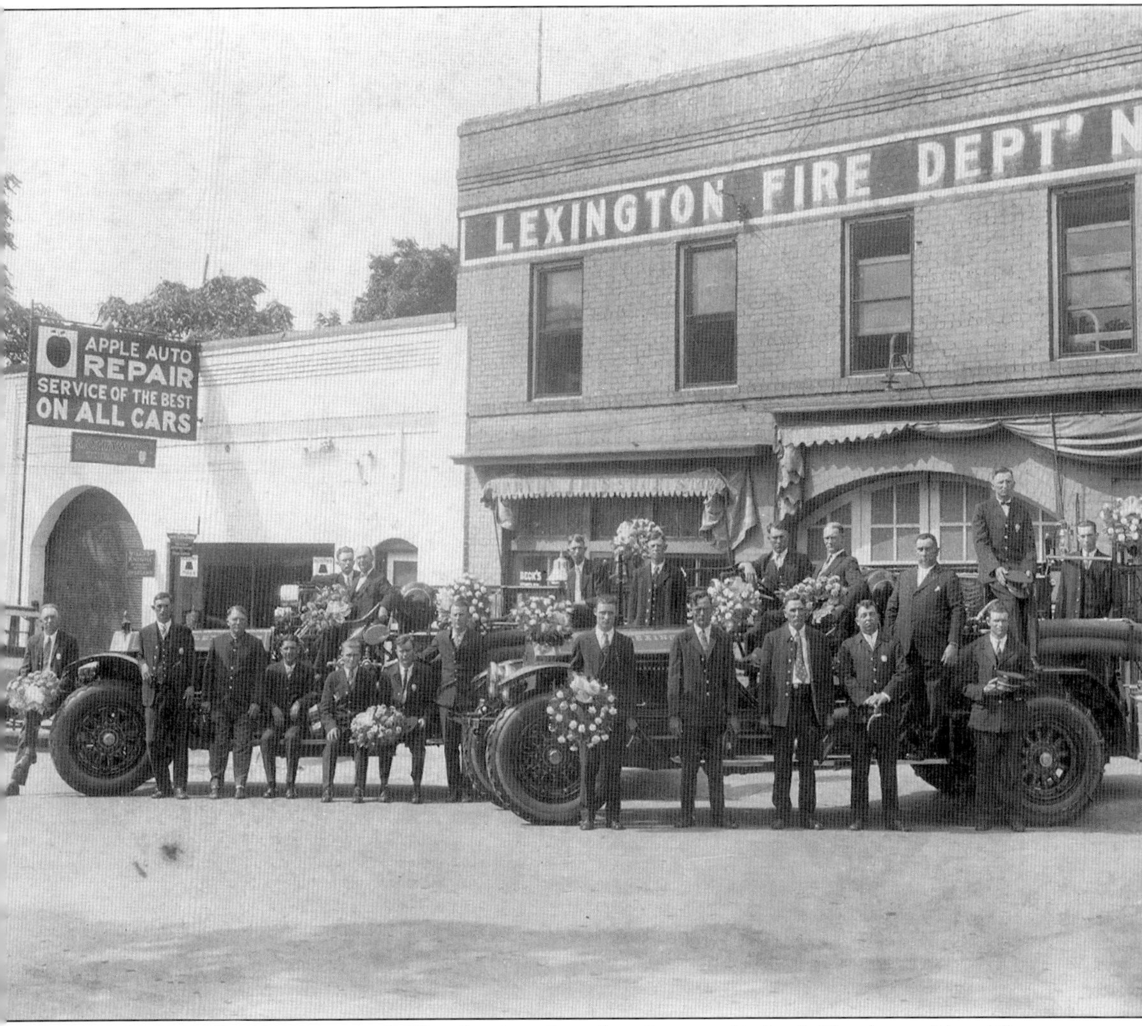

The tragedy was compounded by the fact that the alarm on Raleigh Road was false. There was no fire. Three dedicated firemen were killed. Three women were left widowed. Ten children were left without fathers—all because of a false alarm.